Welcome to the *EVERYTHING*® series!

These handy, accessible books give you all you need to tackle a difficult project, gain a new hobby, comprehend a fascinating topic, prepare for an exam, or even brush up on something you learned back in school but have since forgotten.

You can read an *EVERYTHING*® book from cover-to-cover or just pick out the information you want from our four useful boxes: e-facts, e-ssentials, e-alerts, and e-questions. We literally give you everything you need to know on the subject, but throw in a lot of fun stuff along the way, too.

We now have well over 100 *EVERYTHING*® books in print, spanning such wide-ranging topics as weddings, pregnancy, wine, learning guitar, one-pot cooking, managing people, and so much more. When you're done reading them all, you can finally say you know *EVERYTHING*®!

FACTS

Important sound bytes of information

SSENTIALS

Quick handy tips

ALERT

Urgent warnings

QUESTIONS?

Solutions to common problems

THE
EVERYTHING
Series

Dear Reader:

What you hold in your hands is clearly not an encyclopedia. Weighty Encyclopedia-sized histories of philosophy do exist. Weighty in more ways than one, they are also often most effective as sleep aids.

The Everything® Philosophy Book is an introduction that covers the cast of characters and schools of thought that have shaped the way we look at the world. These people have asked the musical question "What's it all about?" and arrived at myriad conclusions. Some ideas may resonate with you; others may seem bizarre, if not downright comical. Recall the old adage that the only stupid question is the one that remains unasked. Herein I present history's Great Questioners.

It's a Philosophy 101 course without the hefty per-credit fee. But unlike a dry academic affair that would leave you alternately agitated and somnolent, I hope you find this tome to be humorous and entertaining as well as informative.

Descartes changed the world when he said, "I think, therefore I am." To paraphrase one of the many masters you will find between the covers of this modest primer, may I say, "You read, therefore I eat." So, dear reader, buy this book!

Sincerely,

James Mannion

THE
EVERYTHING
PHILOSOPHY
BOOK

Understand the basic
concepts of great thinkers—from
Socrates to Sartre

James Mannion

Adams Media Corporation
Avon, Massachusetts

EDITORIAL
Publishing Director: Gary M. Krebs
Managing Editor: Kate McBride
Copy Chief: Laura MacLaughlin
Acquisitions Editor: Allison Carpenter Yoder
Development Editor: Kelly Ewing

PRODUCTION
Production Director: Susan Beale
Production Manager: Michelle Roy Kelly
Series Designer: Daria Perreault
Layout and Graphics: Brooke Camfield,
Colleen Cunningham, Michelle Roy Kelly,
Daria Perreault

An Everything® Series Book.
Everything® is a registered trademark of Adams Media Corporation.

Published by Adams Media Corporation
57 Littlefield Street, Avon, MA 02322 U.S.A.
www.adamsmedia.com

ISBN: 1-58062-644-0
Printed in the United States of America.

J I H G F E D C B A

Library of Congress Cataloging-in-Publication Data

Mannion, James.
The everything philosophy book: understanding the basic concepts of
great thinkers–from Socrates to Sartre / by James Mannion.
p. cm. -- (An everything series book)
Includes index.
ISBN 1-58062-644-0
1. Philosophy–Introductions. 2. Religion–Philosophy. I. Title. II.
BD21 .M25 2002
100–dc21
2002003934

This publication is designed to provide accurate and authoritative information with regard to the subject matter covered. It is sold with the understanding that the publisher is not engaged in rendering legal, accounting, or other professional advice. If legal advice or other expert assistance is required, the services of a competent professional person should be sought.
—From a *Declaration of Principles* jointly adopted by a Committee of the American Bar Association and a Committee of Publishers and Associations

Illustrations by Barry Littmann.

This book is available at quantity discounts for bulk purchases.
For information, call 1-800-872-5627.

Visit the entire Everything® series at everything.com

Contents

INTRODUCTION xi

CHAPTER 1 *It's Greek to Me* 1
Presocratic Efforts 2
Pluralists: All Kinds of Stuff 6
Leucippus and Democritus: The Atomic Duo. 7
Spin City-States: The Sophists. 8

CHAPTER 2 *The Three Sages: Socrates, Plato, and Aristotle* . . . 11
Socrates 12
Plato 18
Plato's Republic 21
Aristotle. 22

CHAPTER 3 *The Decline and Fall of the Hellenistic Period*. 27
The End of Greek Prominence. 28
The Cynics. 28
Epicureanism: The Pleasure Principle 30
Stoicism. 33
Skepticism: Perception Is Reality 36
Cicero and the Eclectics 37
Neoplatonism: End of an Epoch 39

CHAPTER 4 *The Medieval Mind* 41
The Christian Church and Philosophy. 42
Augustine of Hippo 43
Anselm's Ontological Argument. 45
Thomas Aquinas 46
John Duns Scotus 49
Roger Bacon. 50
William of Ockham 50

CHAPTER 5 *The Renaissance Period* 53
Creativity Abounds. 54

Cosimo de Medici 54
Nicholas of Cusa 55
Bernardino Telesio 55
Giordano Bruno. 56
Niccolò Machiavelli. 57

CHAPTER 6 *Humanism* **59**
What's It All About? 60
Francesco Petrarca. 60
Desiderius Erasmus 61
Sir Thomas More. 61

CHAPTER 7 *The Protestant Reformation* **63**
The Fall of the Catholic Church 64
Martin Luther 64
John Calvin 65
The Catholic Counter-Reformation 67

CHAPTER 8 *The Scientific Revolution* **69**
The Heliocentric Theory 70
The Return of Skepticism. 71
The Invention of the Printing Press 71

CHAPTER 9 *Approaching Modern Times* **73**
Francis Bacon 74
René Descartes 75
Thomas Hobbes 77
Baruch Spinoza 79
Gottfried Leibniz 80

CHAPTER 10 *British Empiricism* **81**
The Concept of Innateness 82
John Locke 82
George Berkeley 84
David Hume. 85

CHAPTER 11 *The French Enlightenment* **87**
    The *Philosophes* 88
    Montesquieu. 89
    Voltaire 89
    Jean Jacques Rousseau 91

CHAPTER 12 *German Idealism*. **95**
    Immanuel Kant 96
    Johann Gottlieb Fichte 98
    Friedrich Wilhelm Josef von Schelling 99
    George W. F. Hegel 99
    Arthur Schopenhauer. 101
    Friedrich Wilhelm Nietzsche 104

CHAPTER 13 *Utilitarianism* **111**
    Jeremy Bentham. 112
    John Stuart Mill 113
    The Feminist 115

CHAPTER 14 *The American Transcendentalists* **117**
    Transcendentalism Today 118
    Ralph Waldo Emerson 118
    Henry David Thoreau 120
    William Ellery Channing. 121
    Amos Bronson Alcott 122

CHAPTER 15 *Phenomenology and Existentialism*. **123**
    Edmund Husserl. 124
    Søren Kierkegaard. 124
    Martin Heidegger 127
    Albert Camus. 128
    Jean-Paul Sartre 130

CHAPTER 16 *Modern and Postmodern Philosophers* **133**
    Bertrand Russell. 134

Ludwig Josef Johan Wittgenstein 136
Michel Foucault 137
Jacques Derrida 139

CHAPTER 17 *Sociology and Anthropology* 141
Sociology 142
Karl Marx 142
Max Weber 144
Emile Durkheim 145
Anthropology 146

CHAPTER 18 *Psychology* 149
The Roots of Psychology 150
Sigmund Freud 150
Carl Gustav Jung 154
Behaviorism 158
Humanistic Psychology 159
And the Rest 159

CHAPTER 19 *Eastern Schools of Thought* 163
Hinduism 164
Buddhism 167
Taoism 172
Confucianism 177
Shinto 180
Sufism 181

CHAPTER 20 *The Big Three Religions* 183
For Better and for Worse 184
Judaism 184
Christianity 186
Islam 189
Final Thought 193

CHAPTER 21 *Objectivism and the Right Livelihood*..........195
    Objectivism: Looking Out for No. 1 196
    Right Livelihood: Doing the Right Thing. 199

CHAPTER 22 *The Forgotten Philosophers*..................207
    "Primitive" Cultures 208
    African Philosophy 208
    Native American Philosophy 210
    Black Elk Speaks 212
    The Medicine Wheel 213

CHAPTER 23 *Twelve Steps to a Better Life* 219
    Alcohol in Society 220
    The Affects of Alcohol. 220
    The Path to Rehabilitation 220
    New Hope for the Alcoholic 221
    The Philosophy Behind AA 223
    The Twelve Steps 227
    AA and God 228
    Twelve Traditions 229
    Anonymity as a Philosophy 229
    Remaining Financially Independent. 230
    Adaptation by Other Organizations 231

CHAPTER 24 *Everything Old Is New Age Again* 233
    So Just What Is New Age? 234
    It's Not New at All 234
    Reincarnation 234
    Soul Mates 237
    I Ching 240
    Astrology 241
    Numerology. 244
    Mandala Drawing 246

CHAPTER 25 *Philosophy and the Couch Potato* **249**
    Philosophy Beyond the Classroom 250
    Star Trek 250
    The Prisoner 256
    The Fugitive 259
    Emma Peel: Feminist Icon 259

APPENDIX A *Glossary of Philosophical Terms* **261**

APPENDIX B *Who's Who in Philosophy* **269**

INDEX **283**

Introduction:
What's It All About?

Those familiar with the opening scenes of Stanley Kubrick's *2001: A Space Odyssey* know that for eons, mankind was just another player scratching for survival in a cruel primordial ecosystem, living and dying instinctually in the unrelenting circle of life. Humans were apelike hominids, foraging for food and warring with rival packs. Suffice it to say, there were no philosophers in that crowd. Or were there?

Neanderthal Man (and woman) was the Big Kahuna from about 200,000 B.C.–40,000 B.C. Neanderthals were, until very recently, perceived as the stereotypical cavemen from the movies, bedecked in fur, sporting the proverbial big stick, and only able to counter a Socratic query with an insouciant "Ugh!" Yet there was much more to these heavy-browed ancestors than heretofore known.

Recent archeological findings indicate that the Neanderthals comprised a complex culture. Ancient burial sites reveal that ceremonies were performed, and that these rituals included floral arrangements and the placement of the body in a fetal position. These rituals clearly indicate a faith of some kind and a regard for fallen comrades and loved ones. In the animal kingdom, a body is simply left to decompose. For millions of years, human descendents did the same thing. Yet somewhere along the line, this tradition changed. Mankind had developed a sense of spirituality and an appreciation of the mysteries of life.

Around 10,000 B.C., the wandering hunter-gatherers started to settle down in communities. They began to plant crops and domesticate livestock. It was in these ancient civilizations that man's first forays into mathematics, astronomy, and the written word began. Within these communities, social classes developed. Agriculture and animal husbandry allowed for the gradual development of leisure time. This free time was certainly not an idolatry of indolence—theirs was, by today's standards, still a struggle fraught with dangers. Yet with this chance to stop and smell the roses, as it were, philosophizing naturally followed. Leisure time was not filled with Sony

PlayStations and cyberchat rooms. People thought and probed, and the human mind continued to expand and grow.

Ancient man's attempt to explain the world and his place in it took the form of what you might consider primitive superstition, but everything old is new age again. As you venture forth into the new millennium, you may find that the wisdom of the ancients was no mere mumbo-jumbo. Closeness to, and a reverence for, nature are sadly missed in the modern age. The gods, each with their singular characteristics and foibles, are archetypes of human personalities. And the fact that gods from divergent cultures are so similar indicates that they sprang from the depths of the human psyche; the kingdom of the gods was within.

A rich oral tradition of myths and tall tales began even before the written word. The epic of Gilgamesh, Homer's *Odyssey and Iliad*, and no doubt countless others that have not survived were an attempt to explain what the human experience was all about, or at least to pose pertinent questions. From this rich mythology, superstition, and nature worship, the first philosophers emerged and attempted to look at the world from a more scientific and human-centric perspective. Perhaps the sun was just the sun and not a god; maybe man was not a mere puppet of the fates but rather a creature in control of his own destiny. Mythology was followed by philosophy, upon which the sciences were founded, and a schism split the mystical and the empirical.

Now, in this new millennium, the chasm between spirituality and science is closing. Quantum physics reveals that the atom is not the smallest particle measurable, and at the subatomic level, those fascinating little bits of matter do things that defy the laws of space and time. Science and spirituality may not be mutually exclusive after all.

In this book, you hear from the experts, from the Presocratics of ancient Milesia to the twentieth-century thinkers. From the robed sages of antiquity to the denizens of your local diner, everyone's a philosopher. You don't need an advanced degree and a string of letters after your name to ask the big question, "What's it all about?"

Philosophy means "love of wisdom," from the ancient words *philos* (love) and *sophia* (wisdom). I hope this primer may inspire your love of wisdom and prompt you to delve deeper into the great minds of the ages.

CHAPTER 1
It's Greek to Me

From the quasimystical Monists to the comparatively contemporary atomists, the evolution of thought among the ancient Greeks was a giant leap in the thinking processes of mankind. Chuckle though you may at some of their theories, at the time they were cutting edge and innovative, and a big influence on those that followed.

Presocratic Efforts

We label as *Presocratics* the world's first official philosophers, a group of men who taught and expounded mostly in the Greek city-states of Ionia beginning in the seventh-century B.C. While many of their theories may seem naïve, primitive, and just plain wrong, these thinkers deserve a great deal of credit for taking the mind of man into an exciting direction.

While entrenched in a rich mythic tradition involving anthropomorphic gods and monsters and the orally transmitted tales of Homer and others, the Presocratics took baby steps into natural law. They sought to explain what it's all about via a scientific method. The Presocratics are sometimes called *Monists,* meaning that they sought to isolate one thing, usually one of the elements (earth, air, fire, and water) as the basic stuff to which all reality could be reduced.

FACTS

The Presocratic philosophers, while their theories may seem ridiculous today, should be given credit for their efforts to move away from primitive explanations of gods and demons to explain nature and reality. Their ancient efforts paved the way for the scientific method.

The ideas and philosophies of the Presocratics were literally written in stone. Unfortunately, only fragments of these slabs survive. In fact, no complete work of any Presocratic philosopher remains intact. All that's left are snippets and fragments, the ancient equivalent of little yellow sticky memo sheets stuck to your computer monitor or refrigerator.

Yet their efforts should not be underestimated. The evolution from superstition to science was a quantum leap in thinking, and their philosophy formed a genesis that grew into many of the truths we now hold to be self-evident.

Thales: Water, Water Everywhere

Thales of Miletus is often designated as the first official philosopher. He is regarded as the founder of natural philosophy. He proposed that everything is composed of water. On a visceral level, Thales saw water as the source of life, an indispensable necessity for survival. In the form of floods and torrents, water could take life as well as sustain it. It could also change form. Even metals and rock could be reduced to a molten, or liquid state. Water and other liquidities were a formidable force of nature.

Though Thales could not have known that the human body is composed of mostly water, he was on to something, simplistic as his theories may seem today. His rational approach of not attributing anything and everything to "the gods" paved the way for the scientific method. He was revered as a sage in his lifetime and long after his death.

Anaximander: A Philosopher of Boundless Energy

Anaximander, a younger contemporary of Thales, didn't believe that water was one of the four familiar elements that was the basic stuff of the world. Instead, he believed that all those elements and more comprised a common element he called *ápeiron,* or "*The Boundless.*" All things arise from ápeiron, and all things return to ápeiron. This belief foreshadows Einstein's dictum that "Matter can neither be created nor destroyed."

Anaximenes: Air Apparent

Anaximenes was a pupil of Anaximander. He digressed from his mentor's theory by singling out air as the root of all things. Humans need air as much as water. He believed that the soul was composed of air.

While water could change its composition, air is capable of rarefication and condensation. Air in its densest form would be solid matter. In its most ephemeral form, it would be the atmosphere itself. Modern scientists (and New Age gurus) will tell you that solid matter is simply energy in its densest form.

Though Anaximenes called his stuff *du jour* "air," and this may seem a ridiculous proposition, what is important is the principle. It was a movement away from the supernatural and an attempt, like his fellow Milesian scholars and thinkers, to look at things from a scientific perspective. This perspective is what makes the Presocratics important figures in the history of the world.

Anaximenes had another theory that was heading in a more sophisticated direction. In those days, the breath, because it exhales from the body, was linked to the concept of the soul, which was and is believed to dwell within the body. In olden days, when people sneezed, they believed the soul was in danger of being expelled from the body, which is why people say, "Bless you" or some equivalent when someone sneezes. It was originally a call for the soul to skootch back inside the body. Perhaps, and no one knows for sure, old Anaximenes was talking about more than mere air when he espoused this Monist philosophy.

The Presocratic philosophers are also called Monists. By definition, this means that, in their philosophy, they determined that the basic "stuff" of reality, such as water, air, fire, and so on, was one thing, though Pythagoras thought it was numbers.

Pythagoras: By the Numbers

Rather than suggest that the basic stuff of reality was an element of nature, Pythagoras proposed that life was a numbers game. He taught that everything could be explained through mathematical theorems and formulae. He also made a connection between mathematical order and music, even going as far as to state that the orbits of celestial bodies were accompanied by tuneful harmonies he dubbed the "Music of the Spheres." This one was quite a claim, because Pythagoras never popped his ear above the stratosphere to verify this theory.

The Pythagorean school of thought was enormously popular and lasted hundreds of years. In his lifetime, Pythagoras was a cult figure whose disciples were sworn to secrecy upon pain of death. He also believed in reincarnation, and his followers were vegetarians.

Heraclitus and Parmenides: Ionian Odd Couple

Nicknamed the Obscure, Heraclitus was a philosopher who was known as something of a downer. His theory that everything is composed of fire, if taken metaphorically, is expressed in his belief that everything is in flux. There is no constancy in the universe. There was no living in the moment for Heraclitus. You could not even step into the same river twice, he said, because the flowing water was not the same water you dipped your big toe into mere seconds before. Life is a never-ending sequence of birth and death, creation and destruction.

Heraclitus felt that this cycle of combustibility is also applicable to the human spirit. Are you the same person at age forty that you were at twenty? Probably not. If taken to heart, this philosophy can lead to melancholy: Youth fades, loved ones die, you were dust, and unto dust you shall return.

FACTS

Pythagoras and his followers believed in reincarnation and were practicing vegetarians. He was also one of the first cult leaders. His followers were penalized if they revealed his numerical secrets. Rumor has it that some found themselves sleeping with the Aegean fishes when they crossed the No. 1 guy.

Heraclitus lived much of his life as an eccentric hermit. He had contempt for society and the feeling was mutual. He is also famous for the oft-quoted maxim that "Character is destiny."

Parmenides was the anti-Heraclitus; he wrote in direct response to him. Simply put, he believed that there is no flux and that, in fact, everything is stagnant. "It is" was his credo. Being is immutable and constant, and change is an illusion.

Parmenides wrote an epic poem called "Truth," which like everything else from the Presocratics, exists only in fragments. Enough survives, however, to piece together the basics of Parmenidian philosophy.

According to Parmenides, you can look at the world in two ways: You ask yourself whether "it is" or "it is not." If it "is not," you cannot be thinking about it, because you can only think about something that exists.

Parmenides also believed that all this coming and going and blossoming and fading away that you see in your daily life is an illusion of the senses. The more things change, the more they remain the same.

Zeno: The Tortoise and the Hero

Zeno is best known for a couple of famous paradoxes, which in the real world make no sense whatsoever, but were extremely popular in their day. The first one explains how, sitting in your room, you can never really reach the door. If the distance between two points is composed of an infinite number of points, then you can bisect that line. And you can keep bisecting the areas you previously bisected *ad infinitum.* Hence, you potentially have an infinite amount of space in a finite distance between two points and can never really get anywhere. Think about that as you get out of your chair, walk to the door, and leave the room.

The second Zeno paradox deals with motion. When you move from one place to another, you reach the midway point before the final destination. And before you get to the halfway mark, you reach the halfway mark of the midway point. Ergo, you have to travel an infinite number of points in a finite amount of time. And that is impossible, right?

The example Zeno uses to make this argument is a race between the mighty hero Achilles (of *Iliad* and heel fame) and a tortoise. If Achilles graciously gave the tortoise a head start, he could never catch up with the turtle based on the preceding argument. Nevertheless, if you're a gambler, you would be ill advised to bet on the tortoise.

Pluralists: All Kinds of Stuff

The next group of philosophers are called Pluralists. They differed from the Monists in that they believed reality could not be reduced to one thing, whether it be an element, a mathematical equation, or a theory of flux or constancy. As they saw it, the world was composed of many elements.

Empedocles: The Root of the Matter

Empedocles can be compared to Pythagoras in that he combined the scientific and spiritual, yet his area of expertise was medicine rather than mathematics. Legend has it that he was a charismatic celebrity who performed medical "miracles" that astounded the populace and was a gifted poet and orator.

Empedocles also offered the theory that it was not one element at the center of it all, but rather that the roots of all four elements—fire, air, earth, and water—could be found in everything. The four roots would exist in different degrees. Obviously water would have a preponderance of water "roots," but the others would be there to a lesser degree. And in an ancient Greek variation on the yin/yang belief of coexisting complementary opposites, he added that the entities he called Love and Strife were complementary forces that impacted on the world as they knew it.

Anaxagoras: Seeds of Knowledge

Anaxagoras took the theories of four roots a step further by declaring that reality can be reduced to an infinite number of "seeds." Not unlike Empedocles's hypothesis, these seeds contain elements of everything and are in everything, yet certain elements are there in greater abundance, creating life's myriad diversity.

And in lieu of Empedocles's Love and Strife theory, Anaxagoras postulated on the existence of a "Nous" or omniscient yet impersonal Mind that gave order and constancy to the universe.

Leucippus and Democritus: The Atomic Duo

The philosophers Leucippus and Democritus were the first to theorize that the world was composed of tiny particles called atoms. These particles were invisible to the human eye yet ubiquitous in their myriad combinations, comprising what is commonly called reality. Between the two, Democritus was apparently the one with the better sense of humor, because he was nicknamed "The Laughing Philosopher" and "the mocker." He was allegedly never without a quip or a cackle at the expense of his fellow citizens.

Democritus built on the theories of Leucippus by suggesting that atoms were indivisible. This was accepted as fact until August 1945, when mankind split the atom and unleashed a conflagration, changing the world forever. And quantum physics has proven that there are things even smaller than the atom. But this theory had a good several millennia's worth of fashionability.

Spin City-States: The Sophists

The next school of philosophy, the Sophists, is as modern as the Pluralists with its contemporary blend of philosophy, politics, opportunism, and cynicism. The quest for wisdom, the growth of a political system, and a good old entrepreneurial spirit brought forth a professional class of wandering educrats known as the Sophists. Sophistry has a negative connotation these days, and it is largely deserved. In this day and age, the Sophists would be in competing infomercials, pitching their platitudes with manic intensity.

The word *sophistry* entered the English language with a decidedly negative definition courtesy of the Sophists. These ancient equivalent of self-help gurus were more motivational speakers than philosophers. For a fee, they would help people use tools of rhetoric and debating skills to help advance one's career.

The Sophists did things that other philosophers found unconscionable: They charged for their services, and they could spin philosophy to accommodate any political situation. Linguistic legerdemain was their stock in trade. They could prove day is night and black is white and leave the toga-clad throng awestruck. They had impressive powers of persuasion, and ambitious young men paid to learn these skills. The Sophists had their pulse on the Grecian *zeitgeist* and were enormously popular and influential celebrities.

However, as with the Presocratics, very little if any information and writings by and about the Sophists survive. The primary source is Plato, a man who hated the Sophists and everything for which they stood. What has come down through the millennia is a distinctly one-sided view of the Sophists.

To put a positive spin on the notorious Sophists, they considered themselves to be teachers and businessmen. They felt that they had a skill to impart on others, and they charged a fee for their service. That's a respectable deal, a fair trade of good and/or services for money.

Or is their belief mere Sophistry? There is a spiritual principle that something that was freely given to you should not then be imparted to someone else for a fee. The Sophists, however, did not deal in notions of Truth, Beauty, Logic, and the like. They were pragmatists helping ambitious men learn and use very earthly skills to find happiness, romance, and success in ancient Athens. A lot of average citizens got valuable skills from the Sophists.

Protagoras

Protagoras is generally regarded as the first Sophist. He had a successful career and enjoyed great fame in his lifetime. Posthumous acclaim would mean little to a Sophist. The Sophists were not all that interested in spiritual matters. In fact, Protagoras was charged with impiety, a serious offense in those days and one that hastened the end of the mighty Socrates.

"Man is the measure of all things" was the credo of Protagoras, which was not to suggest the nobility and evolutionary superiority of the species. It is actually an extreme case of relativism, moral and otherwise. It's a dismissal of Big Picture Universal Truths, where what's true for me may not be true to you, and vice versa. "Anything goes" was the natural devolution of such a principle. If it feels good, do it. If it gets you ahead even at the expense of another, go for it anyway.

Protagoras also had an apathetic view toward the gods. His attitude was that you can't really know if they exist, and because you can never know, they do not really matter much in your day-to-day life so you might as well forget about them—hence the "impiety" charge and subsequent death sentence.

Gorgias

Gorgias, a.k.a. The Nihilist, was an accomplished public speaker. He didn't put much stock in the notion of virtue and instead felt that the power of persuasion was key: Master that and the world was your proverbial oyster.

His philosophy is summed up in this three-pronged theory:

- Nothing exists.
- If anything did exist, you could not know about it.
- If something existed and you knew about it, you couldn't communicate that awareness to others.

Gorgias also wrote a satirical poem mocking Parmenides called "That Which Is Not." In the poem, he demonstrates the many things that you can think about that do not exist and never will.

Prodicus

Prodicus was a rhetorician who, according to most accounts, was unabashedly in it for the money. Plato frequently satirized him as a pedantic lecturer on the niceties of language above all else. His fate is proof that if you can't do the time, don't do the crime. Eloquent and popular as he was, the officials of Athens saw fit to execute him for corrupting the youth, a charge that would also be leveled at the nobler Socrates.

CHAPTER 2

The Three Sages: Socrates, Plato, and Aristotle

As the old adage says, "When the student is ready, the teacher will appear." After the Sophists, perhaps ancient Greece was ready to raise the bar on philosophy and take it to the next plateau. Ready or not, along came three of the most influential and revered thinkers of theirs or any age.

Socrates

The ancient world had become an ethically arbitrary place, rife with moral relativism and a lack of regard for the Eternal Truths when Socrates (469–399 B.C.) came on to the scene. This dynamic and controversial Athenian figure spent a lifetime in the public square, engaging in dialogues with the young men of Athens. Socrates was your classic eccentric philosopher type: Not concerned with his appearance and by all reports not very handsome, but eager to engage in a philosophical debate anytime, anywhere.

His Background

Socrates was from what would be considered a middle-class family in ancient Athens. His father was a stonemason, and his mother was a midwife. We know virtually nothing about his youth. We know that he served in the military during the Peloponnesian War and distinguished himself on the battlefield with great courage and Herculean physical endurance. He also performed mandatory public service, as was the case with most Athenians. Athens was a city-state, which is what it sounds like—a city in size but also a self-contained nation. Loyalty and service to the state were mandatory, and for the most part undertaken without complaint. Socrates had a wife but almost nothing is known about her, other than her name, which was Xanthippe.

FACTS

Socrates compared himself to a *gadfly,* a nasty insect that torments horses by stinging their buttocks. The horse would flick his tail and shoo the gadfly away, but gadfly always returns. In the analogy, society was the horse's rear end, and Socrates was the relentless gadfly. Unfortunately, society eventually turned the flyswatter on Socrates.

As a young man, Socrates had apparently studied the naturalist philosophers, including Empedocles and other Presocratics. Of course, they were not called Presocratics at the time, since Socrates had not yet become a pivotal focal point in the classical age. Socrates was also well versed in the work of the Sophists and could employ their techniques with aplomb if he so chose. He ultimately rejected both schools of thought, believing that Truth did not lie in the natural world, nor was Truth something that could be manipulated through verbal and intellectual trickery.

What we know of Socrates's life is from about age forty until his death at the age of seventy. Living modestly and relying on an inheritance and state subsidies, Socrates was able to live the life of a gentleman of leisure and journeyman philosopher. He was also the most prominent example of "local color" in Athens. He wandered about town conversing with any and all who would engage him.

Socratic Dialogue

Socrates's singular method of posing questions to his intellectual quarry and drawing responses, which made people think for themselves, is called *Socratic Dialogue*. This form of question and answer and the logical debate of opposing views is called *dialectic*.

Socrates served as a coach and mentor to the young men of Athens. His dialogues often made the fellow conversationalist squirm and writhe in intellectual discomfort. Socrates was adept at showing ideas to be foolish, or more accurately, making his subject figure it out for himself. He did not do this out of malice or an attempt to feel superior. He was interested in truth for truth's sake. Of course, not everyone likes to be exposed as a philosophical lightweight, even with the noblest of intentions. Hence, Socrates made a few enemies along the way.

Socrates fancied himself a midwife to ideas. He probably liked the analogy because he saw his mother make a living as a literal midwife. He did not originate deep thoughts, he maintained. Rather, he drew them out of the person with whom he was conversing.

His Demeanor

Because Socrates never put quill to papyrus, all we have is Plato's reportage and interpretation of Socrates the man. It is generally accepted that the early Socratic dialogues are a truer picture of Socrates. The Socrates of the later dialogues serves more as a fictional character, serving as the mouthpiece for Plato's philosophy.

Socrates in essence was using a form of Sophistry to further his points. But Socrates never accepted a drachma for the wisdom he imparted. This lack of payment distinguishes him from the mercenary Sophists. And Socrates didn't gloat when he handily bested his debating opponent. He was in search of Truth with a capital T. He was not in it for the self-aggrandizement, wealth, fame, and power cravenly craved by the Sophists. He also modestly claimed no wisdom, only ignorance and an ever-questioning nature. The Oracle at Delphi preternaturally pronounced Socrates to be the wisest man in the world. Socrates countered that if he was indeed a wise guy, it was only because the truly wise person admits that they really know nothing at all.

Socrates's uncompromising manner and penchant for making the pompous appear foolish made Socrates many enemies among the Athenian upper crust. And that awful specter of impiety loomed large over his activities. Certain people were out to get him, and they ultimately succeeded. But old Socrates had the philosophical last laugh, staying true to his principles to the bitter end.

Socrates's Apology

Brought to trial on charges of impiety and corrupting the Athenian youth, Socrates defended himself in an eloquent speech Plato preserved as the "Apology." In ancient Greek, the word was more accurately defined as "defense," because Socrates was hardly apologetic during the course of this speech. It contains the essence of Socrates's character and philosophy. It purports to be the speech that Socrates gave in his defense at his trial. Plato probably took poetic license, but it is likely that the essence of Socrates the man is depicted in the Apology.

Socrates in Athens

Athens was a democracy, but for a brief time it was taken over by nearby Sparta after many years of warfare. A government of what came to be known as the "Thirty Tyrants" terrorized the populace for about a year before being overthrown. One of those despots was a former pupil of Socrates, and the re-established democracy used this as an excuse to prosecute Socrates. He was an enormously popular local celebrity but intensely disliked by powerful elements in the political establishment.

Socrates was linked to both the Atomists and the Sophists, the scientific approach of the former being interpreted as a rejection of the gods and the latter being charlatans of the worst order. Socrates acknowledged that libelous rumors had been following him for years but denied the charges. Though once interested in the natural sciences, his philosophy changed direction, focusing on mankind and his myriad complexities, which Socrates found far more interesting than the dry notions of the Presocratics. He also distanced himself from the Sophists, stating that he didn't charge for his services nor did he presume to inform or enlighten. He merely brought that which is dormant within a person to the surface and got them thinking. After a lifetime of cross-examining a cross section of Athens, from politicians to poets to craftsmen, he observed that, while everyone has pretensions to insight and wisdom, they were as ignorant as he—more so because they thought they knew something. Socrates repeated the story of his encounter with the Oracle of Delphi wherein he claims he knows nothing. This is called the *Socratic Disavowal of Knowledge*.

The Trial

Socrates, in his opportunity to cross-examine his accusers, used his tried-and-true method to systematically punch holes in their arguments. As he scored points in logic and rationality, he continued to antagonize those who were about to decide his fate.

In the course of the Apology, Socrates went on to explain the central core of his belief system: The most important thing is to live a virtuous life. Doing the right thing and avoiding wrongdoing was what life was all about. Being virtuous is its own reward; doing wrong is its own punishment. There is nothing worse than being a bad person. Thus, if Socrates is convinced that he is a virtuous man, nothing his enemies can do to him can truly harm him so long as he sticks to his guns. Socrates also expressed no fear of death during his speech. Why fear an eternity in Paradise, and why fear nothingness?

Despite being an independent thinker and self-proclaimed gadfly, a big part of virtue is loyalty to the state. In fact, both Socrates and Plato were distrustful of democracies. The class-conscious Greeks believed that a certain type of specially trained, enlightened citizen should be in charge (as in Plato's upcoming concept of the "Philosopher King").

During the lengthy defense, Socrates seemed well aware that this kangaroo court would not rule in his favor, and he was prepared for their verdict. He did not resort to throwing himself on the mercy of the court. He faced his accusers unbowed and unapologetically. He continued doing the right thing as he saw it, no matter how unpleasant the consequences.

SSENTIALS Socrates's credo was "The unexamined life is not worth living." This has been the rallying cry of every philosopher who followed Socrates. Similarly, he is also quoted as saying, "Know thyself." Wisdom comes not only from observation, but also through introspection.

It was no surprise when the jurors returned a guilty verdict. As was the custom of the day, the condemned man was obliged to suggest his own punishment. Socrates proposed that he be given free room and board and be supported by the state for the rest of his natural life. Needless to say, this punishment was summarily rejected. He then proposed a nominal fine and then a larger one. He also announced that, if allowed to live, he would not stop practicing philosophy. It is here that Socrates utters the words for which he is most famous, a motto that should be every philosopher's raison d'être: "The unexamined life is not worth living. Doing what is right is the only path to goodness, and introspection and self-awareness are the ways to learn what is right."

Socrates was sentenced to death. In his final address to the court, he reiterates the themes he discussed during the Apology. He is ready to die because to die is better than to betray yourself. And he correctly predicts that though his individual voice may be extinguished, philosophers will continue to philosophize.

His Death

Socrates met his end like a secular martyr. Rather than face censure and silence, he took this belief to its logical conclusion. Systematically making his persecutors look foolish did little to guarantee him an acquittal. He did not throw himself on the mercy of the court as the powers-that-be had hoped or beg for exile instead of execution. After his sentence, word was filtered down to him that should he choose to fly the coop, the government would not aggressively hunt him down. The politicians were now confronted with executing an extremely popular national treasure. Ignoring pleas from some of his followers to split the scene, Socrates took hemlock and died in the company of his adoring entourage. It is a deeply moving scene as described in Plato's dialogue *Phaedo*. Socrates is quite serene as he says his good-byes to his friends and students. It is actually an assisted suicide, because one of the assembly concocts the hemlock potion for Socrates to drink.

Socrates tries to ease the grief of the despondent group by reminding them that only his body will die. His children are brought to him. He shoos the women out of the room and gently rebukes the men for their tears, urging them not to grieve. He takes a nice long bath and exchanges pleasantries with the prison guard with whom he has enjoyed conversing. His friend Crito asks him to wait until after sunset. It is his right to enjoy the rest of his last day, but Socrates would just as soon get it over with. Socrates drinks the poison without hesitation and without fear. He asks his weeping friends to settle down so that he can die in peace. He covers himself as his body grows numb, but manages to say his famous, and very mundane for so great a philosopher, last words, "Crito, I owe a cock to Asclepius; will you remember to pay the debt?" And then, as Shakespeare said, now cracked a noble heart.

His Legacy

Socrates was a larger than life person in his time on earth. After his death, he achieved mythic proportions. Many schools of philosophy arose after his death that claimed to corner the market on Socratic teachings.

They were often of conflicting philosophies. Most, however, stressed one aspect of Socrates's teaching:

- The Megarians focused on logic.
- The Elian School continued working with the technique of the Socratic dialogue, or dialectic.
- The Cynics rejected formal education and saw the road to wisdom as an inside job.
- The Cyrenaic School was the forerunner of the philosophy of *hedonism*, or the pursuit of pleasure.

All these schools, however, were mere pieces of the giant philosophical jigsaw puzzle that was Socratic thought. It was only Plato who kept the definitive Socratic tradition alive, as well as establishing himself as one of the great minds of antiquity.

Plato

Plato was Socrates's most famous protégé. He continued the Socratic legacy while building on it with his own theories. He also founded a school of philosophy, rather generically called The Academy. The basis of his mission and his goals can be found in his allegory of The Cave.

The Cave

This story is meant to illustrate how the majority of people live with a veil over their eyes, with only a distorted and shadowy notion of such things as Truth and Beauty. Imagine a group of shackled individuals in a dimly lit cave illuminated only by a large fire behind them. These cave people can only see shadows of themselves and other images flickering on a wall before them. This is their reality.

Most are either unimaginative or apathetic and simply accept this reality without speculation. The more inquiring minds observe the patterns more clearly and try to understand their world. Yet Truth eludes them.

One of the prisoners manages to break free from his shackles and escape the cave. Emerging into the light of day, this escapee is blinded by the light, again only seeing a shadowy representation of reality. Over time, however, this person will acclimate his senses to his surroundings and see things more clearly: the landscape, the sky, and the sun's illumination.

Eventually, this newly enlightened soul returns to the cave and tries to spread word of the brave new world that exists beyond the claustrophobic confines of the cave. What will the response of the cave dwellers be? Will they boldly go where this citizen had gone before and take the arduous yet rewarding journey out of darkness and into the light? No, according to Plato. They are more likely to kill the prophet, because he is a threat to the status quo.

This is an obvious reference to Plato's mentor Socrates, and a commentary on humanity's predilection to choose the fogbound existence, the easier and the softer way, the don't-rock-the-boat mentality. And the philosophers that lead the way are usually denounced, derided, and often end up dead.

Forms

In his eighty years (a very long life in those days), Plato established himself as the philosopher all other philosophers look to for inspiration. Some concurred with, adapted, and expanded upon his theories, others disputed and countered them, but all were influenced by him.

Plato was a firm believer in Ideas with a capital I or, as they are also called, Forms. Plato believed that while we can admire the beauty of a windswept beach, or the buff bods on said beach, there exists, out there in the ether, the Form of Beauty. The Idea of Beauty was an entity that imbues all the beauty we see in physical reality. The cast of *Baywatch: Hawaii* are mere shadows of the Form of Beauty that we can never perceive in its ephemeral splendor. Of course, Plato could never prove that in some unearthly realm, Beauty and Truth and Love and Virtue are floating around casting their shadows on us mere mortals who see them only as flickering, tantalizingly transient images in the cave wall. Man, who according to Plato is by nature a seeker of truth, struggles to grasp these Forms, but his perception falls short. Plato does, however, catalogue the various modes of knowledge available for the perceiving.

Knowledge is fourfold, according to Plato.

- The knowledge from imagination, dreams, and what was later called the unconscious
- Our perceptions of the outside world
- Mathematical knowledge
- Philosophical knowledge, which was Big Picture knowledge, an awareness of absolutes, universal truths in the form of those elusive Forms

Plato called the first two mere opinions, because while perception may be reality, things are perceived differently by different people. The second two were True Knowledge, because Plato believed that two plus two will never equal five, and Forms are immutable, eternal truths not to be messed with.

Where does God fit in this picture, you may ask? Plato believed that there was one Form among the Forms called the Good, and this has been interpreted as God. This mysterious realm where the Forms dwell is the true reality, according to Plato, and we poor creatures merely loom in the shadowy cave of our reality.

Reincarnation

Plato, like Pythagoras before him, also believed in reincarnation. We have all lived before and will live again. And in the meantime, in between time, in the period after death and before rebirth, we have access to the realm of the Forms and we can finally "get it." Aye, but there's a rub, as there always is. Once we return to the earthbound realm, we forget about all we can comprehend in the heavenly realm, only retaining a dim and nagging awareness that there is something greater than ourselves out there. And this never-ending quest to reclaim that lost knowledge is what makes potential philosophers of us all. For those seeking a little hellfire and brimstone in their theology, it is worth noting that Plato believed that the truly evil among us do not have the option to return in another life. They are condemned forever.

The world of the senses, and of sensual pleasure, actually inhibits finding true happiness, because it makes us more grounded in the real world, which is, according to Plato, not the highest reality.

Plato's Republic

One of Plato's most famous works is called *The Republic,* wherein he puts forth his political philosophy. Plato, having seen his beloved mentor Socrates unjustly murdered by an out-of-control democracy, has little use for that form of government. After reviewing the following, think about whether you would like to live in Plato's "ideal" sociopolitical state.

Plato did not believe in rugged individualism. He felt that everyone needed to be part of the state and a contributing member of the state. He felt that citizens were cells within a body politic, and that the jobs and responsibilities that people held were to be determined by the state. Plato conveniently assigns classes, or more accurately castes, within which citizens will be organized. Given his chosen profession, it is not a surprise that Plato made the Philosopher class the highest on his societal totem pole. The Philosopher class will rule the state, the Warrior class will protect the state, and the Producer class will serve the state with goods and services and skills.

This "republic" doesn't sound very democratic, does it? It isn't. A ruling class of philosophical aristocrats would be directing the affairs of state, with the famous Platonic concept of the Philosopher-King at its head. The Philosopher class guides the other classes, keeping the military in check and keeping the producers honest, while they contemplate the world of the Forms and try to make reality as Form-friendly as possible.

In a bit of upper-class snobbery toward the workers, the Producer class would be denied the benefits of public schooling. This would be reserved for the Philosopher and Warrior classes.

Though people would study the arts in Plato's Republic, he did not have much respect for the arts. Art was a copy of reality, which in turn is a pale representation of the exalted Forms. He believed that art did not belong in an ideal state. "No Artists Beyond this Point" would be prominently displayed at the gates of Plato's Republic.

Poetry would be banned as well. It speaks of the heart and inflames emotions, things that further entrench people in the material world. And the objective of the citizenry is to strive for the Ideal and avoid the animal passions that enslave people to this seriously flawed reality. Plato did not see art and poetry as inspiring and uplifting the human spirit. He viewed them as corrupting influences.

You probably would not want to live in Plato's Republic, his Utopian vision of the perfect society. There would be a rigid caste system with no upward mobility and all arts would be banned, because they are pale imitations of Truth. The cry "I want my MTV!" would fall on deaf aristocratic ears.

Plato would also have children taken away from their parents and raised in state-run foster homes supervised by the Philosopher class. He believed that the state could do a better job raising (and indoctrinating) children than could their own parents. He also believed in no private property. This applied only to the Philosopher and Warrior classes. The Producer class, the manual laborers and the workers, could keep their kids and their meager possessions, because they did not really matter in any area other than what they could contribute.

Oh, yes, Plato not only believed in community property, but also the communal sharing of wives! Plato's "ideal" hardly sounds ideal to modern ears, yet nevertheless he remains one of the three great sages of antiquity. And just as Socrates mentored Plato, Plato in turned mentored Aristotle.

Aristotle

Aristotle studied under Plato as a student at the latter's Academy for twenty years. He was a prodigy and generally regarded as Plato's heir apparent. However, Aristotle disagreed with the master on several key points. After Plato's death, Aristotle traveled the known world, and spent five years as the tutor of a precocious thirteen-year-old who went on to make a name for himself in an area other than philosophy—that of world conqueror. Aristotle's pupil was none other than Alexander the Great, who went on to capture the known world before dying at a young age.

Aristotle eventually established his own academy and called it the Lyceum. Aristotle liked to walk as he philosophized, eager students in tow. His students became known as *peripatetics*, which means "to walk."

Aristotle's Challenges to Plato

Aristotle disagreed with Plato on many theories. Though some may consider it "bad form" to challenge one's mentor, Aristotle did just that on the Platonic notion of Forms.

Plato believed that a whole other dimension was out there with a bunch of Forms floating around. Truth, Beauty, Love, and other concepts were actual entities that existed separate of the humanly perceived concepts of these ideas. Aristotle thought the theory of Forms to be illogical and impossible to prove. Plato believed that what we call reality was less real than the ethereal realm of the Forms. Aristotle held that the substantial here and now was quite real and that Forms are not separate things, but characteristics embodied in what we can perceive with our senses. He called his revised version of the Forms, *Universals*. There were universal truths, but they could be found without our own space-time continuum.

Plato believed that there were Ideals and their pale imitations. The Presocratic Parmenides and Heraclitus believed respectively that everything was stagnant and everything was in flux. Aristotle was able to draw upon and adapt these opposing viewpoints and come up with his own, a radical belief at the time and perhaps his major contribution to philosophy. This is the theory of *potentiality*.

The Theory of Potentiality

Potentiality means that within everything, people included, there exists a natural evolution toward fulfilling its own potential, in essence becoming its own Form. A movement in nature and in humans from imperfection to perfection, or as close as anything can get to perfection. This is a hardwired component in all things that is an involuntary process, according to Aristotle. The universe is in a constant progression of being and becoming, from the Big Bang to the inevitable Big Chill on a cosmic scale to the cycle of birth and death in the human condition.

Aristotle speaks of causes in the process from potentiality to actuality and identifies four:

- The material cause means that an external force is creating or initiating the new thing.
- The efficient cause is the process of creation.
- The formal cause is that certain something in its natural state.
- The final cause is what it can become when it fulfills its potential.

The first cause of all things is what Aristotle defines as God. God is what Aristotle calls the Unmoved Mover. God is the first thing ever to exist, separate from all other matter, and is the ultimate (and only, as far as Aristotle is concerned) Form. God, by Aristotle's reckoning, is pure mind, or what he calls Nous. God essentially looms around out there somewhere, removed and not especially concerned with the doings on planet Earth, spending all its time in endless, eternal self-contemplation. Totally self-absorbed is the Aristotelian God. Perhaps you have met more than a few people like that in your life.

Aristotle viewed the human soul as an integral part of the body, not a separate entity. He believed in what is now called the "bodymind" concept— that is, we are one human organism comprised of physical and spiritual matter. Hence, the soul did not exist after death. However, each soul is imbued with a piece of the Nous, or universal mind, and that Nous within you would fly off into the ether at the time of physical death.

Happiness and Friendship

Aristotle's ethical philosophy is that happiness is the ultimate goal of humankind. This does not mean "anything goes," however. For Aristotle, true happiness can only come from leading a virtuous life. He believed in a happy medium in all things. Moderation was a major virtue. It kept one free from vice and free to work toward one's potentiality. In this goal-oriented age, people may mistake this for ambition and getting ahead in the material world. Aristotle was referring to an innate forward motion of potentiality that unconsciously drove all things in the universe, people included. So, we are constantly "potentializing," whether we know it or not. This is the path and the goal of the person living the truly virtuous and happy life.

FACTS

Aristotle is famous for the syllogism, an argument that takes two truths, connects them, arriving at a third truth. The most celebrated syllogism is "All men are mortal. Socrates is a man. Therefore, Socrates is mortal." Aristotle believed that the syllogism was the best means to lead to absolute knowledge.

Aristotle places a high premium on friendship as well. True friendships are to be cultivated and treasured. Your true friend is almost like your *doppelganger*, your spiritual double. A true friend is there "to hold, as 'twere, the mirror up to nature; to show virtue her own feature, scorn her own image, and the very age and body of the time his form and pressure." In other words, Aristotle advocates a virtuous buddy system.

In politics, Aristotle sees humankind as a naturally social animal that seeks out community. The society is like an extended family and certain rules apply. The rules of Aristotle's day are different from ours. Aristotle accepted slavery and felt that the slave was a piece of property that had no rights. In commercial dealings, he said that usury, or collecting interest on a loan, was an egregious obscenity—as many modern men and women will attest as they pay their credit card bills.

Government

Aristotle stated that the three best forms of government are monarchy, aristocracy, and constitutional republic, and when perverted, they degenerated into tyranny, oligarchy, and democracy. Yes, democracy was a negative in Aristotle's mindset. He believed it to be a chaotic rule

THE EVERYTHING PHILOSOPHY BOOK

of the masses, just as oligarchy means a rule by a few rich elitists. America is a constitutional republic, not a democracy.

Art and Drama

Aristotle differed from Plato in yet another area: art appreciation. Imitation is the sincerest form of flattery, and humankind likes representations of reality from everything from Manet and Monet to Elvis on velvet and bulldogs playing poker. Aristotle, unlike Plato, did not believe that art was a weak imitation of reality (itself a weak imitation of a higher reality). Aristotle saw art as a means to enhance and idealize reality, therefore striving in our limited human way to touch the Ideal. He though it was ennobling and not a waste of time.

In drama, Aristotle believed that comedy helped people see human absurdity and foolishness and tragedy in the classical sense allowed the audience to achieve a catharsis—that is, a cleansing emotional response within the safe confines of the Greek amphitheater. Seeing mankind represented in all its splendor and stupidity had a therapeutic effect, according to Aristotle.

CHAPTER 3

The Decline and Fall of the Hellenistic Period

The glory days of the Greek philosophers ended with the death of Aristotle, but the intellectual life of humankind was just beginning. The four main philosophies of the Roman world (Epicureanism, Stoicism, Skepticism, and Neoplatonism) sprang from the rich Greek philosophical tradition. Though we now look to Rome, the age is still referred to as the Hellenistic (or Greek) period.

The End of Greek Prominence

The deaths of Aristotle and Alexander the Great more or less coincided with the beginning of the end of Greek prominence in world affairs. Alexander the Great, a Macedonian ruler and a former student of Aristotle, conquered most of the known world before his early death. While invaders overran the Greek world, the Greek culture and philosophical tradition survived, courtesy of Alexander's education and immersion in the Greek classics.

After Alexander's death, political chaos and plagues crippled this once thriving civilization. When the dust settled, the Roman Empire was now the predominant power in the Mediterranean. Though the Greeks were reduced to second-class citizenry in the global village, Greek philosophy, mythology, and culture influenced the Roman world. The Roman gods are simply the Greek gods with new names.

FACTS

Hellenic schools of philosophy introduced many words that have stayed with us to the present day. Epicurean, Stoic, Skeptic, and Cynic were all schools of philosophy whose names are now in common usage to describe types of personalities that are more or less similar to their philosophical forbears.

The Cynics

The Cynics were a Socratic sect who had a very radical approach to life and philosophy. The word *cynic* comes from the Greek word for "dog." It was believed that the Cynics were called this because they had a freedom of expression that was more like that of the animal kingdom than was deemed appropriate in polite society.

The Cynics were not philosophers in the sense that they put their system on papyrus. They were more a living testament to a philosophy of nonconformity. They were believed to be wandering wise guys and sarcastic stand-up comics, poking fun at the hypocrisies of society.

Stoicism, a more formal philosophy, embraced many of the tenets of the wacky Cynics.

Antisthenes

Antisthenes was the founding Cynic. He studied with the Sophist Gorgias but eventually embraced Socratic principles. Antisthenes would travel far to listen to the wise Socrates hold court. He was a shabby young man with a shaggy beard and rags for clothes. The always wise and shrewd Socrates, keen to expose pretensions, accused him of reverse narcissism and affectation with this ancient variation of the "grunge" look. Nevertheless, the Cynics who followed him also affected a dirty demeanor.

Antisthenes followed the Socratic precept that Virtue is the key to a happy life and was its own reward. He believed in a divine force that governs the universe, but this force was an amalgam of many gods; his was not a monotheistic religious view. Like many other philosophers, he believed this divine world was inherently unknowable and hence not to be given much thought.

He also practiced what he preached, living a simple and primitive lifestyle, wearing a ratty old cloak, and never shaving. Antisthenes was rebelling against what he felt were the extravagances of his age. Cynics were, in many ways, the hippies of the Hellenistic era.

Diogenes

Diogenes was the most famous of the Cynics. He desperately wanted to be a disciple of Antisthenes, but the latter initially chased him out of his house with a stick. Antisthenes was eventually charmed by Diogenes's dogged desire to study under the master, so he was accepted into the Cynical fold.

Diogenes lived the life of a homeless man, wearing tattered robes, begging for food, sleeping on the street, and occasionally in a pithos, which is a large tub or barrel. As an old man, he was on a sea voyage when he was captured by pirates and sold into slavery. On the auction block, he announced that he was a natural leader, so he should be purchased by someone who wanted a master. A wealthy man in the crowd found this to be hilarious and promptly bought him, freed him, and made Diogenes the tutor of his children. During this period, it is said that he met Alexander the Great, and the eccentric Cynic asked the world conqueror to move because he was blocking the sun. This apparently thoroughly charmed Alexander.

If all these anecdotes seem like tall tales, they very well may be. Poets and playwrights such as Juvenal and Plutarch recounted much these long after the fact. Even the story of Diogenes's death may be apocryphal. Legend has it he lived to the ripe old age of ninety, and the monument of a dog was erected at his gravesite.

Epicureanism: The Pleasure Principle

Epicurus (341–270 B.C.) is perhaps one of the most misinterpreted philosophers in the pantheon of great thinkers. His name and philosophy became synonymous with wanton hedonism. The Epicurean lifestyle is widely considered to be a celebration of sensuality, the indulgence in pleasure for pleasure's sake, a shameless enjoyment in all manner of debauchery and gluttony.

True Epicureanism

The humble, quiet, and retiring Epicurus would be aghast at the revelry that went on and continues to go on in his name. While it is true that Epicurus put great stock in the pursuit of pleasure, his definition of pleasure would be more akin to the delights enjoyed by the couch potato as opposed to the libertine.

Epicurus led a restful, contemplative life, eating modestly, drinking moderately, and philosophizing for the most part from a prone position on his hammock. Though he would have considered himself an Atomist, following Democritus's dictum that reality can be reduced to indivisible particles he called atoms, science was not Epicurus's main area of interest. Epicurus can in no way be called a man of spiritual belief. His rational, Atomist mind told him that, upon death, the body is reduced to a decomposing collection of atoms that return to the earth. No mention is made of the existence of the soul after death. You were atoms, and unto atoms you shall return. Still, this did not distress Epicurus. There is no pain in nothingness, and when you're dead, you're dead. You will not be aware of it because you will no longer exist, so there is no reason to fear death.

Epicureanism actually means the opposite of its common usage today. While the original philosophy did mean a pursuit of pleasure, pleasure was defined as moderation, reading, and introspection, not the sensual indulgences that the word implies today.

The religious leaders of the day thought Epicurus's philosophy carried with it the whiff of atheism. Epicureans steadfastly denied their fearless leader's lack of religiosity. This controversy may explain while almost none of his writing survives today, and we must rely on secondhand sources. When Christianity became the pre-eminent faith and philosophy of the Roman Empire, it is possible that the early Church fathers, in their never-ending quest to stamp out heresy, may have tried to consign Epicurus to the ash heap of history.

The Role of the Senses

Epicurus believed that everything we know we get from the senses alone, and he thought the senses are trustworthy, unlike the Skeptics, who held precisely the opposite opinion.

La dolce vita was the name of the game for Epicurus: Living the good life was what it was all about. He felt that mankind's modus operandi should be the pursuit of pleasure and the avoidance of pain.

Epicurus believed that desires could be divided into the following categories:

- Natural desires that are essential and mandatory for survival (food and shelter)
- Natural desires that you can live without (sex)
- Narcissistic desire (wealth and fame) that should be avoided

The natural desires are relatively easy to satisfy, and the vain desires are difficult to achieve and indicative of a shallow personality. The vain desires should be expunged from your character because they are an obstacle to true inner peace.

Leisure Time

Epicurus also was a big proponent of quiet time, pleasant conversation with a small circle of like-minded friends, and the joys of reading. The pleasures of sex were, for the most part, to be avoided, because its charms usually come at an exacting price. The rocky road of romance is fraught with many minefields, and the potential for profound angst and crushing heartbreak was not worth the effort, as far as Epicurus was concerned. Such anxiety would interfere with his quest for inner peace. It is safe to say that he rarely, if ever, invited a guest to swing with him on his ever-present hammock.

One of the worst things you can do, according to Epicurus, is fret about the uncertain future. If we can live in the now and achieve tranquility one day at a time, then we are in the best possible "space," and the elusive yet eminently desirable *ataraxia* (inner peace) will be ours.

Justice, according to Epicurus, can be reduced to the simple adage, "do unto others." People assemble in communities to live in peace and to observe this precursor to "The Golden Rule."

One of the most important and wonderful things is friendship. The ordinarily passive Epicurus believes in laying down your life for a friend, if necessary. Friends are the only people you can count on, and they are to be held in your heart of hearts. The pleasures of sex are fleeting, while the rewards of friendship are immense.

Live Unnoticed

Epicurus was not a political animal. His definition of happiness dramatically differed from Aristotle's ethical and social activism. Epicurus saw the political life as adding to the *agita* that would detract from his serene pursuit of modest pleasures. He was a stay-at-home kind of guy.

"Live unnoticed" was a main precept of Epicureanism. He and his followers were laid-back and low profile.

Epicurus lived and died quietly in a home with a garden outside of Athens, where he received guests and taught students. The Garden and its teachings and traditions lasted for almost 500 years.

Epicurean communes were quite egalitarian. Men and women were treated as equals, and socioeconomic distinctions were ignored. Even the slaves were treated with equanimity. This was unheard of in the Greco-Roman world, and some might argue that it isn't even completely practiced today. Needless to say, they were regarded as outcasts and oddballs, but they probably did not worry too much about that because they had little use for mainstream society.

Meanwhile, over in Rome, Epicureanism was taking on a decidedly different bent—the one it continues to be known for to this day. However, whether it be an orgy in Caligula's palace or a toga-party in a contemporary frat house, those who would call themselves Epicureans bear no resemblance to the man or his philosophy.

Stoicism

Zeno of Cyprus (334–262 B.C.) founded the Stoic school. He used to lecture from his porch, called a stoa, hence the name Stoic. As was the case with the Epicureans, Stoicism took its cue from the Presocratics (as the Epicureans were Atomists, the Stoics sided with Heraclitus in the belief that everything could be reduced to fire). The word *stoic* has remained in the language and defines a person who accepts life's slings and arrows without whining about it.

Knowledge and Wisdom

A Stoic would have agreed with an Epicurean that all knowledge comes from sensory experience. They did not accept the Platonic notion of Forms. The mind is a *tabula rasa,* or blank slate, upon which experiences are imprinted. And because all knowledge is subjective, so is truth. There is no Eternal Truth in the Stoic handbook.

The Stoics saw wisdom as the greatest virtue, and from wisdom came bravery, self-restraint, and justice. There were no shades of gray in the Stoic philosophy. People are either totally good or utterly evil, completely wise or perfectly foolish. And those who decry the decline of civilization can identify with the Stoics, who were saying the same thing 2,000 years ago.

The Divine

The Stoics believed in a Divinity that shapes our ends. This Divinity, however, like the Stoics themselves, was not of the warm-fuzzy variety. It was called Logos, or Mind, and the path to happiness was to get with the Logos's program and stay on the same page with the Divine Mind. The Stoics also introduced the word *pneuma,* or breath, which is the soul of the universe. The individual souls all derive from this breathy Oversoul. This is an early form of monotheism, with a dash of Presocratic monism thrown into the mix.

Stoics put no great stock in worldly pleasures; they were a hindrance on the path to wisdom. Passionate emotions got in the way as well. They were to be kept in check. An ascetic lifestyle was the ideal. It promoted the good orderly direction and avoided distracting histrionics.

SSENTIALS

The most famous Stoic was also a Roman emperor. Marcus Aurelius was a foremost Stoic whose collection of journal entries, written in between vanquishing barbarian hordes, *Meditations*, is a quintessential distillation of Stoic thought and practice.

"Everything happens for the best, and you can usually expect the worst" was the Stoic philosophy. If a Stoic saw a loved one in peril, the response would naturally be to try to save their life. But if the attempt was unsuccessful and the loved one perished—*c'est la vie!* Because the Divine governs all, and the person died, then this death must have been for the best. To respond with sadness would be illogical. If you have done your best in this world and you still fail, so be it. Doing your best is its own reward.

The Stoic Ideal

The Stoics took a principle of Aristotle to an extreme degree. Aristotle said that passions have their place in the human psyche, but that reason should rule. The Stoics, on the other hand, saw the passionate side of human nature as evil and something to be eradicated. In later centuries, modern psychologists like Freud and Jung would see this as an impossibility, and an unhealthy thing to even attempt. You can never rid yourself of these impulses and if you try, they will only lay dormant, poised to surface at inappropriate moments.

For the Stoic, if you were consigned to a life of suffering, you could deal with it and still live a life of goodness. In fact, you had the advantage over your wealthy counterpart, because material things often got in the way. One of the famous Stoics, Epictetus, was in fact a slave. He believed in virtue and did not lament his lot in life. He made do with the deck he was dealt, as did Marcus Aurelius, an emperor. Stoicism worked for those at both ends of the scale. Pleasure is not good. Pain is not evil. Virtue is the only good and vice the only evil. And duty is everything.

The Greek expression for negative emotions, such as fear, was *pathe*. Stoics were antipathe, and the word used to describe their approach to these emotions has come to us through the ages. The Stoics were big time advocates of apathy. The truly wise and good man was apathetic.

Stoics were also not averse to suicide under certain conditions. Seneca, the Roman playwright and noted Stoic, took his own life when he fell out of favor with the notorious emperor Nero. If you have a perfectly indifferent and apathetic outlook, which was the Stoic ideal, your life is meaningless and a small loss if it is snuffed out.

The Stoics were also pantheists. Pantheism is the belief that God is present in everything, not a bearded figure seated imperiously on his throne on the other side of the Pearly Gates.

Both the Epicureans and the Stoics sought the principle of *ataraxia*, or inner peace. The Epicureans sought it through withdrawal from society and the pursuit of pleasure. The Stoics found it in a Clint Eastwood demeanor and a grim fatalism, perceiving themselves as inconsequential cogs in a cold and indifferent mechanism. Some Stoic principles were adapted by the newly emerging religion of Christianity. Others, including pantheism and the advocacy of suicide, were obviously rejected. And, of course, Christianity found nothing nice to say about Epicureanism.

QUESTIONS?

Is Hannibal Lecter a Stoic?
Hannibal tutors Clarice in *The Silence of the Lambs* by introducing her to Stoicism 101, "First Principles, Clarice. Simplicity. Read Marcus Aurelius. Of each particular thing, ask what is it itself. What is its nature?" It would seem that even cannibals read the classics.

The person who lived the Stoic ideal to the fullest was called a Sage. A Sage was a rare bird indeed, and when discovered, followers flocked around him. Nowadays, sage simply means a wise man or woman, but the word has its genesis in the Stoic tradition.

Skepticism: Perception Is Reality

The Skeptics have also contributed a word to the English language. And the Skeptics were indeed a skeptical lot. They believed that you could not know anything about anything. The only thing you can know is what your perceptions tell you, and your perception is highly suspect and not to be trusted.

Think of it in terms of witnesses of a crime scene. One person may report having seen a culprit of medium height; another might say he was taller than average. One witness may tell the police that the suspect had brown hair; another may claim to have seen a blond-haired suspect. He fled the scene in a sky blue Audi, or was it a gray BMW? There are usually as many descriptions of such events as there are witnesses.

Consider the classic Japanese film *Rashomon*, where three different participants in a robbery and rape tell the story three different ways, each equally valid to the individual telling the story. For those of you unfamiliar with this film, you may recall the episode of *The Odd Couple* that has the same plot. This is the basic premise of Skepticism.

The founder of the Skeptic school was Pyrrho of Elis (c. 360–272 B.C.). He, like Epicurus, saw the road to happiness as doing as little as possible. Because we wander largely clueless through life, a world where black is white and day is night (or maybe not), one might as well not do much. Repose was the only recourse for the truly wise man. The only path to peace was to suspend judgment, because no worldview is any better than another. Do not believe anything you see or hear. Do not have any opinions. There is no such thing as good or evil. Rather than promote chaos and confusion, Pyrrho believed that to accept them is the only way to live. Nothing can be proved, so what is all the fuss about?

FACTS

A humorous and probably apocryphal legend has Pyrrho, founder of the Skeptics, wandering around like an ancient Mr. Magoo, oblivious to the world around him as his disciples protect him from charging chariots, wild beasts, and assorted other perils of antiquity.

Cicero and the Eclectics

Cicero was a famous Roman senator, lawyer, orator, and philosopher who lived and died during some of the most turbulent times in ancient history. In a time when power was reserved for the aristocracy, he rose from the less exalted classes to the Roman senate. He favored the Republican form of government in a society that was headed toward dictatorship. He was exiled and almost executed more than once. He witnessed the assassination of Julius Caesar and was eventually executed under the orders of Mark Antony.

Even though it was a culture in decline, Greece still had the monopoly on philosophy in the ancient world. Cicero "Romanized" the Greek philosophers in Latin translations designed to bring the classics to the Romans. It is said he was inventive in his translations, and as a lifelong lawyer and politician, he had ulterior motives in his efforts to bring philosophy, to the Roman Empire. Ever the pragmatist, he intended to use philosophy as a tool to further his political goals and advance the glory that was Rome. Though he was largely linked to the

Roman branch of Skepticism, he was also a premier practitioner of Eclecticism.

"When you eliminate the impossible, whatever remains, however improbable, must be the truth," was the philosophy of detection employed by Sherlock Holmes. This is essentially what the Eclectics had in mind. Wading through the weighty thoughts of the Epicureans, Stoics, and Skeptics, the Eclectics sought to find Truth amidst that conflicting jumble. Cicero examined the major philosophies of the day and, politician that he was, selected his belief systems from the philosophical salad bar.

QUESTIONS?

Who were the Eclectics?
The Eclectics, as the name suggests, were a group of thinkers who picked and chose from a variety of philosophical schools of thought, in an effort to devise a new and improved philosophy.

Cicero had little use for Epicureanism. And that makes sense. Why would a career politician embrace a philosophy that calls for a rejection of public life and recommends a life of anonymous and quiet contemplation? In fact, Cicero was largely responsible, through his translations, for the misrepresentation of Epicurean thought, giving it its undeserved reputation as a coven of party animals.

Cicero embraced certain aspects of Stoic teaching when it came to politics. The extreme Skeptic advocates total inaction, because one cannot trust his own perceptions, and that, of course, is anathema to a politico. So Cicero took one from Column A and one from Column B in his philosophy.

Cicero believed that chaos would ensue if everyone casually did his own thing and did not wholeheartedly embrace the rule of law. There would be no Roman Empire if people did that, and Cicero was a Roman first, philosopher a distant second. Hence, when it was convenient, the heck with the Skeptics—it was time for a little good old-fashioned Stoicism. It was often, however, Stoicism according to Cicero. He incorporated the Roman gods and the active role they played in human affairs, bestowing blessings and afflicting punishment. And he endorsed the pursuit of pleasure in moderation as opposed to the ideal of ascetic self-denial. Of course, Cicero was diluting the message by adapting it to his own ends. This adaptation of philosophy is not unlike our old friends, the Sophists. Sophistry is almost as eternal as one of Plato's Forms. It appears in many faces and guises through the millennia, whether it be in ancient Greece or Rome, right up to and including the current sociocultural climate.

Neoplatonism: End of an Epoch

Plotinus of Alexandria (A.D. 205–270) was the founder of Neoplatonist thought. He established a school in Rome. Neoplatonism was the last shout of ancient Greek philosophizing. It, as the name suggests, relied heavily on the teaching of Plato and lasted well into the sixth century A.D. It spoke of the dichotomy between the spirit and the flesh. And it was a belief designed to help you prepare to meet your maker, which in its interpretation was a perfect divinity, the One.

It sounds like Christianity, doesn't it? However, Neoplatonism was pagan monotheism, and it was major competition to Christianity. Christianity won out eventually, of course, but Neoplatonism gave it a run for its money.

Neoplatonists believed that the One blesses creation with Nous (divine intelligence), and this animates the universe. Human souls are parts of this universal soul, just as cells in the body, and are created in the image of the One. Sounds like "God created Man in his own image," doesn't it? God is an unknowable mystery beyond human understanding, and we must have faith. Again, this is very familiar to Christian precepts. No wonder there was a hostile rivalry and also a cross-pollinating of ideas. Augustine, later St. Augustine, acknowledged the influence of Neoplatonism in the shaping of his theology.

In a world where religion was poised to become the driving force in shaping world affairs, Neoplatonism was a bridge between the old and the new. It was a combination of the principles of Plato and the influence of eastern religions and the emerging Christian Church.

CHAPTER 4
The Medieval Mind

When the Roman Empire fell in A.D. 476, the subsequent Dark Ages were not a time when philosophy thrived. To say that life was nasty, brutish, and short would be an understatement. Rome was Christianized in A.D. 313, and the giant shadow of this new and fast-growing faith loomed ominously over independent thinkers.

The Christian Church and Philosophy

During the Dark Ages, the Christian Church firmly established itself as the pre-eminent religion of the Western world. Christianity is a theology that professes a *dogma*. Dogma is a doctrine of belief presented as absolute truth in an authoritarian manner.

The rise to prominence of the Christian Church can be divided into three periods:

- The Evangelization Period, as the name suggests, was when the faith spread through the known world by missionaries. The word by and large spread like wildfire, ultimately becoming the official Church of Rome, formerly its chief nemesis.
- The Patristic Period comprises the second through the eighth centuries. The Church leaders codified and systematized church dogma. They picked a wealth of gospels (chronicles of the life of Jesus) and chose four "official" gospels. Depending on your bent, the Church was either "defending" itself against the pagans and the heretics or crushing all those who disagreed with them by branding them as blasphemers and lighting a fire under their bad heathen selves.
- The Scholastic Period lasted from approximately the ninth to the sixteenth century. In this period, Christian philosophy evolved, based on Platonic and Aristotelian principles, and yet designed to be harmonious with Church dogma. This synthesis between philosophy and theology was the main school of thought of the Medieval Age and forever changed the world.

FACTS

Scholasticism began at the University of Paris and Oxford University in England. The rallying cry was "Learn everything," a noble and open-minded goal. These universities established first courses of study from which modern liberal arts programs are derived. It was in these schools that the shift from Plato to Aristotle took place.

Augustine of Hippo

During this time, many a philosopher prudently kept his thoughts to himself. However, some deep thinkers appeared in those dark days. The first major philosopher of the Christian era was Augustine of Hippo (A.D. 354–430). He was born and died in the last days of the Roman Empire, and he serves as a bridge between the classical and the medieval worlds.

His Background

Augustine was a pagan born in North Africa who, though a scholar and a teacher, led the life of a libertine in his misspent youth. He was not without guilt and he wrestled with his sensual nature, embracing a faith called Manichaeanism. Manichaeanism was an amalgam of Christian and Persian philosophies and emphasized the eternal struggle between good and evil. Augustine's candid autobiography, *Confessions,* chronicles his struggles in this arena and contains the famous and ironic prayer, "God grant me chastity . . . but not yet."

As Augustine got a little older, Manichaeanism no longer satisfied him, and he began to study Neoplatonism, the popular rival of early Christianity. He eventually converted to Christianity, became a priest, and was ultimately installed as the Bishop of Hippo, in what is now Algeria in North Africa.

As is always the case, once a thing becomes institutionalized, it becomes stale and rigid over time. Such was the fate of Scholasticism. It would get quite a shake-up, however, and old Plato would get a revival of his own, as the Middle Ages drew to a close.

Augustine used Neoplatonic philosophy to defend, endorse, and affirm Christian theology. Philosophy and faith would be intermingled throughout the Middle Ages. Augustine attempted to explain some of the many mysteries of Christianity through the philosophies of Plato. Of course, he adapted Platonic principles to neatly fit into Christian dogma. Remember, he was operating from a faith-based starting point, and for him, the precepts of Holy Mother Church were inviolate. That was the starting point for his philosophy and not a source of speculation, rumination, or debate. Augustine sought to "Christianize" Plato, just as a future philosopher-saint, Thomas Aquinas, sought to Christianize Aristotle.

Plato spoke of the Forms, Eternal Truths, and The Good; Augustine says they all spring forth from God. More important than speculation and intellectual pursuits, there must be divine illumination. In other words, Augustine believed that real insight does not come from mankind's brainpower alone. A little divine intervention goes a long way.

God and Free Will

One of the age-old enigmas that has had theologians and laymen alike scratching their heads is this: If God is all knowing and all-powerful, how does this gibe with the notion of free will and the existence of evil in the world? If God knows in advance what people will do and allows it to happen, then God allows evil to exist and people should not be held responsible for their actions, for those actions existed in the mind of God eons before they were born.

Augustine suggests that time, as we measure it, is meaningless to God. God exists in an Eternal realm where linear time has no meaning. There is no past and no future. There is only an Eternal Present, the Big Now.

In today's hectic world, it is fashionable for the New Age sages to exhort us to "live in the moment." People often try in vain to stay in the now. Yesterday is history, and tomorrow is a mystery, the old adage tells us. According to Augustine, this is God's natural state. Linear time is an illusion and a limitation that does not afflict God. God's infinite wisdom and omniscience has no bearing on our free will. Personal responsibility still rules in the human condition. Yet God is there to guide us if we seek Him out. Hence, we can only take partial credit when we are good and assume all the blame when we are evil.

Original Sin

Given his lustful youth, Augustine was keenly aware of the sins of the flesh. He was a firm believer in Original Sin. Original Sin is, of course, the unwelcome gift bestowed upon us by Adam and Eve in the Garden, as described in the Old Testament's Book of Genesis. Eve ate the apple at the prompting of that snake, Satan. Augustine, while endorsing the concept of Original Sin, has a different take on the nature of evil.

Again, the big question is this: If a perfect and perfectly good God created the world, how can such rampant naughtiness flourish? Taking a page from Plato, Augustine espoused that evil is not a diabolical force ravaging the souls of the sinful, but rather the absence of good.

FACTS

Augustine, later St. Augustine, was the first Christian philosopher and theologian who sought to take the philosophy of Plato and, in essence, Christianize it to conform to Church dogma. He was a libertine in his youth and is famous for the prayer, "God grant me chastity . . . but not yet."

Not every Christian agrees with this idea. Even today, depending on whom you talk to, modern Christians still maintain that Hell is either the fire-and-brimstone inferno of legend or merely the absence of God. The inability to bask in the warmth and love of God for eternity is in itself a terrifying and abysmal prospect to men and women of faith. We have the free will to embrace the light, and if we eschew its beacon and skulk in the darkness of sin and despond, we have no one to blame but ourselves. Such is the price of free will. Just as goodness is its own reward, sin is its own punishment—a descent into the maelstrom of nothingness—because, according to Augustine, sin, the absence of good, is a terrible void. The sinner is more harmed than anyone he may afflict through his actions, and it is only through God's grace that we can be saved.

Anselm's Ontological Argument

Anselm of Canterbury (1033–1109) was a Benedictine monk and teacher who ultimately became the Archbishop of Canterbury, the highest religious office in England. He is the most significant philosopher of his century. He sought to distinguish between philosophy and theology. The famous maxim of Anselm was "Credo ut intelligam," which means "I believe that I may understand." Faith comes first; understanding the world around you is secondary and must be infused with faith in order to truly get to the bottom of things.

Anselm continued the faith-based philosophy of Augustine and took it to the next level. He is most famous for his argument which "proves" the existence of God. This argument has fascinated the philosophers that followed Anselm. It is called Anselm's Ontological Argument. The word "ontological" is defined as "Of or relating to the argument for the existence of God holding that the existence of the concept of God entails the existence of God." In other words, thinking about it makes it so.

Anselm starts off with a quote from Psalm 14: "Fools say in their hearts, 'There is no god.'" Anselm then says that even a fool can conceive of the notion of something "than which nothing greater can be conceived." If it can be conceived in the mind of man, it can exist. Even a fool, or a heretic, has some conception of what God might be like. Naturally, for the sake of argument, they called God the most perfect being that could possibly exist. Anselm is suggesting that there is an inherent contradiction in denying the existence of God. In order to deny the existence of God, we must have a conception of what God is. If the limited mind of man can speculate on the existence of so perfect a being, then that said being must in fact exist.

Thomas Aquinas

Thomas Aquinas (1225–1274) was a primary Catholic thinker who sought to Christianize Aristotle just as Augustine adapted Neoplatonism. He also, to the satisfaction of many, reconciled the dilemma of Faith versus Reason.

Augustinian thinking was the accepted school of the day, and it did not see any distinction between philosophy and theology, yet steadfastly stuck to the theory of illumination. In other words, divine intervention was necessary for profound intellectual advancements.

Thomas Aquinas rejected both illumination and the Double Truth. In regard to Averroism, he believed that religion and reason did not each represent a separate truth. There cannot be two opposing and competing truths—there is one Truth. Philosophy and theology are not in opposition; they are on parallel courses. Some things are self-evident, and others require a leap of faith.

The Averroist theory of the Double Truth stated that philosophy and theology were mutually exclusive. There is truth that comes from philosophy, and the truth that comes from theology, but they are parallel truths.

Thomas Aquinas gave more credit to the human intellect than Augustine did. Mankind did not need divine intervention to think profound thoughts. One can ascertain the Form by observation of the reality. We can conceive of the exalted notions of Truth and Beauty without a celestial nudge. In fact, mankind cannot truly grasp the Forms, because like Aristotle, Thomas Aquinas felt the Form was embedded in the corporeal reality and was not a free-floating entity out there in the ether. Harkening back to Aristotle, and with a little Christian pride, Thomas Aquinas believed that if a "pagan" like Aristotle can figure all this out, Christians certainly could. Old Aristotle did not have the advantage of divine assistance, pagan that he was.

Another welcome contribution of Thomas Aquinas was his holistic approach to the body-mind-spirit that makes a human being. There was less of "the spirit is willing, but the flesh is weak" thinking in his philosophy than in Augustine's and Plato's.

Thomas Aquinas also postulated five ways that we can prove the existence of God:

- Motion is a reality, at least to human perception. For every motion, there is a prior impetus that set it in motion. Go back far enough, and you have the Primary Mover. This is God.
- Similarly, new things come into being all the time. For each of these events, there must be a cause. Regress cause after cause until you get to the first. There you will find God.

- All things change, and all things are contingent upon something else for their existence. Ultimately there will be something original that is not contingent on anything else for its existence. Therein lies God.
- Thomas Aquinas suggests that you take a look around you and note that there is an inherent perfection to the nature of things, to greater and lesser degrees. There must be something that is purely perfect, from which all other things descend in a perfection pecking order. Mr. Perfect himself is God.
- Order exists everywhere. There is a profound order to the universe. Ergo, there must exist an intelligence responsible for this magnificent orderliness. This is God.

Motion, cause, contingency, perfection, and order are Thomas Aquinas's five proofs for the existence of God. Many have disagreed with it, but it was a big hit in its day.

Thomas Aquinas did for Aristotle what Augustine did for Plato, making the "pagan" philosopher appear to seamlessly blend right in with the teachings of the Christian Church. Aquinas is regarded by many as the man who successfully ended the discrepancy between faith and reason.

In addition to the dilemma of Faith versus Reason, the other problem in medieval philosophy was the problem of the Universals. Universals are Aristotle's attempt to make sense of the Platonic Forms. Plato believed that Forms were divine entities (called Truth, Beauty, and so on) that are floating around out there in the ether, and that earthly notions of truth and beauty are mere shadows of the forms. Aristotle felt that there were Universals within substantial objects, and that these Universals were not separate entities.

Because much of the classical writings of Plato and Aristotle were lost during the Dark and Middle Ages, to be rediscovered later during the Renaissance, the medieval philosophers were debating this notion all over again. Aquinas comes to the same conclusion as Aristotle, some 900 years later.

Aquinas also concurs with the Aristotelian view that physical reality is simultaneously composed of both its actuality (what it is) and potentiality (what it will become). This is an Aristotelian/Aquinian principle. Also, physical reality is composed of both matter and form—Aristotle's Universals theory.

Aquinas divided knowledge into two stages, sensitive and intelligent. Sensitive knowledge is simple awareness of something, such as a rock. Intelligence is grasping the abstract concept of "rock." He divided intelligence into three processes: abstraction, judgment, and reasoning.

Though Aquinas died young (he was only fifty), his legacy in both philosophy and theology is significant. His body of work is enormous, as was his physical girth. Rewarded posthumously with sainthood by the Catholic Church, even secular humanists continue to marvel at his keen intellect and contribution to philosophy.

John Duns Scotus

There were other contributors to the expansion of the medieval mind. One of them was John Duns Scotus (c. 1265–1308) He was nicknamed The Subtle Doctor.

Scotus was a Franciscan monk who endorsed many of the precepts of Augustine, yet differed on other key elements, including the necessity of "illumination." Humans have the intellect to comprehend God and his wonders without a celestial cheat sheet. Being a cleric and a man of his time, dogma rules as far as Scotus is concerned. He spins the notion of Universals by suggesting that they exist as Forms (to be found in the mind of God) and as part of the physical things they represent (as perceived in the mind of man). Aquinas has the intellect pre-eminent over the human will; Scotus said that will is more important than intellect. This led to a great medieval debate known as the Thomist-Scotist controversy.

Roger Bacon

Another important philosopher of the age was Roger Bacon (c. 1214–1294). Bacon was a Franciscan monk who is regarded as a forerunner of the modern scientist. He sought to incorporate the academic disciplines of mathematics and language into theology and philosophy though his book *Opus Major*.

Bacon proposed that there are three ways to gain knowledge: authority, reason, and experience. He breaks experience into the realms of the internal and external. External experience is awareness of physical reality and the world of the senses. Internal experience is similar to Augustine's "illumination," a little help from the person upstairs.

William of Ockham

William of Ockham (c. 1300–1349) is most famous for the theory known as Ockham's Razor. This is the belief that when all is said and done in this crazy world, the simplest answer is usually the right one.

 **SSENTIALS**

Ockham's Razor, simply put, is the belief that when all things are considered, the simplest explanation is the truest one. This theory is reiterated numerous times in the Jodie Foster science-fiction movie *Contact*.

In a little more detail, what Ockham was saying—and it was a radical viewpoint to have in the Middle Ages—was that the Platonic Forms and Aristotelian Universals were a lot of nonsense. There is a physical reality of concrete things, both animate and inanimate. They exist in and of themselves. Any significance or importance that humans assign them comes solely from the human mind. Any knowledge to be acquired from man would be from direct sensory experiences and certain logical conclusions, like the instinctual sense not to step off a cliff or stick your hand in a fire. This philosophy was a form of nominalism. *Nominalism* means that things like Universals and Forms are names that man gives things after the fact. They are not pre-existing entities.

This very contemporary belief had Ockham skirting the peripheries of heresy throughout his lifetime. He was, however, a devout Christian who defied the worldliness of the papacy of his day and believed in a draconian vow of poverty in the style of St. Francis of Assisi. He also had other very forward thinking and hence heretical views, including the following:

- The Church was not infallible.
- A pope should be able to be impeached.
- Women should be permitted to play a more active role in Church affairs.
- Rulers and royalty are not there by divine right and should get the boot if they become tyrants.

William of Ockham had the misfortune of succumbing to the Black Plague, but had he not, these views may have guaranteed him a more fiery fate.

CHAPTER 5

The Renaissance Period

Europe emerged from the dismal Dark Ages into the Renaissance Period with a big bang. Within a generation, an explosive transformation of consciousness and creativity occurred, ushering in the modern age. The big names of antiquity were revived and revered all over again.

Creativity Abounds

During the Renaissance, advancements in all areas and disciplines were nothing short of quantum leaps out of the depths of medievalism into the heights of human potential. The list of giants who enriched the world during the Renaissance is an impressive who's who of genius: Leonardo da Vinci, Michelangelo, Galileo, Christopher Columbus, and Shakespeare, to name just a few.

And not only the mind of man was expanded. The New World was discovered, leading to unprecedented economic potential and a race to exploit the natural resources of paradise, forever to the detriment of the natives.

Neoplatonism ruled, for the second time since the original Plato philosophized. Greater contact with the Byzantine Empire and the Far East allowed for increased exposure to the ancient classics by the Europeans. More of these texts survived in the East, having been spared the destructive barbarian hordes and the draconian censorship of the emerging Church.

The philosophy of Aristotle and his followers received renewed interest, as did that of the Stoics, the Epicureans, the Atomists, and just about every famous philosophy from the philosophical golden age. There was little in the way of a new philosophical movement during the Renaissance. The intellectual genesis that was the Renaissance was imbued with the classical concepts, and as it grew and reached maturity, Western thinkers began to proffer bold new visions about mankind, the universe, and our place therein.

Cosimo de Medici

The notorious Florentine politico Cosimo de Medici founded a Platonic Academy wherein the most famous alumnus, a philosopher called Marsilio Ficino, wrote a volume called the *Platonic Theology*. Ficino argued that Plato was a kind of pagan saint, a heathen harbinger of the Christian principles that were to follow. This is similar to the writings and teachings of St. Augustine, another formidable Plato-phile. The Catholic Church has a tradition of sanctifying mere mortals. People are posthumously made saints and prayed to as if they were demigods. So it is not surprising that a Renaissance Catholic might want to ascribe an otherworldly quality to one of the great thinkers of the classical age.

Nicholas of Cusa

Nicholas of Cusa (1401–1464) challenged the rigidity of Scholasticism. He theorized that there are three stages to knowledge. He called two of the three fantasy and reason and found them lacking. Cusa, a Cardinal of the Church, called the third form of knowledge *intellective,* which he describes as divinely inspired intuition. Similarly to Augustine, Cusa believed true knowledge needs a divine jumpstart.

FACTS

Despite the advances of the Renaissance, it was not a barrel of laughs for most people. Life was nasty, brutish, and short for the majority of the populace. The Black Plague alone wiped out a third of the people of Europe.

Nicholas of Cusa employed a paradox that he called *learned ignorance.* It is a Renaissance spin on Socrates's belief that the wise man is only wise when he admits to himself that he really knows nothing at all. Cusa said that God was an essentially unknowable entity. How can mere humans comprehend the ultimately perfect being? Yet he also claimed that God was the only truth in town, the only thing we could truly rely on.

Bernardino Telesio

Bernardino Telesio (1509–1588) divided reality between the concepts of matter and force. Like the Monists of antiquity, he reduced things to the simple elements of heat and cold. Life thrives on heat and knowledge is gained through turning up the heat. The inherent flaw in this argument is that, according to Telesio, Albert Einstein is hotter than Jennifer Lopez, a philosophical absurdity if ever there was one.

Giordano Bruno

Giordano Bruno (1548–1600) was an Italian priest who adapted and expanded upon the astronomy of Copernicus. (You can find out more about Copernicus and the Scientific Revolution a little later.) In brief, the theory is *heliocentric,* meaning that the Earth was not the center of the universe. This theory, now a matter of fact, maintained that the Earth and the other planets revolved around the sun. This theory challenged the accepted belief that went back to ancient times and was an adamantine dogmatic doctrine of the Catholic Church. Of Copernicus, Galileo, and Bruno (the first two being more familiar names to modern readers), Bruno bore the brunt of the Church's formidable wrath.

ALERT

Heliocentricism says that the sun is the center of the solar system and the Earth and other planets revolve around it. This theory is now accepted as fact, but a few hundred years ago, you could have been burned at the stake for teaching it.

Though he was not part of the Protestant Reformation, Bruno was highly critical of Catholic dogma, a most dangerous view to be voiced in those days. In addition to the belief that the sun was the center of the solar system and the Earth and the other planets revolved around it, Bruno posited that there were an infinite number of solar systems supporting an infinite number of planets, many of which supported life, both like and unlike life on Earth.

A radical notion? It is the commonly accepted belief today. Both scientists and the public at large readily accept that we are very likely not alone in the vast universe.

Bruno's views on the cosmos are being validated by modern science. He was way ahead of his time, not a household name like the more famous Galileo, and there have been many attempts over the centuries to discredit him and dismiss him as simply a Renaissance magician. While it is true he had a great interest in magic, there was a scientific method to this magus. Bruno believed that there were more things in Heaven and Earth, as the poet said. There were unseen elements and untapped energies governing the cosmos that, if comprehended and perhaps even harnessed, could have world-transforming results. Unfortunately, there were established political and religions institutions who were quite cozy in their exalted and controlling status quo and who did not take kindly to the notion of a transformed world. Giordano Bruno was imprisoned by the Catholic Church, tortured, and eventually burned at the stake for his beliefs. Such was sadly and often the case for great thinkers who wanted to push the envelope of human knowledge and achievement.

Bruno's statement that someone who fancies himself a philosopher must be ready to doubt everything ranks up there along with Socrates's "Know thyself" and "An unexamined life is not worth living" as a cardinal rule for a philosopher to live by. It was later made better known by Descartes many decades later.

Niccolò Machiavelli

The name Niccolò Machiavelli (1469–1527) conjures all manner of unethical political chicanery. The man's name has entered the vernacular with a decidedly unsavory definition. He has been reviled by many, studied by as many more, and no doubt publicly disavowed by those who clandestinely practice his principles.

SSENTIALS

Machiavellianism, named for the Renaissance political philosopher Niccolo Machiavelli, has come to mean any form of political ruthlessness wherein the end justifies the means. It has a thoroughly negative connotation these days and is hurled as an epithet to attack one's opponents.

His political philosophy can be reduced to the credo, "The end justifies the means." Machiavelli rejected the Platonic and Aristotelian notions of the ideal state as fanciful and unattainable. He also believed that the infusion of a Christian ethos into the mix was impractical and counterproductive. His most famous work, *The Prince,* is a basic primer for the Renaissance ruler and has been studied by everyone from the Robber Barons to Wall Street yuppies.

According to Machiavelli, power and control were the objectives of a prince, not compassion and justice. Lying was perfectly acceptable; arguing about what the definition of "is" is would be just fine. The name of the game was to do what thou wilt and not get caught. Inspiring respect was secondary to instilling fear. Of course, the argument is that all this is done for the greater good of the citizenry.

The Prince should not be without ethics, Machiavelli maintained, but they were not ethics of the Christian perspective. Patriotism was the premier morality of the Prince, and "my country right or wrong" meant wrongdoing was perfectly all right if it furthered the goals of the state.

Shakespeare's Richard III boasts that he can "set the murderous Machiavel [sic] to school." There is no evidence that Machiavelli ever killed anyone, but this homage from the venerable Bard of Avon a few short decades after Machiavelli's death indicates how fast the political philosopher's reputation had grown and how his name became synonymous with all things unsavory.

CHAPTER 6
Humanism

Humanism was a philosophy that took a page from the Stoic songbook, in that it posited, though not quite, that man is the measure of all things—not quite because Holy Mother Church still ruled the societal roost, and those who defied the Old World Order still found themselves in danger of being branded heretics.

What's It All About?

If you've taken a Humanities class, you can thank the Humanists for the introduction of those courses into the curriculum. Humanists stressed history, literature, philosophy, and other liberal arts, particularly the study of new translations of ancient texts. The classical world of ancient Greece and Rome was rediscovered and celebrated. Just as the medieval mind fell in love with Aristotle as interpreted by Aquinas and the scholastics that followed him, so the Humanists loved Old Plato, and he enjoyed a renaissance of his own thousands of years after his death.

ESSENTIALS

Humanism is the belief in, and celebration of, the potential and abilities of man, without dependence on divine intervention to solve our problems.

There was much resistance to the introduction of these courses into the great universities of the day. Scholasticism stressed theology, medicine, and the law, and the Humanists sought to broaden the educational spectrum. Innovative thought was stagnating in the stodgy groves of academe, where the Scholastics reigned supreme, and they had to be dragged kicking and screaming into the fifteenth century.

Francesco Petrarca

One of the first and most famous proponents of Humanism was Francesco Petrarca, more commonly known as Petrarch (1304–1374). Petrarch actually predates the official Renaissance by a few years, but his influence helped shaped the coming rebirth.

FACTS

Francesco Petrarca was also a poet who created the *sonnet,* the poetical format of fourteen rhyming lines also used to great effect by Chaucer, Shakespeare, and others.

Petrarch and his disciples spearheaded the renewed interest in the classics, ushering in the era of Renaissance Humanism. Lest we think Humanism and Christianity were mutually exclusive, two of the most famous Humanists were also devout Catholics.

Desiderius Erasmus

Desiderius Erasmus (1466–1536) was a Dutch Humanist. He was also the illegitimate son of a priest who in turn became a priest. Erasmus was well aware of the circumstances from which he sprang, and, though a priest, he satirized and condemned the hypocrisies of his time in his book *In Praise of Folly* and essays that comprise his *Colloquia*. In fact, the priestly life was not to his liking, so he looked for a regular job where he could don civilian garb. He ultimately needed permission from the pope himself to live and work as a secular humanist and humorist. He also is famous for his Latin and Greek translation of the New Testament.

Erasmus was a premier tutor, scholar, and professor and knew most of the great thinkers of his day. He was ahead of his time in that, in addition to his social satire and calls for reform, he also wrote treatises against the severe discipline of children and advocated adding physical education into school curricula. Because he never renounced the Catholic Church, when Martin Luther and the Reformation were in full swing, he ended up being embraced by neither side. The Church saw him as a gifted royal pain, and the reformers saw him as an apologist for an outdated and corrupt institution. His work eventually ended on the Church's notorious Index of Forbidden Books. Fortunately for Erasmus, he didn't lose his head for his heady arguments, unlike his contemporary and friend Sir Thomas More.

Sir Thomas More

Some may say you have lost your head if you are willing to die for a principle, but Thomas More (1478–1535) is best known for doing just that. His satirical work, *Utopia*, describes life in the titular and imaginary island where, to quote Mr. Spock's favorite axiom, "The needs of the many outweigh the needs of the few, or the one." He was contrasting what is an ideal communist state with the inequities of his own society. Of course, no such perfect communist state has ever existed and probably never will. The communist countries that emerged and collapsed in the twentieth century were the brutal and barbaric totalitarian antithesis of this idyllic ideal.

To learn more about the tribulations and the trial of Thomas More, rent the 1966 version of *A Man for All Seasons* at your local video store. The Oscar-winning film entertainingly tells the inspiring story of a man who took his ethical code very seriously, paying the ultimate price for his convictions.

More studied Greek, Latin, and law, but also wrote comedies and was interested in the humanities. He attempted to live within a monastic order but gave that up after about four years. He eschewed ascetic self-denial for the very worldly realm of politics. He became a member of England's House of Commons and eventually an intimate of King Henry VIII.

Mutual admiration between the two men turned sour when More refused to side with Henry when the monarch sought to divorce his wife, Catherine of Aragon, and marry Anne Boylen. Henry's first wife could not have children, and Henry wanted a male heir to his throne.

Catholic law, of course, forbade divorce, and the pope had refused to accommodate the King in this matter. More, a devout Catholic, would not defy the Church and was beheaded for his beliefs. The Catholic Church canonized him 400 years later, a symbolic pat on his back for a job well done.

Henry VIII defied the Catholic Church and thus the Church of England was established. A faith founded on the fact that a man wanted a divorce might seem to be a faith built on a foundation of sand, but in truth the winds of Reformation had been stirring for some time, and the resultant tsunami reshaped the face of Christendom.

CHAPTER 7

The Protestant Reformation

The growing celebration of the individual that was Humanism and the less than holy conduct of the Renaissance papacy conspired to create a schism among Christians. Throughout the Dark and Middle Ages, one Church grew into a sociopolitical entity of pre-eminent influence in Europe.

The Fall of the Catholic Church

The Catholic Church had the monopoly on God, and its leaders sought to monopolize all other aspects of culture as well. Kings bowed before popes, and those who dared defy the Church were threatened with the awful specter of excommunication. An excommunicated Catholic in those days was the ultimate pariah, a spiritual leper to be shunned in this life and consigned to the infernal regions in the next. In order words, one did not mess with the Holy Mother Church.

ALERT

The Protestant Reformation was in part a response to the rampant corruption that had spread through the papacy. Martin Luther was outraged by the selling of indulgences—in other words, paying a monetary fee for the sacrament of confession.

The Renaissance made Europeans a little cocky, and they started to openly disagree with many of the papal practices of the day. One of the more outrageous examples of the abuse of religious authority was the selling of indulgences. The Catholic Church has a sacrament called Confession (nowadays given the more hip and politically correct name of Reconciliation), and it was, for most of the millennium, offered free of charge to those who sought to remain in God's good graces. This started to change during the Renaissance when the Church needed money to fund its various enterprises.

Martin Luther

Martin Luther (1483–1546) testily bristled at what he saw as egregious injustices enacted by the Church. He felt that the message was obscured by men with earthly ambitions and goals and decidedly secular desires. Luther emphasized the "internal experience" of faith. In other words, these bejeweled, well-to-do middlemen who lived in ornate palaces were muddying the spiritual waters. Luther sought an ecumenical downsizing by eliminating the middlemen. The individual could have a direct experience with God through prayer, meditation, and going back to basics. In other words, everything you need to know is in the Old and New Testament, and thanks to Gutenberg and his moveable type, the Bible was now available to the masses.

Luther had other problems with the Church, and these were removed from the table in the Protestant tradition. Less attention was given to the tradition of the Virgin Mary. She does not hold the special place of reverence in the Protestant tradition that she does in the hearts of Catholics. Luther also did not buy the notion of the transubstantiation of the Eucharist (that the bread and wine transforms into the literal body and blood of Christ during Mass). Luther believed it was a symbolic ritual. And then there was the vow of celibacy. Luther eventually left his religious order, married an ex-nun, and had a family.

FACTS

An interesting note about Luther and Calvin is their contribution to their respective languages. This was an age where the educated spoke Latin. With the Humanist movement and the Reformation, nations came to celebrate their uniqueness and their languages. Luther and Calvin's voluminous writings in their native languages helped contributed to the evolution of modern German and French.

The Church did not take Luther seriously at first. The Pope could not be bothered with "a monk's quarrel," as he called it. The Church regarded itself as untouchable. It took three years to respond to Luther after he nailed his written protests on the door of his local church. But it was too little too late. The winds of change were sweeping across Europe. Backed by German and other Northern European princes and politicians who stood to benefit in the power and financial arenas by a break with Rome, the Reformation was a crusading juggernaut.

John Calvin

In France, another radical reformer was raising a ruckus. His philosophy not only reshaped religion, but also influenced economic thinking for all time. John Calvin (1509–1564) was a French theologian and humanist who joined the Reformation bandwagon and was influential in much more than spiritual pursuits. When he embraced the reform movement and began to write extensively about his beliefs, he was forced to live a life on the run to avoid angry church fathers. His seminal tract *Institutes of the Christian Religion* cemented his reputation as a major proponent of Protestantism.

QUESTIONS?

What is predestination?
Predestination is the belief, put forth by Protestant Reformer John Calvin, that God has already decided in advance who goes to Heaven and who goes to Hell, and nothing you can do in this life will change that. Consequently, followers of Calvin became austere, industrious, and frugal.

Like Luther, Calvin emphasized the individual's spiritual experience and reiterated that everything you need to know can be found in the Scriptures, unfiltered by Catholic dogma. Calvin, like Luther, believed in a literal interpretation of the Bible. He felt that not only the religious institutions should be guided by this principle, but also society as a whole should be structured around and held accountable to a literal interpretation of the Scriptures. This is called a *theocracy,* or a government ruled by religious authorities. The leaders of this theocracy would be, rather than governors, senators, and congressmen, modeled on the organizational structure of the early Christian Church as described in the New Testament book in the Acts of the Apostles, and divided into four categories:

- Pastors: These five men were in charge of all religious matters.
- Teachers: This group would teach Church doctrine to the citizenry.
- Elders: Twelve men (as in the twelve Apostles), chosen by the municipal bureaucracy, who would oversee everything that everyone did in the city.
- Deacons: This group would be appointed to tend to the sick, widowed, orphaned, and poor.

Calvin tried to put this theocratic government into practice in the Swiss city of Geneva, but the residents soon rejected it, and Calvin and his followers were run out of town.

Unlike Luther, Calvin emphasized the concept of predestination. Predestination means that, before we were born and through no fault of our own, God has decided who is going to go to Heaven and who is destined for Hell. Predestination was also called the "doctrine of the elect" and the "doctrine of living saints."

Along with this notion of predestination, there came a sense of frugality and spirituality that became known as the Protestant Work Ethic. God's grace would be gained through hard work, modest living, and financial success. The vow of poverty that is common among many Catholic religious orders was nowhere to be found in Calvinism. This spiritual philosophy had transformative results in much more than mere matters of the soul. It ushered in the age of capitalism and the free market economy in Europe.

FACTS

Calvinism brought about the Protestant Work Ethic, which directly led to the emergence of capitalism (private ownership, free markets, and no shame in turning a profit) as the major economic system of Europe. Capitalism replaced feudalism, the system in which the local lord controlled all aspects of the lives of the peasants in his territory.

The Catholic Counter-Reformation

Not to be outdone, the Catholic Church entered into a Reformation of its own with what came to be called the Counter-Reformation. The free lunch was over for wealthy priests and fat bishops. The wanton worldliness of many of the Renaissance clergy was giving Holy Mother Church a bad name. It was time to bite the bullet and return to a more Spartan and ascetic lifestyle, or at the very least cultivate that image via good public relations and an Inquisition or two. Like the Internal Affairs

Division of a law enforcement agency, the Catholic Church began to police itself from within.

In 1534, Pope Paul III encouraged the development of new religious orders, most notable being the Society of Jesus, or the Jesuits. Founded by St. Ignatius Loyola, they were an elite corps of clerics dedicated to the propagation of the faith, most famously through education. Many Jesuit universities were established in Europe and eventually the New World.

ESSENTIALS

The Catholic Church initiated a Counter-Reformation in response to the Protestant Reformation. As slow to action as any bloated bureaucracy, the Church took years to finally set a meeting to discuss their reforms. And the eventual meeting, called the Council of Trent, was eighteen years long.

The Counter-Reformation had its dark side. The nefarious Spanish Inquisition came into existence. The Inquisitors had a unique way of fostering faith among the flock. A hot poker makes a stronger statement than a stern sermon. Censorship was also institutionalized in the form of the Index of Forbidden Books. Volumes of literature were now deemed inappropriate for public consumption, and the penalties for having one of the forbidden volumes in your possession was severe.

Another element of the Counter-Reformation was evangelical. The Good News was spread to the New World. The Church came on a little strong and did not really know how to take "no" for an answer. Like the Borg Collective, resistance proved futile for the indigenous peoples of the Americas.

The Counter-Reformation was also not especially forward thinking in the area of the sciences. Having already burned Giordano Bruno at the stake, they went after other inquiring minds in an attempt to thwart what would prove to be a major milestone in mankind's brief tenure on the planet.

CHAPTER 8

The Scientific Revolution

ankind assumed that he, second to God, was the center of the universe. Earth was the center of it all, and the sun and all celestial bodies revolved around it. The Aristotelian view held that the heavens were immutable, or absolute, and the moon, other planets, and stars were smooth, pristine orbs. This view was the one adopted by the Catholic Church.

The Heliocentric Theory

This long-held belief was eventually challenged by Nicolas Copernicus (1473–1543) and mathematically confirmed by Johannes Kepler (1571–1630). Their theory was called heliocentric, meaning that the sun was the center of our solar system, and Earth and the other planets revolved around it. This theory was regarded as poppycock and ultimately turned into heresy. Great controversy surrounded the hypothesis while it was still only mere speculation. When Galileo invented a telescope and was able to prove the theory via empirical and indisputable observation, things really hit the fan.

Galileo Galilei (1564–1642) was an Italian mathematician and scientist who proved the heliocentric theory. His telescope also showed that the moon had peaks and valleys, crags and craters, and that the sun had spots that appeared and disappeared, disproving the Aristotelian/Christian belief of pristine heavens. In 1616, he was called before the Inquisition and forbidden to teach the heliocentric theory. Knowing what fate befell those who defied the Inquisition, he sensibly consented to this demand. You cannot keep a good scientist down, however, and in 1623, he published a work called "The Appraiser," which reiterated his heliocentric belief. He was tried and found guilty, but he recanted, and his life was spared.

FACTS

Legend has it that Galileo offered the then-pope the opportunity to look through his telescope and see for himself the true nature of the cosmos. The pope refused. He had no need to look through the telescope because his mind was already made up.

The Catholic Church ultimately suffered as a result of their stubborn condemnation of the Copernican heliocentric view of the cosmos and the persecution of Galileo, not to mention the murder of Bruno and numerous other "heretics." In 1993, Pope John Paul II more or less apologized for past indiscretions and acknowledged that the Earth did indeed revolve around the sun.

The Return of Skepticism

One of the many ancient philosophies to become fashionable during the Renaissance was Skepticism. This was brought about due to the rediscovered writings of a Roman Skeptic called Sextus Empiricus. Just as the old Skeptics had, the neo-Skeptics believed that people should suspend belief when confronted with a situation that can be doubted.

The most famous Skeptic of the Renaissance was Michel de Montaigne (1533–1592), who espoused the philosophy in his celebrated and influential *Essays*. In fact, Montaigne created the literary conceit of the essay, introducing a new genre to the literary world.

Montaigne believed that our senses were inherently suspect, hence we should doubt just about everything. People were entitled to their opinions, and all opinions were valid because we can never be really sure of facts. Montaigne had little faith in the Scientific Revolution, either. He believed that such knowledge was transitory and would eventually be usurped and disproved by subsequent generations. His philosophy was a variation of "can't we all just get along?" or perhaps, more accurately, there is no reason why we should not get along, because none of us really know which end is up. Life is a grand and glorious guessing game.

The Invention of the Printing Press

The printing press, invented by Johannes Gutenberg, has been called the most significant invention of all time. Born in 1395 in the German city of Mainz, Gutenberg was a goldsmith and a gem cutter, all the while acquiring knowledge about the properties of metals. Gutenberg was a master of metallurgy.

With financial backing from a partner, Johann Fust, Gutenberg perfected a movable type cast in metal that could be evenly spaced and set on a printing press. This was a revolutionary advancement in 1440, the year Gutenberg completed his wooden printing press and his new-fashioned metal type. This new type consisted of the metals lead, antimony, and tin and was fashioned into 290 separate symbols. Gutenberg even formulated special ink from boiled linseed oil and soot to enhance the visual appeal of the mass printing of words, which turned into pages and pages, and then whole books. He so finely tuned his invention that it enabled him to squeeze water out of the paper, while simultaneously printing on it.

FACTS

Clay type had been invented and utilized in China 400 years earlier, but it was inefficient and cumbersome compared to the durable metal type employed in the Gutenberg machine. In the past, a craftsman carved a block of wood, leaving raised the section to be printed. One page of text often required that several blocks of wood be joined together.

Gutenberg's movable metal type has earned him the title of the Father of Modern Printing. His *Gutenberg Bible* was printed in 1455. It contained forty-two lines per page and took over two years to complete. It also was the first "modern" book ever printed in Europe.

The printing press and its moveable type had a profound impact on the spread of philosophy. "Knowledge is power," as the saying goes, and the proliferation of great thoughts by great thinkers had the potential to make philosophers out of Everyman. The big, wide, wonderful world of ideas was suddenly open to all, something the powers-that-be were not entirely crazy about. Kings and politicians lost their luster, and the Church found its mystical power diminished. Ideas were read and savored and inspired by the mass production of the printed word. The New Age had begun.

CHAPTER 9
Approaching Modern Times

The philosophers of the Renaissance drew from a rich ancient tradition and enhanced and expanded upon it. These adventurers of the mind spread themselves over a variety of disciplines: science, mathematics, medicine, religion, and so on. Now you are entering an age where philosophy reasserted itself as a singularly significant discipline.

Francis Bacon

British politician and businessman Francis Bacon (1561–1626) took a scientific approach to philosophy. He studied the world as an empirical observer would and attempted to avoid bringing his preconceptions and prejudices into the proceedings.

Bacon proposed that, in order to truly understand the world, we must first be aware of the various obstacles and distractions that prevent us from seeing things clearly. He identified these impediments as Idols.

Idols of the Tribe refers to the sense of self-importance that people have about their place in the grand design of things and their penchant to take at face value the observations of our senses. In other words, everything may not be what it appears to be, and we should be aware of that.

Idols of the Cave speaks to our tendencies to make generalizations about the world at large based on our limited experience in our little corner of the world. Put in laymen's terms, never assume anything.

Idols of the Marketplace deals with the imperfections of language as a means of communication. By attempting to understand the wonders around us and describing them via the limits of language, we do not do them justice nor are we fully able to comprehend them.

Idols of the Theatre are the inherent flaws of philosophy itself. Great thinkers devise and put forth lofty notions about things, but these are beliefs built on the shaky foundation of our own faulty perceptions.

Once we notice the effects that these Idols have upon us, Bacon supposed, we are in a position to avoid them, and our knowledge of nature will accordingly improve. Just as many people fall for the bogus gossip and urban legends that flood the Internet, so, too, were people thoroughly captivated by the explosion of information available courtesy of the printing press and the proliferation of books. Bacon was highly suspicious of this cascade of paper and the massive amount of disinformation therein. It was not to be trusted. Bacon exhorted fellow philosophers to discard their books and set about scientifically and empirically exploring their environs.

René Descartes

French philosopher René Descartes (1596–1650) is often called the Father of Modern Philosophy. He started out his career as a mathematician and is credited with discovering the concept of Analytic Geometry. He also was a physicist of great repute. Descartes was a faithful Catholic, but he privately knew the Church was wrongheaded in its resistance to and persecution of men of science. He knew that these men and their philosophies were the way of the future, and if the Church did not adapt, it would suffer as a result.

Doubt Everything

Descartes sought nothing less than the formidable task of a radically revisionist look at knowledge. He started with the premise of doubt. He decided to doubt everything. He believed that everything that he knew, or believed he knew, came from his senses, and sensory experience is inherently suspect. This is the classic Skeptic starting point.

FACTS

Descartes was hesitant to publish much of his work because it supported the findings of Galileo. He eventually "hid" his controversial theories in a philosophy book called *Meditations,* which he dedicated to the local Church leaders in an effort to curry favor.

Descartes quickly discovered that to doubt absolutely everything is to be poised on the precipice of madness. Is it real, or is it a dream? Descartes came to believe that he could not even know if he was awake or if he was dreaming things. There is no absolute certainty, not even in the realm of mathematics. This was called the Dream Hypothesis and is radical skepticism taken to the max.

Descartes went on to speculate that there might not be an all-loving God orchestrating things from a celestial perch. Perhaps there was an Evil Demon who had brainwashed us into believing that all we see and sense is reality, but is really an illusion devised by this diabolical entity. This is called the Demon Hypothesis.

Cogito, Ergo Sum

You have heard the Latin phrase "Cogito, ergo sum" in its English translation. It is perhaps the most famous sentence in the history of philosophy. "I think, therefore I am," became the rallying cry of the modern philosophical age.

Everything could be questioned, but one thing remained a fact: the thinking of the thinker. Self-awareness. You can count on at least one thing in this wacky world, according to Descartes: Wherever you go, there you are.

Descartes then tried to use this newfound certainty to prove the existence of God. It is an ontological argument similar to the one employed by St. Anselm a few centuries earlier. Descartes used the following arguments to "prove" the existence of God:

- "'I think, therefore I am' proves that I exist, but I am an imperfect, flawed mortal man. If I were my own creator, naturally I would have made myself perfect. This proves that I did not create myself, and if I did not, than who did? God."
- "I have a conception of what perfection is, though I am not perfect. Okay, so where does this idea of perfection come from? Not from me, of course. After all, I'm imperfect, and perfection cannot come from something as so patently imperfect as I. So there must be a perfect being, and that is God."

Having proved that he existed and having "proved" the existence of God, at least to his satisfaction, Descartes turned his sights on the nature of reality. According to Descartes, two elements compose reality, as we know it. He called them substances. *Thinking* substances are our minds, and *extended* substances are our physical bodies. He adds that not all ideas come from sensory experience, but other ideas dwell within the mind, ready for the accessing. Descartes calls these ideas *innate*. Notions of morality, mathematics, logic, and the idea of God are all innate ideas. They are similar to the Platonic theory of Forms. There are also, according to Descartes, two other types of ideas: adventitious, which come from what we experience through our senses, and fictitious, which are what the name implies.

Though a scientist and mathematician, Descartes sounds like St. Paul when he speaks of the body-mind disconnection, or *dualism*. He had a mechanistic view of the physical world and viewed the mind as being imbued with spirit. Descartes believed that a body without spirit could still be a walking, talking, animated entity, like an android. Feelings, or *passions* as he called them, are generated by the body. They are not to be trusted, and they are best kept under control. This is a philosophical spin on the New Testament's "spirit is willing, flesh is weak" belief. That the mind can know things without actually experiencing them is called *rationalism*.

Descartes was a Rationalist, meaning that he believed that you can know things without having to rely on sense experience. These are called innate ideas, or primary ideas. Other information gathered from experience is called secondary.

Descartes was initially hesitant to publish his theories because they strongly resembled those of Galileo, and he did not want Torquemada, the Grand Inquisitor, knocking on his door. But he ultimately did so and further shook the foundations of the Church, which was reeling from the one-two punch of the Protestant Reformation and the Scientific Revolution.

Thomas Hobbes

Englishman Thomas Hobbes (1588–1679) rejected Descartes's dualism and touted the theory that ours is a mechanistic and materialistic universe. An attempt to synthesize Empiricism and Rationalism, it is also quite a pessimistic viewpoint and paints man as a less than noble piece of work. Though it was not a prudent time in history to announce from the rooftops that you were an atheist, Hobbes certainly sounds like one, and his worldview is dreary indeed. This bewigged Brit would not be inclined to do exuberant pirouettes on Bosworth Field while singing that the hills were alive with the sound of music.

Hobbes's most famous work is called *The Leviathan.* In Biblical parlance, a leviathan is a great beast, not unlike the one that swallowed Jonah. (The Bible never actually specifies that it was a whale, the King James edition actually says "great fish.") The titular leviathan of Hobbes's tome is a society without order. Hobbes felt that without order, society would violently self-destruct. He felt that order was essential—the order of a decidedly fascistic bent under a strong ruler. In his day the rulers were monarchs: Kings, Queens, and assorted potentates who lived off the hard labor of others and called it their Divine Right. Why should the privileged few enjoy the amenities while the rest of the nasty and brutish folk led short lives? Because God deemed it so was the convenient explanation.

FACTS

Thomas Hobbes is famous for the remark that life is "nasty, brutish, and short," as well as for the book called *The Leviathan.* Hobbes's leviathan is a society without order. Hobbes felt that without order, society would violently self-destruct, and that the best order was a dictatorship.

In an age where many monarchies were uneasy on their purple cushions while ominous winds of change ruffled their ornate tapestries, Hobbes alienated everyone. He did not make any friends among the friends of Liberty because he endorsed monarchies, and he displeased the royalty because he dismissed the Divine Right theory. He believed that strong rulers were chosen by a collective and unconscious mandate rather than by God. This was what he called a *social contract.* It is necessary for the survival of society and must be sufficiently stern to keep the genetically predisposed barbaric humans under control. Hobbes's world was racked by civil war, and he believed that a draconian dictatorship would save mankind from himself.

Hobbes maintained that the *modus operandi* of mankind was rooted in selfishness. Life was all about survival of the selfish and achievement at the expense of your neighbors. Even altruism is a myth. *Altruism,* or a philosophy of charity and helping one's fellows, was denounced by Hobbes. There is, according to Hobbes, no such thing as an unselfish act. Being charitable feeds your own ego. Good Samaritan activities increase your standing in the community or prevent social ostracism.

Hobbes lived to the ripe old age of ninety, no doubt remaining a cynical and cranky old coot who chased neighbors' kids out of his yard. To him, they must have been a microcosm of man's natural state, which he viewed as savage anarchy.

Baruch Spinoza

Baruch Spinoza (1632–1677) believed in *pantheism,* meaning that God is present in all things. It is believed that the ancient Druids were pantheists of a sort. So, too, is the contemporary New Age tree hugger. It is a form of nature worship that naturally made him suspect by the then all-seeing eyes of the Christian authorities. The fact that he was also raised as an Orthodox Jew did not endear him to the Church authorities, either. The Jewish leaders cast him out for his pantheistic beliefs as well, so Spinoza was a man without an organized religion.

Like Descartes, Spinoza wrestled with the idea of Substance. Descartes called the infinite substance God; Spinoza called it Nature. His belief that God is Nature and that nature is one substance that can shape-shift into various forms that he called *modes* is not unlike the Monist philosophies of the Presocratics.

ESSENTIALS

Pantheism is the belief that God is Nature, in everything and around us all the time. Baruch Spinoza's brand of pantheism captured the worst of all possible spiritual beliefs. He denied the existence of the soul after death, yet the world was governed by predestination.

Like Descartes, Spinoza eschewed the passions, believing that they got in the way of inner peace. He believed in acceptance of your lot in life, and that you are part (however inconsequential) of a cosmic Big Picture (however impersonal), and that you are a happy anonymous mode among a myriad of other modes should provide at least a modicum of serenity. Needless to say, many disagreed with this philosophy.

Gottfried Leibniz

Gottfried Leibniz (1646–1716) rejected Spinoza's pantheism and dismissal of man as one mere mode in the universe. While Spinoza spoke of modes, Leibniz believed that reality was made up of what he called monads. Leibniz posited that the one entity who had access to all the monads was God. Hence, God has all the answers, and so much of life is a bitter mystery to humans. We only have access to a piece of the elaborate puzzle that is reality, but God has a Big Picture view of it all.

Like Descartes and Spinoza, Leibniz had a mathematical mindset and found animal passions to be a hindrance. Descartes, Spinoza, and Leibniz all revered logic.

Leibniz posited a few rules of logic that he believed governed reality:

- The principle of noncontradiction: Contradictions are inherently false.
- The principle of sufficient reason: Everything happens for a reason, though it may remain a mystery to you.
- The principle of predication: Everything that predicates a thing is also part of what that thing is, not just something that happens to it.
- The principle of the identity of indiscernibles: Everything is unique. Nothing is exactly alike. If two things were identical, they would be the same thing.
- The principle of the best world: This is the best of all possible worlds. God designed it to be the ultimate in logic and simplicity. By suggesting that this was "the best of all possible worlds," Leibniz did not mean that the world was a grand and glorious Utopia. He meant that the world was like a highly logical, perfectly functioning supercomputer.

CHAPTER 10

British Empiricism

British Empiricism proposes that all knowledge comes entirely from experience. This philosophical school strongly opposed the notion of innate ideas and maintained that knowledge derives from sensory input as well as emotional responses and self-generated thought. The Empiricists did not, however, summarily reject the concept of innateness.

The Concept of Innateness

Though they may not have called it such, British Empiricists knew there was an autonomic nervous system because many bodily functions go on without thought. Breathing, digestion, and the pumping of the heart occur all by themselves, without a philosopher to speculate and theorize on how and why. They simply happen. These functions are innate.

FACTS

The school of Empiricism rejects Descartes and the Rationalist notion of innate ideas. They believed that everything we can know must come from sensory experiences and observations of the physical world.

However, the Empiricists did not accept that they were born with, in essence, preloaded software. Knowledge was installed over time through life experience. The three main British Empiricists of the eighteenth century are John Locke, George Berkeley, and David Hume.

The British Empiricists certainly got people thinking with their controversial revisioning of what it means to be human. Of the three, Locke's philosophy proved to be the most successful and influential.

John Locke

John Locke (1632–1704) believed that all knowledge was gained through experience. While Descartes and other Rationalists maintained that ideas can be generated by the mind or inspired by the soul, independent of practical experience, Locke dismissed such notions as unprovable. There was no such thing as innate ideas. He put forth his philosophy in a book called *An Essay Concerning the Human Understanding*.

SSENTIALS

Tabula rasa is Latin for "blank slate." The theory is that a baby is born with a void for a brain, and information is imprinted on the empty mind as the child is exposed to all manner of sensory experiences.

Locke Versus Hobbes

Locke and his more irascible predecessor, Thomas Hobbes, have much in common. There is no evidence that either was an atheist, but much of their belief system infers that they were. As previously noted, it would have been career (and perhaps literal) suicide to aggressively espouse such a view in those days. Suffice it to say, they minimized, if not outright dismissed, all matters metaphysical. They also had little use for the imperious notion of the Divine Right of Kings.

FACTS

The Founding Fathers of the United States were deeply influenced by the philosophy of John Locke, especially his notion of social contract and his belief that mankind is endowed with certain inalienable rights, including life, liberty, and the pursuit of happiness.

Whereas Hobbes felt the natural law of man was survival at any cost and the "state of nature" was one of violence and barbarism, Locke believed in a natural law where people had, to paraphrase another famous writer, "certain inalienable rights" such as life, liberty, and the pursuit of happiness. And these rights are to be gained by working for them, not by the *noblesse oblige* of the sitting liege or from a welfare state. The system of capitalism is an economic expression of Lockean principles. Capitalism, of course, is the system of providing goods and services for a financial profit.

A Social Contract

Locke, like Hobbes, is also famous for his notion of a *social contract*. Locke saw the contract as between society and the government to protect the rights of the individual. Basically, Locke feels that a citizenry's silence is consent. If they are displeased, they have the right to pack up and leave, or change it. The architects of the American and French Revolutions picked up on this idea and ran with it.

The nagging question of substances led to certain inconsistencies in Lockean theory. After going on and on about how all knowledge is gained from experience alone, he was left with the question of substances, which he did not satisfactorily address.

What is the difference between Hobbes's and Locke's social contract?
Thomas Hobbes believed that a social contract existed between the ruler and the masses in an effort, by any means necessary, to keep civilization from reverting to its natural state, which Hobbes believed was savage anarchy. Locke believed that the contract is there for the greater good of society and to uphold the inherent rights of the individual.

Two subsequent British empiricists, both Locke supporters, added their unique voices to the Lockean theory.

George Berkeley

George Berkeley (1685–1753) was awash in the world of ideas. He believed that everything was an idea, even physical matter. Only minds and the ideas they generate are real, according to this Irish clergyman. He is considered to be the founder of the modern version of Idealism, a belief that goes back to Plato in its original presentation. Unlike the closet atheism of Locke, Berkeley flatly states that God is responsible for the introduction and dissemination of perceptions into the human brain. These things we perceive do not exist outside the mind. They have no substantial reality of their own.

His Treatise

Berkeley's major work is the *Treatise Concerning the Principles of Human Knowledge.* When a thunderous "Say What?!?" came forth from his philosophical peers, Berkeley attempted to give it a more populist spin in a version called *The Three Dialogues Between Hylas and Philonous.*

Berkeley's controversial philosophy was a response to the skepticism and atheism of the day. He lauded much of Locke's work but not the antispiritual element. Referring to Descartes's primary and secondary ideas (the mind and the physical world), Berkeley states that the only way to grasp the primary qualities is through the secondary qualities. And no matter how you look at it, it's all in your mind.

Direct and Indirect Perception

Berkeley made the distinction between direct perception and indirect perception. *Direct perception* is the sensory input of things, and *indirect perception* is how they are interpreted by the mind. Berkeley insists that we all exist in our subjective realities with language being the only thing that can bridge the gap between isolated realities. Hence, sensory experiences and communication through language are the only way we can know things. But, of course, there is one exception to the rule: God. Berkeley was once asked the age-old philosophical question, "If a tree falls in the forest and no one is there to hear it, does it make a noise?" Given his view of reality, you would think that the answer would be no. The answer is yes, according to Bishop Berkeley, because God is there to hear it.

Berkeley did not gain many converts with his outlandish notion, but he certainly prompted many a lively debate among those who get excited about discussing such mind-blowing matters.

David Hume

David Hume (1711–1776) was a Scottish philosopher and the third man in the troika of British Empiricists. He was influenced by and expanded upon the ideas of John Locke and George Berkeley. Hume not only denied the existence of the material substances of Locke, but also the spiritual world of ideas proposed by Berkeley. Hume also rejected the existence of the individual self. You do not exist. According to Hume, you are nothing more than what he called "a collection of different perceptions." He dismisses the scientific principle of cause and effect and states that knowledge of anything as certainty is just plain impossible, except maybe mathematics.

Hume explained his position as follows: "Reason can never show us the connexion of one object with another, tho' aided by experience, and the observation of their conjunction in all past instances. When the mind, therefore, passes from the idea or impression of one object to the idea or belief of another, it is not determined by reason, but by certain principles, which associate together the ideas of these objects and unite them in the imagination."

Being obliged to at least pretend he existed in the real world, Hume wrote extensively about economics as well as philosophy. He also wrote a highly regarded history of England that looks at historical events from an economic perspective.

CHAPTER 11
The French Enlightenment

This philosophical period centered in France and influenced not only the philosophy, but also the literature and politics of the period. Both the American and French Revolutions were products of this era. The flamboyant philosophers did not wait for posterity to call their age the Age of Enlightenment—they did so themselves.

The *Philosophes*

The *philosophes* (French for philosophers) were rational men. They valued the human mind and reason above all, and this often got them into hot water with the Catholic Church, still a formidable social and political institution in Europe. Just as we now believe that only 10 percent of the brain is utilized and the remaining untapped potential is enormous, the *philosophes* believed that the development and deployment of human reason could and should unleash a Golden Age, with advancements in every field of human endeavor. Nature took precedence over classical philosophy and the Bible in the theories of these men. They believed that people should be active and engaged in this life, and not fretting or planning for either damnation or paradise in the next. They assaulted the Church with caustic tongues and quill pens dipped in vitriol and often found themselves locked up or on the run as a result.

These *philosophes* were more than deep thinkers. In the age of powdered wigs and pantaloons, they were flashy showmen and celebrities in their lifetimes. They sought to aggressively change the world through word and deed and not merely passively sit in the pose of Rodin's sculpture of the Thinker and speculate on what it was all about.

Be careful what you put on paper. All the great thinkers of the enlightenment paid a price for espousing their beliefs. Those were the days when the powers-that-be could have your head for expressing a dissenting opinion. Many spent time in prison and exile for their writings.

The American Revolution was hailed as an example of their theories put into practice. In their own homeland, the French Revolution was a bloody and barbaric affair and led to the rise of Napoleon. Love him or hate him, it is safe to say that Bonaparte was not an aficionado of democracy. Though the terrors of the French Revolution were used by the Enlightenment's detractors to denounce it as a failed philosophy, its success across the pond in America vindicated the *Illuminists,* as they are also called. The philosophers of the Enlightenment left a legacy that continued to inspire and illuminate the minds and hearts of humankind in the nineteenth and twentieth centuries. The three most noteworthy *philosophes* are Montesquieu, Voltaire, and Rousseau.

Montesquieu ✓ *good man*

Montesquieu, whose full name is Charles-Louis, Baron de Montesquieu (1689–1755), poked fun at the French society of his day with *Persian Letters,* a book written in the form of correspondence between two Persian visitors to Europe. This device of the stranger in a strange land quipping about what he observes has been used many times. The satiric piece was a big hit and is considered one of the first classics of the Enlightenment.

Montesquieu was also a noted jurist who spoke of *relativism* as it pertains to the law. Relativism is the belief that what is good for the goose may not necessarily be good for the gander.

FACTS

Montesquieu believed in a political system that separated the powers of the government and provided a series of checks and balances so that one branch could not gain too much power and become a tyranny. This philosophy directly influenced the Founding Fathers when they were framing the United States Constitution. ✓

The Baron of Montesquieu concerned himself with legal relativism. Good and bad, legal and illegal were not absolutes to Montesquieu. What is an appropriate and good law for one society may be inappropriate for another. Montesquieu's tolerance did not extend to what are called *despots*, monarchs who do not have the best interests of the people at heart and abuse the privileges of power to indulge their own vices.

Voltaire

Voltaire is the pen name for the man who began life as François Marie Arouet (1694–1778) and who became one of the most famous and infamous philosophers of the Enlightenment. Voltaire was a celebrity and a controversial figure in his lifetime. His satirical pieces landed him in the Bastille on more than one occasion, but these incarcerations did not cause his quill pen to run dry.

Voltaire was virulently anti-Christian and considered himself to be a Deist. Voltaire bounced around Europe for many years. Invited to leave his native France, he crossed the Channel to England where he learned and wrote in the language. Back in France, he wrote *The Philosophical Letters*, which got him into more trouble with the Church and political authorities.

In his life, Voltaire was in and out of favor, alternately locked up and the toast of the royal court. He was a prolific writer in a variety of genres, from philosophy to fiction to verse. He was feted in Prussia and run out of Berlin. He finally returned to France where he lived out his remaining years and wrote his magnum opus, *Essay on General History and on the Customs and the Character of Nations.* This work condemns religion and the Catholic Church.

ESSENTIALS

Deism, a popular belief of the time, is a religious philosophy that believes that, while there is a God, it is an extremely impersonal entity and not the micromanaging and often cantankerous Christian God. Deists often compared the universe to a well-ordered grandfather clock designed by God and then left to tick-tock, and occasionally cuckoo, more or less on its own. The divine manufacturer has no obligations or warranty plan.

Voltaire's most famous work is *Candide.* It is a scathing satire that lampoons the philosophy of Gottfried Wilhelm Leibniz, who believed that we live in "the best of all possible worlds." Voltaire did not believe the cliché that "Everything happens for a reason and everything happens for the best." Voltaire mocks the naïve optimism of his hero, but also champions the indomitable human spirit that can endure such trials and tribulations and emerge sometimes broken, but always unbowed. After learning the hard way that this is not the best of all possible worlds, Candide and his compatriots go off to live simply on an isolated farm, and the lesson learned is straight out of Buddhist philosophy—everyone should simply tend to their own garden, and the world will be a better place.

Voltaire, through his dismissal of metaphysics and his championing of the human spirit, and his belief that fiction and literature should be used as vehicles to promote philosophy and social change, was a precursor to the twentieth-century French existentialists, including Albert Camus and Jean-Paul Sartre. But Voltaire, unlike the existentialists, believed in God. He affirmed his faith with characteristic wit when he proclaimed that "If God did not exist, it would be necessary to invent Him. But all nature proclaims that He exists."

Jean Jacques Rousseau

Jean Jacques Rousseau (1712–1778) was another French philosopher and social critic who also was one of the earliest practitioners of the tell-all memoir. His candor was shocking in his day.

Confessions

Rousseau's famous book *Confessions* is a distillation of a lifetime of philosophizing and also a very frank memoir. Rousseau's book is a forerunner of the psychobiography. Early on, he tells the story of being infatuated by his childhood governess, the fetching Mademoiselle Lambercier. The young woman gave the precocious eight-year-old Jean Jacques a spanking, and this seemingly innocuous event in the course of child-rearing had a profound effect and forever shaped the philosopher's personality and sexual proclivities. For the rest of his life, he sought the company of dominant, usually older, women. Rousseau announced in the very first sentence of *Confessions* that there had never been a book of its kind before and never would be one again, a claim that is not entirely accurate on either count. However, *Confessions* did introduce a new candor to literature, and it influenced the literature of Romanticism that flourished in the early nineteenth century.

Other Writings

In less titillating philosophizing, Rousseau wrote many treatises, dramas, operas, and novels, all of which included his theories and observations on the human condition. In his book *Discourse on the Origin and Foundation of Inequality among Mankind,* he condemned the corrosive influence of polite society, including the arts and politics, suggesting that they were deleterious to mankind. He professed that the primitive people of the world were in every way superior to "civilized" societies. The more sophisticated the civilization, the more rampant were vice and corruption, according to Rousseau. Voltaire, for one, roundly mocked this belief, and the two men became enemies thereafter. For his own part, Rousseau did not elect to leave Europe, thus he was not a philosopher who applied his own words to actual practice. He later refined what he meant by a return to nature to mean an internal trek, adopting the virtues of innocence and spirituality.

Rousseau's Social Contract

Like Brits Hobbes and Locke, Rousseau took a crack at his version of the social contract, in a political treatise of the same name. Unlike the irascible Hobbes but kindred to the egalitarian Locke, Rousseau preached for the cause of liberty for the citizenry and against the oppressive divine right theory of monarchies. Just as Locke's writing inspired the Founding Fathers of the American Revolution, Rousseau's tome lit the fires of insurgency that prompted the French Revolution of the late 1700s. Unlike the French, however, the Americans got it right.

Rousseau opens *The Social Contract* with the famous line, "Man was born free, yet everywhere he is in chains." In *The Social Contract,* Rousseau proposes that all men were created equal and endowed with certain inalienable rights. Sound familiar? Ironically, others see *The Social Contract* as a model for a totalitarian state.

Rousseau speaks of general will and the will of all. The *general will* is the inalienable right of every man. No king can bestow these rights upon you—you already have them. Governments can repress them, however, and often do. The *will of all* is a different matter. This is the will of certain factions of a society, whether they be the king or the aristocracy or any special interest groups. It is the rule of the powers-that-be, not really the "will of all" at all.

 **ESSENTIALS**

Rousseau sees freedom and liberty not as a license to do whatever you want, but rather, the opportunity to do the right thing. This includes obedience to authority—not an authority that is imposed on you, but one that governs by the assent of the citizens.

Education Reform

If Rousseau was a tad authoritarian even in his defense of liberty, he was a reformer regarding education. Rousseau's novel *Émile* was a vehicle to state his case for a new paradigm in education. It was critical of the rigidity of the time and proposed more freedom of expression in the learning process instead of learning by rote at the hands of a stern schoolmistress. Rousseau opposed what he felt was the stifling nature of the schooling of the time. Little ones, still in their natural and uncorrupted state, should have their spontaneous natures encouraged, not thwarted. The novel was burned and banned in France and Switzerland, and Rousseau found that he had a price on his head in many provinces.

His Final Years

Like his rival Voltaire, Rousseau often found himself on the lam from his native France and adopting aliases to escape angry authorities. He spent some time with Scottish philosopher David Hume, but as philosophers are wont to do, they feuded and thenceforth denounced one another in print. He romanced a succession of wealthy aristocratic women, yet he fathered five children with a simple peasant woman whom he eventually married late in life. While being a celebrated man of letters, he also managed to antagonize every religious and political authority of the time and spent his last years never settling anywhere too long, always being run out of town by the powers-that-be. He paid a hefty price to enrich the world with his philosophy.

CHAPTER 12
German Idealism

England had the Empiricists, France had the Illuminists, and the Germans spawned the school of philosophers we call the Idealists. While the British and French emphasized the senses as the only path to knowledge, the Germans placed the focus on the mind, thoughts, and ideas. A big influence on this movement was Liebniz.

Immanuel Kant

Immanuel Kant (1724–1804) was the first of the German Idealists. His most well-known work is *Critique of Pure Reason*. In this book, Kant sets forth his philosophy, called *critical philosophy*.

What Lies Beyond

Kant was interested in *metaphysics,* which is what lies beyond our ability to perceive. We only get tantalizing flashes of the metaphysical world. According to Kant, we can never really grasp the true nature of the material world. Things such as the soul or the existence of God were unknowable and unprovable. They were matters of faith. Kant was influenced by the philosopher David Hume and by the scientist Sir Isaac Newton, even though the former said that nothing is real and we cannot grasp it anyway, and the other "proved" the laws of gravity and other scientific "realities."

Science Versus Faith

Kant, who had more or less been a follower of Liebniz, read a book by David Hume in middle age and claimed to have awakened from a "dogmatic slumber." Hume's view that there were no certainties in life and that we were all merely a mishmash of sensory impressions rattled old Kant, a fusspot old bachelor and apparently a rigid creature of routine. He sought to make sense of it all and resolve the seeming conflict between science and faith, an age-old philosophical dilemma.

One thing that even the most skeptical philosopher could agree on is that two plus two equals four. For the most part, mathematics was regarded a constant in a chaotic universe. Kant sought to do nothing less than reconcile the conflicting philosophies of rationalism and empiricism.

In his book *Critique of Pure Reason,* Kant defined two types of judgments, the *analytic* and the *synthetic*. The analytic judgment is one where the truth can be determined within itself; that is, the definitions of the words within the statement of truth affirm the truth. The famous example of this is "All black houses are houses." Of course, a black house is a house. An example of a synthetic truth is simply "The house is black." This needs to be determined by the action of looking at the house in question to see if it is indeed black.

Two other ways of judgments are what Kant called *a priori* and *a posteriori*. These are simply the Latin words for "before" and "after." "All black houses are houses is an *a priori* judgment—you do not have to see the houses to know this. "The house is black" is an *a posteriori* judgment—you have to see the house to determine its color.

The German philosopher Immanuel Kant called the world that we experience through our senses the *phenomenal* world and the reality beyond that the *noumenal* world. The German word for this is translated approximately as "of things in themselves."

Two more terms in this Kantian point-counterpoint are Transcendental and Empirical. Transcendental would be *a priori* knowledge—it is a given, and you just know it to be true. Empirical is *a posteriori* knowledge—you need to observe it to ascertain its truthfulness.

Following this logically, there would be one column of analytic, a priori, and transcendental, and another column of synthetic, a posteriori, and empirical. Kant sought to take one from Column A and one from Column B and see what he came up with. Through mixing and matching, Kant found that some combinations were illogical, but he liked the notion of the synthetic a priori. This concept would be nothing less than a Universal Truth arrived at through a scientific method.

Reality

Kant proposed that reality is not an ordered universe waiting to be perceived by the human mind. Rather, the human mind takes the chaos out there and orders and structures it into the reality that we perceive. Time and space as we understand them are not concepts external to us; they are intrinsic mechanisms that enable us to make sense of reality. We create our own reality not out of mental illness or egotism; it is simply the way of things.

Reality, if we were to see it without the filter of our own mind and perception, would be something like a preschooler's scribbling in crayon. In other words, it's a nebulous jumble in which we would be unable to maneuver, and that would probably drive us mad.

Kant speculated on the nature of the noumenal, or metaphysical, world. He looked at the otherworldly realms from an optimistic standpoint. Kant believed we had regular intuitive hints to the nature of the noumenal world. The feeling of awe on a starry night, a spiritual sense of oneness with the cosmos is one such clue. Kant believed that there was a God, a universal justice, and immortality to be found on the "other side."

FACTS

Kant proposed that the mind has "categories of understanding," which catalogue, codify, and make sense of the world. The mind cannot experience anything that is not filtered through the mind's eye. Therefore, we can never know the true nature of reality. In this sense, Kant claims that indeed "perception is reality."

As a result, Kant posited that humankind does not receive all his knowledge from sensory experience alone, as the Empiricists claimed. Nor does he comprehend things through reason alone, as the Rationalists firmly maintained. This was a revolutionary thinking in the history of philosophy, and Kant influenced almost every philosopher that followed. His immediate heirs, the other German Idealists, although deeply affected by Kantian thought, revised, modified, and disagreed with him.

Johann Gottlieb Fichte

Johann Gottlieb Fichte (1762–1814) was a fan of Kant who followed the old adage that imitation is the sincerest form of flattery. His book, *Critique of All Revelation,* in many ways, out-Kanted Kant, and people believed that Kant had actually written it. He agreed with much of Kant, but did not like the idea that the ultimate reality would forever remain unknowable. Fichte sought a way around this, and his solution was nothing if not egotistical.

He stated, boldly and controversially, that not only was he his own creation, the world was his own creation.

It is kind of a variation of Descartes's "I think, therefore I am," but it's more like "I think, therefore everything is." There is both an overweening egotism in this and yet a Horatio Alger determinism in that, if we create ourselves from scratch, we cannot blame anyone else or society as a whole for our troubles. Fichte evolved his view of the ego as focal point to all things as he grew older, eventually coming up with the proposition that there is a Universal Ego of which we are all a part.

Friedrich Wilhelm Josef von Schelling

Friedrich Wilhelm Josef von Schelling (1775–1854) was a follower and eventually a critic of Fichte, as is often the case in the history of mentor and protégé relations.

He never fulfilled his potential as a philosopher and was forever overshadowed by Hegel, whom he accused of stealing his ideas. He was an Idealist sandwiched between two more prominent and influential contemporaries who got lost in the Idealist shuffle. In his later years, after Hegel's death, he had one brief shining moment in the spotlight, and one of his students, Kierkegaard, went on to have a successful career as a philosopher.

George W. F. Hegel

George W. F. Hegel (1770–1831) was another German idealist philosopher who was the most famous disciple of Kant, but disagreed with him on several key points. Hegel's goal was to devise a philosophical school that would explain the totality of experience in terms of the past, present, and future. The explanation and comprehension of Reality as we know it was his goal. His supporters think he achieved this with philosophical aplomb, while his many detractors find his often obscure writings unconvincing and unfathomable.

Hegel called reality the Absolute Spirit, and it was his goal to explain it and chronicle its development. Hegelian philosophy is an amalgam of the monism of the ancient Presocratics and Idealism. Monism proposes that one thing composes the basic stuff of reality. For Hegel, this is the rather nebulously named *Absolute*.

The Absolute

The Absolute in its physical state is nature itself and the world around us. In its spirit or immaterial form, the Absolute is the human mind and its ability to reason. Hegel proposed that the Absolute was constantly evolving, and he called the process dialectic. The evolution of the Absolute is, according to Hegel, brought about by the conflict of opposites.

SSENTIALS

Hegel believed that reality was an Absolute Spirit and that history moved forward through constant acts of synthesis. Thesis meets its opposite, antithesis, and they combine into a synthesis, which then meets its own antithesis to make a new synthesis and so on and so on. . . .

Mankind's ability to reason, however limited and finite it is, enables the inevitable progression of the Absolute toward self-knowledge. Human mental evolution is helping to aid the Absolute in achieving self-consciousness. This is almost like the rather blasphemous notion that Man is in the process of creating God.

Art, Religion, and Philosophy

Hegel rates art, religion, and philosophy as the three best ways humankind spurs the dialectic process along. Art celebrates the material forms of the Absolute, finding beauty in the rational world. Perhaps with more than a little cultural bias, Hegel pronounced Christianity to be the best of the world's religions, seeing the belief that God became man in the person of Jesus Christ as an expression of the finite and infinite aspects of the Absolute achieving the ultimate synthesis. And it is no surprise that, of these three elements, Hegel placed philosophy at the pinnacle. This is because, without the trappings of the arts or faith, philosophy is the vehicle to comprehend the absolute through reason.

An Orderly and Rational Process

Hegel was a big fan of the rational, as are most philosophers. He saw the march of history and the evolution of mankind as an orderly and rational process, and the history of man as an evolution of greater and greater freedom. His was an age where the rights of man and increased freedoms were foremost on the minds of the great thinkers.

Hegel was in tune with the contemporary climate in that he was something of a moral relativist. Yet he adds that social morality must take precedence over personal ethics, and one must conform to the dictates of society.

Hegel was the most influential philosopher of his day. People of diverse ideologies could interpret his beliefs. There were conservative and liberal Hegelians, fundamentalist Christians, and atheist Hegelians. Two notorious leftist Hegelians were Karl Marx and Friedrich Engels, the architects of the Communist Manifesto.

Arthur Schopenhauer

One fellow who didn't think too highly of Hegel, or most philosophers for that matter, is Arthur Schopenhauer (1788–1860). The driving modus operandi of Schopenhauer was to dispute and discredit the very popular philosophy of Hegel. His magnum opus is the influential work *The World as Will and Idea*.

Will

Schopenhauer was like an ancient Monist in his outlook, in that he said that reality was one thing. He called it *will*. While Kant said that we could never really know the true nature of reality, the "thing in itself," Schopenhauer disagreed. If we were merely disembodied minds, perhaps Kant would be right. But we all have physical bodies that are driven and motivated by will. Will is Reality, according to Schopenhauer.

In nature, will is manifested in the survival instinct. This extends beyond humans and the animal kingdoms, to the entire universe itself. In fact, the cosmos itself is an entity evolving and seeking to achieve consciousness, which, so says Schopenhauer, it has through the mind of mankind. The world is nothing short of the physical representation of the will of the universe. Schopenhauer's Will, unlike the warm-fuzzy noumena of Kant and the logical and ethical Absolute of Hegel, is a random, irrational, and often destructive force.

Schopenhauer concludes that life is full of inherent misery. Life is pain. Will inspires desire, and desire is a constant reminder of the things in life that we lack. If we do not satisfy our desires, frustration and pain increase. Unlike inanimate objects and the animals, we are well aware of our rampaging will and suffer from that knowledge. Of course, we all do things that are strange even to ourselves—out of character, self-destructive acts that baffle us after the fact. This is our Will following its own singular path. In this regard, Schopenhauer's philosophy is similar to Freud's psychological theories on the unconscious. The more you know, the more it hurts is Schopenhauer's pessimistic and depressing worldview. Love is an illusion, according to Schopenhauer. It is really the will's desire to survive via procreation of the species.

Making Sense of It All

Schopenhauer, as an older fellow, looked back on his life and saw that what he had believed were random elements, chance meetings, and coincidences, seemed to be perfectly and logically ordered in hindsight. And just as people entered and exited Schopenhauer's life with no seeming rhyme or reason, looking backward he saw the long-term role that people played in his life.

Schopenhauer was intrigued by Indian philosophy and Hinduism, which was only then becoming widely disseminated in the Western world. He was especially fascinated by the notion of the Veil of Maya, which is a retelling of the very familiar philosophical and religious belief that physical reality is merely an illusion.

Life Without Joy

Schopenhauer was an atheist (as was Hegel, though an optimistic one), yet he does advocate ethics and morality, albeit as much of a downer as is his rampaging and irrational Will. There is no joy, no celebration of life in this morality.

Schopenhauer, though his philosophy reeks of nihilism, still sought to create a morality of sorts, designed for such a hostile and insane world. This morality was not a joyous celebration of doing good and avoiding evil for some spiritual satisfaction and promise of posthumous reward. It was a rejection of life itself in a way that falls just short of advocating suicide. He did not endorse suicide, however.

Aesthetics, Ethics, and Ascentics

The three-pronged approach that Schopenhauer proposed to deny life without taking it were aesthetics, ethics, and ascetics. Aesthetics, by Schopenhauer's reckoning, would be a total immersion into the contemplation of beauty. Without thinking about the seven deadly sins or thy neighbor's wife, you repress that naughty Will and keep the focus on the abstract. Of course, you cannot do this twenty-four/seven, so Schopenhauer proposed an ethical system.

Schopenhauer's ethical system grudgingly acknowledges that the individual is part of a community and is, in effect, his brother's keeper. Schopenhauer advocates compassion. One is naturally suspicious of this, given the decidedly negative streak in Schopenhauer's philosophy, but it is not altruism that motivates Schopenhauer. It is self-interest, because if we remain aware of our fellows and are empathetic to their plight, our potentially destructive ego is subdued and the Will is dampened slightly.

Still, this ethical system doesn't completely do the trick, so the third element in Schopenhauer's moral code is ascetics. Complete self-denial would completely neutralize that nasty Will and, in Schopenhauer's worldview, was the only way to fly.

Friedrich Wilhelm Nietzsche

Friedrich Wilhelm Nietzsche (1844–1900) is perhaps the most controversial and most misunderstood philosopher. He was a German who spoke of the Superman (not Clark Kent), which led some to believe that he was a Nazi.

Nietzsche was influenced by the philosophy of Schopenhauer, whom he discovered as a young man. Schopenhauer's pessimism and atheism was right up Friedrich's alley, and he took it to a nihilistic extreme. His controversial phrase "God is dead" also got him into trouble in his lifetime as well as posthumously. However, there is much more to Nietzsche than his provocative views on the Superman and God.

Many dismiss Nietzsche's later works as symptomatic of increasing mental illness. Others hail him as an original and provocative thinker who influenced subsequent generations of philosophers.

High-strung, overly sensitive, and unlucky in love, Nietzsche was plagued with physical and emotional problems throughout his life and tragically went insane, suffering a mental breakdown after watching a man beat a horse. He ran to the defense of the animal and collapsed into a madness from which he never recovered. He spent the last decade of his life under the care of his mother, and upon her death, his sister. His sister was an anti-Semite and a kind of proto-fascist, and her role in promulgating his legacy contributed to tagging Nietzsche with the Nazi moniker.

Nietzsche was not a philosopher who espoused a cohesive theory such as Empiricism or Idealism. He was more like a ranting talk radio host, entertainingly and effectively railing against his pet peeves: Christianity and Western civilization.

The Superman

Nietzsche called Christian morality "slave morality" and believed it to be a destructive societal ill that made sheep out of people. In its place, he advocated the philosophy of the Superman. Nietzsche's Superman would achieve the greatest in human potential. His morality and values would be "beyond good and evil" (a title of one of his many books) and he would rise above "the herd," as Nietzsche called the great-unwashed masses. The Superman does not bow before the power of the church or other authority figures. The Superman does not, lemming-like, follow the throng and conform. He plans each charted course, each careful step along the byway. He is not imprisoned by established mores. He makes his own ethical decisions based on his morality, not one imposed by the Church and society. Nietzsche did not believe that any Supermen had yet burst onto the scene, but he listed Jesus, Socrates, Shakespeare, and Napoleon as role models for any Superman in training.

Nietzsche's Superman rejects the traits of humility and passivity, believing that they are encouraged as virtues by Christianity while they are really devices that the powers-that-be use to control us. The Superman focuses on this world rather than the next.

The Nazis seized upon Nietzsche's Superman principle and hence all the bad press followed. But Nietzsche was not interested in controlling or conquering others. He was advocating mastering yourself and achieving your personal potential without allowing yourself to be inhibited by a repressive society.

The Birth of Tragedy

For a guy with a lot of problems, Nietzsche managed to be a fairly prolific writer. Though he never hit the bestseller lists in his lifetime, he was confident that he would be a philosopher for the ages. His first book, *The Birth of Tragedy,* was a tribute to ancient Greek society and philosophy and set up the differences between Dionysian and Apollonian aspects of human nature. Dionysus was the Greek god of all manner of sensual delights. Nietzsche felt that he would be a better model than Apollo, a rather dour and serious fellow. He believed that European culture was far too Apollonian and a dose of Dionysian debauchery would be beneficial for all.

His Aphorisms

Nietzsche's favorite form of philosophizing was the aphorism. An aphorism is a short proverb-like observation, usually only a few lines. Most of his books are collections of his aphorisms on a variety of topics. His first collection of aphorisms is called *Human, All Too Human*.

Another famous collection of maxims is called *The Gay Science*, refering to the medieval songs of the French troubadours. This book is famous for one famous Nietzsche-ism, his audacious proclamation that "God is dead." This deliberately provocative statement is designed to shake things up, to get people to think more about their freedom and human potential in the real world, and to not dread divine punishment or sacrifice happiness in this life in the hope of being rewarded in the next.

Nietzsche's theory of eternal recurrence is a strange suggestion to come from a staunch atheist. Nietzsche was an accomplished poet and literary figure, and there is much figurative flourish in his prose and his philosophy, so it is possible he did not really believe this to be literally true. Certainly, eternal recurrence is one of the least attractive prospects for an afterlife.

Thus Spoke Zarathustra

Nietzsche's most famous work is called *Thus Spoke Zarathustra*. It is a flowery, frenetic polemic, a flamboyant attack on the Judeo-Christian tradition. It is poetic, metaphoric, and passionate. It is an allegorical tale about the spiritual awakening of the titular Zarathustra. Zarathustra is the quintessential Nietzschean Superman and again brings up eternal recurrence, suggesting that we should strive to create for ourselves the kind of life we could not mind repeating over and over again.

The prologue of *Thus Spoke Zarathustra* begins with a fable that sums up Nietzsche's views on the objective of the individual in society. In the fable, a camel morphs into a lion, the lion slays a dragon named "Thou shalt," and then the lion morphs into a child.

In youth, we are all camels. Born into life cute little blank slates, we have the weight of the world heaped upon us. We are beasts of burden, carrying all that society and Christianity have imposed on our innocent souls, preventing us from achieving our full potential and finding true bliss. In adulthood, we are lions, and we venture out into the world. The more stuff thrown at us by the diabolical forces of society and religion, the stronger we are. It was Nietzsche who uttered the famous aphorism "That which does not kill us makes us stronger."

QUESTIONS?

What is the theory of eternal recurrence?
Eternal recurrence poses the possibility that we may be destined to live our lives over and over again with no variation, no possibility to make changes or right wrongs. Nietzsche, an atheist, was perhaps indulging in poetic license by proposing an alternative myth to what he perceived to be the unhealthy mythology of the Judeo-Christian tradition.

The lion is confronted by a dragon with the curious name "Thou shalt." The fire-breathing, menacing monster is all the "dos and don'ts" of society and religion that have stifled us in our lifetimes. The lion slays the nasty dragon and is transformed into a child, innocent and uncorrupted. Paradoxically, this childlike state should be the goal of the fully matured adult who has survived the slings and arrows, remained broken but unbowed, and slayed the dragon to emerge the triumphant Superman. This is Nietzsche's philosophy in a nutshell.

Beyond Good and Evil

Nietzsche uses the book *Beyond Good and Evil* to express his philosophy on philosophy itself and other philosophers. He holds academic types in disdain and champions a more active and aggressive approach. Nietzsche felt philosophers should be willing to take risks and live life in the philosophical fast lane if they are to make a difference and rattle the cage. The notorious Nietzschean "will to power" is triumphed in this book. He does not believe that the morality imposed on society is a valid one, and real life occurs in a realm beyond good and evil. The will to power, in a relatively benign interpretation, can simply mean "go for the gusto," and "be all that you can be." Its darker side disputes the accepted belief that compassion and protection of the weak and disenfranchised is a virtue. Other people may get hurt along the way as you exert your will to power, and you may get hurt by another's rampaging will, but hey, that's life according to Nietzsche. These notions are ripe for the perverting by everyone from the bully on your block to the bully pulpit of a tyrant. Just as bad things have happened in the name of God, bad things have been done by certain Nietzsche-philes over the years.

On the Genealogy of Morals, A Polemic

On the Genealogy of Morals, A Polemic continues the themes set forth in *Beyond Good and Evil*. Again, Nietzsche accuses Christian morality of being a means to control the cowering populace. Like the stereotype of an overprotective mother, the Church and society successfully use guilt as a weapon and means to control people. Nietzsche also takes the opportunity to launch into a vicious attack on the priesthood, branding them all a craven and cowardly class of men who delight in abusing the power they wield over the even more craven and cowardly flock.

His Other Writings

In *The Case of Wagner, A Musician's Problem*, Nietzsche ostensibly uses the device of musical criticism to attack his former mentor and friend Richard Wagner and everything he represents. Wagner, who is best known today as a classical composer, was also a political activist and by all accounts, a big meanie.

In *Twilight of the Idols,* or *How One Philosophizes with a Hammer*, Nietzsche turns his poison pen on just about every major philosopher: Socrates, Plato, Kant, and Rousseau are called decadent. The angry Nietzsche praises Caesar, Napoleon, and, of all people, the Sophists!

FACTS

Nietzsche was unlucky in love and had several marriage proposals turned down. Yet despite, or perhaps because of, his tormented life, he was able to produce a powerful body of work that rattled the Victorian cage and continues to both inspire and outrage with equal measure.

Becoming progressively provocative, Nietzsche's next book *The Antichrist, Curse on Christianity*, Nietzsche laments the corruption of the Roman Empire by the destructive influence of Christianity and beats the dead horse that Christianity is an unhealthy creed that undermines all that is noble in man.

All about Nietzsche

Nietzsche offers his own "Everything Nietzsche Book" with *Ecce Homo, How One Becomes What One Is* that is part autobiography and part critical study of all the books he had written in his career. He outrageously titles some of the chapters "Why I Am So Wise," "Why I Am So Clever," and "Why I Write Such Good Books." Nietzsche praised himself as a sensitive man, a fellow who knew how to eat right and take good care of himself, and someone who is a bold visionary thinker who will only be appreciated by a few discriminating readers and thinkers. In the last chapter, called "Why I Am a Destiny," he claims that his legacy will be the weapon of mass destruction that will destroy polite society and create a new world order. He hopes that the libertine pagan god Dionysus will usurp Jesus as the influential deity for the next millennium.

Nietzsche wasn't quite the destiny he hoped he would be, but his legacy did deeply influence the twentieth century in both good and bad ways. Of course, the worst exponent of Nietzsche was his sister, who was an anti-Semitic fascist who later became chummy with both Adolf Hitler and Benito Mussolini. Through selective interpretation, it was easy for the Nazis to adapt and corrupt Nietzsche's rants to justify their own ends.

CHAPTER 13
Utilitarianism

Philosophy and social activism merged in the nineteenth-century movement called Utilitarianism. It began in England, and its two most well-known proponents were Jeremy Bentham and John Stuart Mill.

Jeremy Bentham

Following a cue from David Hume, who believed in mankind's gravitation toward things that have a utility, or function, Jeremy Bentham (1748–1832) was a social reformer whose claim to fame is a book called *An Introduction to the Principles of Morals and Legislation.* The gist of it is an old theory, and a somewhat obvious one: Humans seek the pursuit of pleasure and the avoidance of pain.

The Pursuit of Pleasure

Bentham takes this theory from the individual level to the society as a whole. He argued that you can put a precise scientific value on pleasure and pain. What the majority perceives as pleasure and comfort should be the desired status quo, so long as no harm is done. Public policy decisions and laws should be devised to serve that greater good. As far as punishments are concerned, they should be severe enough to be a deterrent and based on the nature of the offense. Thus, the precept "a punishment to fit the crime" is a Utilitarian principle.

Jeremy Bentham's philosophy of Social Hedonism did not mean that everyone was entitled to live on Temptation Island. Like the Epicurean philosophy, Social Hedonism means maximizing pleasure and minimizing pain, not rampant naughtiness.

Bentham advocated the philosophy of Hedonism, but like Epicureanism, it does not mean the reckless pursuit of pleasure. Bentham believed in Social Hedonism, which he called, "The greatest amount of happiness for the greatest number." Bentham associated morality with happiness, and the more happiness an act provided, the more moral he thought it was (and vice versa). Bentham and Utilitarianism took a lot of heat as a libertine philosophy. This philosophy is also called *consequentialism,* meaning that the consequences of your actions determine their morality.

The Calculus of Felicity

Bentham's empirical and scientific application to the pleasure principle resulted in his making a mathematical formula to precisely chart the pleasure and happiness factor of any particular activity. He broke the equation down into seven categories:

- Intensity: How powerful is the pleasure?
- Duration: How long lasting is the pleasure?
- Certainty: How guaranteed is the pleasure?
- Proximity: How close is the pleasure?
- Fecundity: Will this pleasurable activity generate additional pleasures?
- Purity: How pain-free is this particular pleasure?
- Extent: How many other citizens will experience this pleasure?

Bentham believed that people should apply this formula to all the pleasures in their lives. He called this the Calculus of Felicity, which Bentham believed would eventually become second nature.

FACTS

Bentham's mummified body is present at every Board of Trustees meeting of the University of College of London. He bequeathed his fortune to the school with the proviso that he attend every such meeting in perpetuity.

John Stuart Mill

John Stuart Mill (1808–1873) carried on the Utilitarian tradition and became the most famous and effective advocate of the philosophy. Mill's father, James, was also a philosopher of note and was a staunch supporter of Bentham and his beliefs.

John Stuart Mill's book *Utilitarianism* elabortes and improves upon the philosophy espoused by Bentham. Mill agreed with Bentham about pleasure and pain and morality.

Higher and Lower Pleasures

Mill sought to combat the critics who mocked the Utilitarian concept of the statistical analysis of every act to determine the pleasure factor before undertaking the act. He did not agree with the notion and created his own compromise. Mill differed from Bentham on the quality of pleasure, not just the quantity. Mills defined the nature of pleasure into two levels, the higher and the lower. Mill made value judgments on pleasure that Bentham did not, and he believed that a little pain was not a bad thing if, in the long run, it served society as a whole. By making the moral determination that some pleasures are better and more beneficial than others, Mill was attacked for not only elitism but for undermining the very foundation of Utilitarianism.

Mill's most famous book is called *On Liberty*. Considered politically liberal at the time, it now reads like it could be the manifesto of a conservative talk radio host. Mill stresses personal responsibility for yourself and your actions, your pursuit of happiness, and your pleasure. Society is concerned only with Big Picture issues, and minimal government interference into personal lives is the ideal. The state is only expected to intervene in the personal affairs of people when individuals are guilty of gross antisocial behavior and are a danger to others. If the harm you are doing is only to yourself, then that is your business. Of course, there are exceptions to Mill's rules for order. Free speech is a cornerstone, but to incite riot or to encourage people to commit crimes or other assorted acts of mayhem should naturally be restricted.

The Role of Women

Mill was ahead of his time as far as women's rights were concerned, and his utopia had strict laws protecting wives from spousal abuse. And in a time when children worked for hours in unsafe conditions, Mill also championed the rights of the very young. In short, the freedom of the individual is paramount, and state interference should be minimal and infrequent.

Mill also wrote a book called *The Subjection of Women* that predated the modern feminist movement by almost a century. The political and social women's rights movement of the nineteenth and early twentieth centuries was called the suffrage movement, and Mill was a leading advocate of universal suffrage. *Suffrage* literally means the right to vote, and this was the focal point of the women's movement of the day, but it actually encompassed much more.

FACTS

Mill's other famous book is *The Subjection of Women*, which was a passionate call for equal rights for women, long before the modern feminist movement. That a man would write such a treatise in the nineteenth century is amazing.

Mill's book was a passionate polemic attacking the injustices of the patriarchal society of the time. Women did not have the right to vote and were in general treated as second-class citizens. Mill compared the situation of women to slavery, which had been abolished some time before in England and only recently in America. The book was published in 1869, four years after the end of the American Civil War. The mistreatment was a vestige of the caveman epoch of prehistory when brute force ruled. This "might is right" mentality had, Mill argued, been abolished in every other aspect of civilized society except as far as women were concerned.

The Feminist

Although Mary Wollstonecraft (1759–1797) doesn't fall into the Utilitarianism category of philosophers, we've included her in this chapter because her views on women, like Mill's, were truly ahead of her time. Wollstonecraft wrote eloquently about the social and political conditions of her day, including feminism, and her contribution to literature, though not prolific, is formidable.

While working as a schoolteacher and headmistress in London, Wollstonecraft observed that the young women in her charge had already been socialized to a subordinate mindset, and though many were as equally gifted as the young lads, their lives were forever set in stone.

A Vindication of the Rights of Women is Mary Wollstonecraft's powerful feminist anthem, written long before the modern feminist movement. She eloquently makes the case for women's rights almost two hundred years before it became fashionable.

Because this is a philosophy book, we will focus on Wollstonecraft's contribution to the philosophy of feminism, long before it became fashionable. The book is called *A Vindication of the Rights of Women* (1792), in which she takes the *philosophes* of the Enlightenment to task, especially Rousseau, for often misusing their vaunted Reason. She also had many other complaints:

- She decries the "brainwashing" of women of her day, forcing them to fit into a social structure with no room for independence.
- She advocates the education of women to a degree equal to men.
- She laments the state of "spinsters," the pejorative term for women, who for whatever the reason, never married.
- She acknowledges that men are for the most part physically stronger than women, but argues that we have evolved beyond caveman ethics.
- She exhorts women to stop trying to please men.
- She laments the obsession with youth.
- She attacks the double standard where the man can be the playboy.
- She advocates coed schools, maintaining that bringing the sexes together at an early age will bring out the best in both, and break down barriers.

This remarkable woman, long before the appearance of Gloria Steinem and Betty Friedan, made the case for equality more powerfully, and with far more literary flair, than any who followed. Unfortunately, she was a lone lioness in the wilderness with few fans who were eager to hear her roar. But while the chauvinists who denounced her are no longer here, the Romantic Feminist's legacy eventually contributed to changing the world.

CHAPTER 14

The American Transcendentalists

Transcendentalism is a philosophy that began with Plato and his Forms. There is much in the universe that we cannot perceive or comprehend. Some insightful souls may have an inkling of the ephemeral realms, but it is not privy to the average Joe and Jane.

Transcendentalism Today

Transcendentalism in the modern era applies to a school of thought and a cast of characters that wrote and philosophized in America in the first half of the 1800s. Focused primarily in the New England states, these men and women were reacting against the Yankee Puritanism that came with the pilgrims and became entrenched in the culture of the region. They rejected the rituals and dogma of all organized religions and sought a more personal, direct, and secular route to unlock the mysteries of the universe and commune with the divine.

FACTS

It is no surprise that American Transcendentalists emerged in the New England region of the United States as opposed to another part of the country. This area, of course, is where the pilgrims landed, and their rigid Puritanism naturally inspired a forceful backlash among free thinkers and intellectuals of the time.

The American Transcendentalists were a combination of philosophers, psychologists, rugged individualists, naturalists, and literary folk. Their nature-loving ways bordered on pantheism. They called nature the macrocosm, and the human soul the microcosm. They believed that the microcosm perfectly mirrored the macrocosm and called the God of their understanding the Over-Soul. The Transcendentalists valued instinct and insight above intellect. They were into mysticism and the philosophical and spiritual teaching of India and China. They wrote experimental poetry, advocated civil rights, were early feminists, and lived in communes. The most famous Transcendentalists are Ralph Waldo Emerson and Henry David Thoreau, but there were other major players in the Transcendentalist movement as well.

Ralph Waldo Emerson

Ralph Waldo Emerson (1803–1882) is regarded as one of the two leading proponents of American Transcendentalism. A Unitarian preacher who had a transformative crisis after the tragic and premature death of his wife, he gave up his old life and traveled extensively abroad. He met the famous British poets Wordsworth and Coleridge and many other European artists and thinkers before returning home and settling in Concord, Massachusetts.

He was one of the founders of the Transcendental Club in 1836, which included the great Transcendental thinkers covered in this chapter. *The Dial* was their newsletter and some of them lived in a commune they called Brook Farm, in Massachusetts. They championed individualism and self-reliance and the belief that human intuition, not church dogma, contained the key to illumination and insight. Part social club, part support group, part "open mic" where they shared their poetry and philosophy, they were a controversial hotbed of radical thinkers.

QUESTIONS?

What is pantheism?
Pantheism is the belief that God is present in all things. He does not preside from a distance, but is everywhere. A distillation of the Christian belief system is sometimes stated as "God is Love." To the pantheist, it would be more accurately described as "God is Nature."

Emerson was a writer and lecturer whose famous works include *Nature and Self-Reliance,* which expressed the Transcendentalist philosophy. He viewed every individual as having full and free access to the Over-Soul. We are all something like cells in the giant organism that is God/Nature. We can access this collective unconsciousness and experience total interconnectedness with our fellows and the natural world. He believed, like St. Augustine, that evil is not a force unto itself but merely arises from the absence of good. He considered poets to be the modern mystics and prophets and directly influenced and inspired America's greatest poet, Walt Whitman. His influence in philosophy and literature had a profound impact on the American culture. And it did not fade away in the nineteenth century.

Henry David Thoreau

Henry David Thoreau (1817–1862) was no theoretical philosopher; he put his principles into practice and paid whatever price society exacted for his unflinching individualism. His famous book *Walden* is a journal of his solitary existence in a cabin on Walden Pond and an eloquent vehicle for the Transcendentalist philosophy. He was a Harvard grad who studied Emerson and then had the opportunity to meet him. He even lived in Emerson's home for a few years, functioning as a general factotum, everything from editor to handyman. He contributed to the Transcendentalists' journal, *The Dial*. After that, he built the famous cabin at Walden Pond and lived there for two years, writing his book.

Another philosophy that Thoreau espoused, and was later made better known and practiced in the twentieth century, was civil disobedience. He wrote an essay of the same name after spending a night in jail for refusing to pay a tax that went to support the Mexican War. The Mexican War of 1846–48 is a forgotten war in many ways, but it was an outgrowth of America's sense of Manifest Destiny.

FACTS

Manifest Destiny is a term created by a journalist and soon thereafter used as a nationalist rallying cry. It maintained, rather audaciously, that America's expansion from sea to shining sea was not only a grand and glorious juggernaut, but in fact the will of God.

Civil disobedience means to protest what one believes to be an unjust law or an unfair sociopolitical system through nonviolent means, fully aware that the consequence may entail imprisonment and/or brutality by the powers-that-be. *Passive resistance* means that you will turn the other cheek to law enforcement officials in riot gear and that you will do the time if you do the crime. The theory is that if enough people do this, then they will cause a change in society. Conscience before conformity was Thoreau's credo.

Thoreau was one of the original American nonconformists. He rejected materialism, lived modestly, often in near-poverty, and did his own thing despite social pressure and ostracism. And he was a tree-hugger more than a century before it became fashionable. In addition to the observations of the natural world and its mystical beauty in Walden, he also wrote eloquently about the pristine spirituality beauty of Cape Cod and the Maine woods, in books of the same name.

The strength of his resolve and his uncompromising nature eventually alienated those around him, including Emerson. He lived a hardscrabble life, usually alone, isolated by his nature and his attitude. Regarded as an eccentric failure in his lifetime, posterity sees him as a heroic philosopher who walked the walk rather than blithely talking the talk from a position of comfort and security.

William Ellery Channing

William Ellery Channing (1780–1842) was a preacher in the American Unitarian movement in the early nineteenth century. Unitarianism is a branch of Christianity that rejects the belief in the Holy Trinity, which is the conviction that God, Jesus, and the Holy Spirit are separate entities yet simultaneously one God.

ESSENTIALS

Unitarians were often liberal reformers of their day. They were social activists who championed many worthwhile causes, most notably the abolition of slavery. Many of the American Transcendentalists originally came from the ranks of the Unitarian Church.

Channing was also a social reformer who eloquently spoke and wrote, calling for the abolition of slavery and the establishment of a public school system to provide education for the increasing huddled masses yearning to breathe free. Channing's writings influenced the Transcendentalist movement. He believed that man's relationship to God is a personal one. The kingdom of God is within, as it were, and human nature is in fact divine. By "doing unto others," living a good life, and being compassionate, we can touch the divinity within ourselves.

Amos Bronson Alcott

Amos Bronson Alcott (1799–1888) was an academic who had a hard time supporting his family and making ends meet until his daughter, Louisa May Alcott of *Little Women* fame, hit the bestseller lists. He was an abolitionist, an early feminist, and even a vegetarian. Ahead of his time, he was regarded as an affable yet eccentric oddball. As a teacher and lecturer, he was largely a disseminator of others' philosophies, expressed in an endearing New England manner. He was a regular contributor to *The Dial,* the Transcendentalist newsletter of the day. Always broke but largely beloved, he was an influential figure in the Transcendentalist movement.

Do you think your hippie parents, aunts, and uncles were social innovators? Think again. One hundred and twenty years before the tumultuous 1960s, the American Transcendentalists were studying Eastern Philosophy, advocating a vegetarian diet, living in communes, and fighting for civil rights and feminist causes.

CHAPTER 15

Phenomenology and Existentialism

Phenomenology is a twentieth-century school of philosophy that attempts to eliminate theories and preconception and strives to "keep it simple." The existentialists believe that, despite the pessimism and nihilism that a world without spirituality can engender, individuals are capable of profound personal heroism in the face of seeming hopelessness.

Edmund Husserl

The founder of phenomenology, German philosopher Edmund Husserl (1859–1938) studied the mind itself, not the outside world of things and events that the mind perceives. Consciousness is properly studied through the mind, according to Husserl. He called this *phenomenological reduction.* The mind can think of things that do not exist, so this philosophy is similar to Idealism and Immaterialism. He called this the *bracketing of existence,* leaving the reality or unreality of things out of the equation.

QUESTIONS?

What is existentialism?
According to the American Heritage Dictionary, existentialism is "a philosophy that emphasizes the uniqueness and isolation of the individual experience in a hostile or indifferent universe, regards human existence as unexplainable, and stresses freedom of choice and responsibility for the consequences of one's acts."

He defined the essence of consciousness to be what he called *intentionality.* The thought and the thing are inextricably linked. You cannot think without thinking about something. There are absolutes in the mind that he called meanings, and assigning a meaning to a thing was directed intentionality. This is similar to the theory in New Physics that the experimenter cannot help but affect the result of the experiment.

Thinking and rethinking about things in your mind, describing them to yourself, and looking at them in different ways is an aspect of creativity. Phenomenology as a philosophy has influenced many in the creative pursuits of art and literature. Phenomenology also shows us how much our perceptions influence our worldview. Perception is reality, as it were.

Søren Kierkegaard

Regarded as the first existentialist, Søren Kierkegaard wrote in reaction to the popular philosophy of Hegel. A literary figure in Denmark, Kierkegaard used irony to make his points. As a result, it is often hard to tell when he is being serious and when he is pulling our philosophical leg. He was also a writer who introduced himself into his work, breaking down the "fourth wall" between the writer and the reader.

His Goals

Kierkegaard wrote candidly of his desire to be a famous writer. He also announced that he wanted to spread the true message of Christianity within the established Christian community, believing it had lost its way.

Kierkegaard saw paradox as the one constant of his time. A *paradox* is a seemingly contradictory idea that, upon closer examination, makes sense and is not contradictory. Kierkegaard, in many ways, embodied the very paradoxes of which he wrote. He was the Lieutenant Columbo of philosophers; he would often, in his writings and his life, pretend to be a dense, eccentric oddball in public when he was, in reality, a serious and cerebral thinker.

He wrote many books under a pseudonym. Removing the author's name from the work, he believed, would make the message a pure one and prevent the writer from being a fame-seeking egotist, enabling readers to concentrate on the message, not the messenger. Not only did Kierkegaard write a caustic parody of Hegel and his philosophy, he even wrote a satiric lampoon of himself and his own philosophy under an assumed name, just to play devil's advocate.

Kierkegaard celebrated the individual over the crowd; in fact, he believed that in regard to the Big Questions, the opinion of the group is invariably the wrong one. We must think for ourselves and be suspicious of *groupthink*. We should not worry about or be swayed by what our neighbors of society think. We must decide things for ourselves and then have the integrity to stand up for our beliefs despite the inevitable pressure that will be applied by the group.

To live this kind of uncompromising life is naturally a scary prospect. Alienation and social ostracism are sure to result from charting such a course. Living such a life will invariably lead to a sense of anxiety, or dread. With freedom comes fear. He wrote a book called *The Concept of Dread* that proposed that the natural response to living an intellectually independent life is what he called angst, the German word for anxiety and one that has entered the English vernacular. Religion is no help in alleviating anxiety and providing succor, because it is an illogical and unprovable philosophy that requires a giant leap of faith.

Subjective and Objective Truth

Kierkegaard sought to distinguish between what he called subjective and objective truth. Objective truth implies that something is true whether you know it or believe it. Subjective truth means that what is true for you may not be true for your neighbor. Kierkegaard's philosophy of the individual would clearly lead him to lean toward subjective truth as the only way to go. Objective truths are created by the group, and the group is not to be trusted as a source of insight, wisdom, and truth. Kierkegaard believed that a passionate intensity for a subjective truth was better than a lukewarm toeing of the party line to an ostensibly "objective" truth.

This is not to say that Kierkegaard was anti-Christian, In fact, he was deeply Christian, and he sought to cut through the groupthink and dogma to get back to basics and make Christianity once again accessible to the average Christian. He believed that Christianity should not be mediated by the middleman that is organized religion. Religion should be directly between the individual and God. This is done by living your life according to the principles of your faith, not merely going to church on Sunday and mindlessly following church dogma. Your life is like a Master's thesis that you will present to God on Judgment Day. Your life is your magnum opus that will be subject to scrutiny by the Almighty. This is quite a responsibility, and you had better make the most of it.

The Roots of Existentialism

This business of alienation, angst, and absurdity have come to make Kierkegaard regarded as the first of the existentialists. Though the existentialists were atheists who did not follow Kierkegaard's conviction that faith in God is a good and important aspect of life, they did embrace his belief in the importance of individualism against an apathetic if not downright hostile society. Existentialism took off in the twentieth century, but it has its origins in the philosophy of Kierkegaard, and Friedrich Nietzsche as well. Kierkegaard not only influenced future generations of philosophers, including Martin Heidegger and Jean-Paul Sartre, but also literary figures such as Henrik Ibsen and August Strindberg.

Martin Heidegger

Martin Heidegger (1889–1976) was a German philosopher whose existential philosophy influenced Camus, Sartre, and many modern philosophers that followed. He was influenced by Kierkegaard, Nietzsche, and the Presocratics. He shifted the focus from the examination of consciousness to experiencing the state of simply "being there," in his book *Being and Time*. Nothing less than the understanding of Being was his goal. Forget the theories and the speculations and the obtuse arguments and philosophical ruminations. The only thing we really can be sure of is our being, our existence. Hence, Heidegger is regarded as the first twentieth-century existentialist and an influence of Jean-Paul Sartre, the most famous existentialist.

SSENTIALS

Unlike Nietzsche, who posthumously suffered the slander of being labeled a Nazi, Martin Heidegger has earned the title fair and square. He publicly endorsed Hitler and the Nazis in the 1930s.

Heidegger also believed that "being" is not a stagnant state. Existence is constantly changing, which harkens back to the philosophy of Heraclitus. This chaotic world, according to Heidegger, generates far more than mere angst. He took angst one step further to its depressingly logical conclusion called *nihilism*. He felt that this hopelessness and despair and sense of the meaningless of life was a relatively new mindset brought about by the Industrial Age that was turning humanity into a race of lemming-like automatons. He lauded the ancient Greeks for their more positive outlook on "being." This had been dampened and subsumed by a couple of millennia of Western thought.

There is no shortage of philosophical arrogance in this theory. Heidegger infers that those truly "in the know" are the ones tortured with angst and dread about the nature of things and their own eventual demise.

The authentic experience the wonder of it all, in all its beauty and ugliness. The inauthentic are bland camp followers and cookie-cutter ciphers who live their lives without a clue. Heidegger obviously elevates the enlightened "authentic" folk above the great unwashed inauthentic masses, following Socrates's dictum that "an unexamined life is not worth living."

Albert Camus

Twentieth-century existentialist Albert Camus (1913–1960) was a French-Algerian man of letters and Nobel Prize winner. Raised in poverty in the North African country that was then a French colony, he had literary and theatrical ambitions in his youth, flirted briefly with the Communist Party, and eventually became a journalist.

His Background

He was sympathetic to the plight of the Arab natives of Algeria who suffered at the hands of their colonial masters, and his newspaper reports on the subject caused him to lose his job as a reporter. He went to France during World War II and courageously worked with the French Resistance against the Nazi occupying forces.

SSENTIALS

Albert Camus and Jean-Paul Sartre are the two most famous existentialists of the twentieth century. Both these Frenchmen believed that people had to take personal responsibility for their own actions, not to waste time blaming society or God (whom they did not believe in) for their problems, and that dignity, heroism, and even happiness could be found in an absurd world.

Camus is considered an existentialist by everyone except himself and the other famous existentialists. His criticism of Stalinism earned the ire of fellow French thinker Jean-Paul Sartre and other French existentialists. The intelligentsia of Europe and America curiously supported Josef Stalin, the Russian leader who history has proved to be a vicious dictator and mass murderer on the scale of Adolf Hitler.

Camus was given the Nobel Prize for literature in 1957 and died tragically in a car accident in 1960. Although primarily known as a novelist and playwright, it is these very fictional devices that exposed existentialism to a wide audience. Given a choice, most people, then and now, would rather read a novel or see a play than slog through a philosophical tome.

His Writings

The novel *The Stranger* and the essay *The Myth of Sisyphus* are part of what Camus called "the cycle of the absurd." The world is a silly and ridiculous place, and existence is meaningless and absurd, according to Camus. This is not to suggest that life is a raucously merry, feel-good laugh-riot. Camus's writing does not elicit many a warm, fuzzy glow or hearty bellow. People seek order in a cold and chaotic world and find only indifference, despair, and an inexorable trek to a lonely and silent grave, without even an afterlife to provide some posthumous succor.

FACTS

The two famous twentieth-century existentialists, Albert Camus and Jean-Paul Sartre, were both offered the Nobel Prize for literature. Sartre did not believe in dispensing such accolades to authors. He felt it would compromise his integrity as a man of letters. Camus gratefully accepted the honor (and the cash prize).

Alienation is the norm according to Camus. Camus's protagonists strive to find some happiness in their seemingly dismal situations by ultimately resorting to the age-old technique of acceptance. Even though a saint said it, an atheist can practice it. They accept the things they cannot change. The spiritual person asks their God for help to gain acceptance, while the existentialist summons acceptance from his singularly human spark, the life force that he or she would never consider calling a soul.

Camus came of age between the two world wars in the first half of the last century. He sought to find meaning in life despite the despair and malaise that descended upon Europe in those days. With no faith in God, Camus sought the answer in the indomitable human spirit and its ability to survive and thrive while bearing unbearable burdens.

The Struggle of Sisyphus

The myth of Sisyphus is an ancient myth about a man who is condemned by the gods to roll a huge rock up a hill, only to have the boulder roll back down upon reaching the summit. He has to repeat this frustrating process for all eternity. Camus's essay on this myth sees it as a metaphor for the modern human condition. Sisyphus typifies what Camus calls the "absurd hero." Enormous effort and energy are expended on a task that accomplishes nothing. This is often the plight of contemporary people, be they blue- or white-collar laborers. A beast of burden performs such tasks with the luxury of being oblivious to its plight. Mankind is cursed with a consciousness of his unpleasant predicament.

Camus finds solace, even triumph, in this fate. There is, according to Camus, a comfort that comes in knowing you are on your own. Society is of little help, and there is no God. You have only your humanity to rely on, and, according to Camus, that is enough. The indomitable human spirit can endure anything, even the relentless struggle of Sisyphus.

Jean-Paul Sartre

The other French existentialist of the twentieth century was Jean-Paul Sartre (1905–1980), who was also a novelist and dramatist as well as the author of philosophical works and political polemics. Like Camus, he was active in the French Resistance during World War II. A political Leftist, he alternately criticized and lauded the activities of the Soviet Union during the Cold War era. Unlike Camus, he refused the Nobel Prize for literature when it was offered.

Taking Responsibility

In *Being and Nothingness*, Sartre, like Camus, saw humans at their best when rebelling against their impersonal society, by taking responsibility for their own actions and not becoming bogged down by self-victimization and buying into humanity's penchant for blaming others for their problems. Interestingly, his emphasis that self-reliance and rugged individualism are essential to be truly alive and truly human is not particularly encouraged in the Marxist and Communist governments he often publicly championed. His plays and novels also reflect this philosophy.

Sartre's later philosophy shifted to a more Marxist bent. In a later treatise called *Critique of Dialectical Reason*, Sartre switches gears from focusing on the individual to advocating that people join together to affect change in a revolutionary fashion. Only through the group force can individual freedom be achieved. This is quite a departure from his earlier belief, and because no Marxist/Communist government has ever fulfilled the dubious promise of Utopia, Sartre would have been better off continuing to focus on individualism.

If you want to get a feel for existentialist philosophy but just cannot see yourself revisiting required reading from high school and college syllabi, try watching Martin Scorcese's 1976 classic *Taxi Driver*, which creates an existential ambience and displays New York City in all its tarnished beauty as an existential kingdom.

Sartre remarks that mankind is "condemned to be free." By this statement, he means that freedom is both a blessing and a curse. It's a responsibility and a burden, but you can find happiness and hope after a fashion even within the seemingly pessimistic universe of the existentialists.

No Exit

Literature in the form of fiction and drama usually makes a greater impact on the average person than a philosophy book. A philosophy can be more palatably transmitted to an open mind when presented in an entertaining format. Sartre, like Camus, had success as a playwright and novelist, and these works effectively brought his existentialist thought to life.

No Exit includes a famous line of dialogue and, for many, a painful truth. *No Exit* takes the format of a "drawing room drama," popular in the first half of the twentieth century, and makes it a vehicle for his existentialist beliefs. An aristocratic man, a lesbian, and a vacuous beauty are trapped in a well-furnished room. They are all aware that they are dead and in Hell. As is the case in a play set with three characters in one room, there is a great deal of talk.

The man likes the lesbian, who does not like him. The lesbian likes the other woman, who doesn't like her. The "dumb blonde" likes the man, who finds her far from compelling. Thus the man finally utters the often all too true remark at the play's end, "Hell is other people!"

The Story of Roquentin

Nausea tells the tale of Roquentin, an alter ego for Sartre, who narrates the story in the form of journal entries. He lives a basically solitary life and is a writer, grappling with a biography of a historical figure in which he has little or no interest. The crux of the novel is the insight that comes to Roquentin when he realizes that his bouts of "nausea" are his existential epiphany about the meaning of his life and his place in the universe. Dread results with the realization that you are totally alone and on your own. With freedom comes responsibility, as the cliché tells us. Conformity and the comfort of being subsumed by a structured society is a refuge for the cowardly, but that is an illusion anyway. All is chaos in the existential playbook. To accept this lot in life is to live what Sartre called "authentically." And it is only the brave hearts out there that have the courage to live an authentic life, and they heroically struggle to maintain human dignity in a world of bureaucrats and automatons and nothingness.

CHAPTER 16

Modern and Postmodern Philosophers

In the twentieth century, analytic philosophy emerged. This approach included an interest in the natural sciences, linguistics, and logic. Philosophizers were making careers in academia, and cynics suggested that if Universal Truth was ever found, they would be out of jobs. Nevertheless, analytic philosophy was a dominant philosophical strain.

Bertrand Russell

Bertrand Russell (1872–1970) was a British philosopher, Nobel laureate, and one of the most influential philosophers of the twentieth century. His primary focus early in his career was mathematics. His first major work is called *The Principles of Mathematics* (1902) in which he endeavored to make math more accessible.

Russell sought to look at problems in philosophy through the objective eyes of logic and to find solutions to the big philosophical issues with the determination of a man of science.

His Writings

Russell was a longtime collaborator of fellow philosopher and mathematician Alfred North Whitehead. Together, they composed the massive *Principia Mathematica,* a masterpiece that established the interconnection between logic and mathematics. This mammoth volume was considered a work of genius.

FACTS

Russell opposed militarism and warfare under any circumstances. He also lived to be ninety-eight, so he protested every major conflict from World War I to the Vietnam War. He did take a patriotic stand during World War II, but in the Cold War, he remained a staunch antinuclear weapons activist.

In *The Problems of Philosophy,* Russell sought to discredit the philosophy of Idealism, which suggested that physical reality is not real at all, and all objects we perceived through the senses are actually created in the mind. Russell was a realist and felt that this was poppycock in the extreme. Russell was an Empiricist, who believed that everything we know must be acquired through sensory experience. Like the Objectivists and the Empiricists, Russell believed that the outside world had a reality all its own and exists whether we see it or think about it.

His Political Background

Russell was no stranger to the lockup. At the age of eighty-nine, he was arrested at an antinuclear protest. His protests of the World War I caused him to lose his teaching job at Cambridge and end up in prison. Like many intellectuals of the day, he was intrigued by the Russian Revolution and the emergence of the Soviet Union. Unlike many of them, he had the good sense to condemn the form of government that rose to power. The totalitarianism and oppression did not match his notions of what an ideal socialist state should be.

His Attacks on Christianity

In addition to being a philosopher, Russell was primarily an educator. He taught in China and was headmaster of the exclusive Beacon Hill School in England. Among the books that got Russell in hot water with some holier-than-thou American academics were *What I Believe, Why I Am Not a Christian,* and *Manners and Morals.* Russell opined that the millennia worth of "proofs" of the existence of God proposed by philosophers were ineffectual at best. And he was quick to remind the world of the many atrocities committed in the name of God and other deleterious side effects of adhering to the Christian ethic. Russell also spoke candidly, advocating freedom of sexual expression and the hypocrisy and destructiveness of bourgeois morality.

Logical Analysis

Just as pop stars periodically reinvent themselves, Bertrand Russell changed boats in the philosophical stream from time to time. However, he maintained that his philosophies followed a consistent course, and he did remain at heart an Empiricist. He had great respect for science, which he believed was the best source to knowledge. Physical reality was not a realm of Ideas; it was very real and independent and was perceived by, not created by, the mind.

Russell sought to create a system he called *logical analysis,* whereby a particular concept or proposition could be deconstructed and all its parts examined to gain knowledge and understanding. This is also called *Logical Atomism.* Simply put, this means that the world is composed of facts, not unlike the atoms that make up physical reality. A *proposition* is a collection of these "atoms."

In *On the Relations of Universals and Particulars,* Russell was able to use logical analysis to, as he said it, finally have the last word on the nagging problem of Aristotelian Universals. He was able to logically "prove" that both Universals and particulars can exist. Of course there is never a "last word" in the wonderful world of philosophy.

Ludwig Josef Johan Wittgenstein

Ludwig Josef Johan Wittgenstein (1889–1951) studied with Bertrand Russell and became an influential advocate of analytic and linguistic philosophy. In 1918, Wittgenstein had completed *Tractatus Logico-philosophicus,* which he called the "final solution" to all problems of philosophy. In later years, however, Wittgenstein rejected his own conclusions in the *Tractatus* and wrote yet another seminal work of modern philosophy called *Philosophical Investigations.*

Tractatus

In his *Tractatus,* Wittgenstein, like Russell, maintained that language was composed of things he called propositions, which could be broken down to less complex propositions until you arrived at some basic truths. Similarly, the world is composed of myriad complex facts that can be broken down again and again until you arrive at an atomic fact.

Here is Wittgentsein in brief: The world is made up of facts. We perceive facts through turning them into thoughts, which in essence means creating a mental picture of them. Thoughts are expressed in language in what Wittgenstein called propositions. He envisioned boiling language down to what he called atomic sentences, which would successfully, if not poetically, describe reality as we know it.

A Change of Heart

Because language is an expression of facts, it has no meaning. And a truly logical language would not be able to express subjective notions of Beauty and Love. Wittgenstein decided that the massive volume of the *Tractatus* had left him with nothing more to say on the subject of philosophy. He remained philosophically silent for ten years, only to come back with another major work that basically denounced his earlier theories.

QUESTIONS?

What is meant by the term "postmodern" philosophy?
Postmodern philosophy is basically the state of philosophy today. It covers a wide range of thought, and most postmodernists would deny that they are part of such a movement. It is a convenient label for contemporary philosophy.

Logical analysis is an exact science, and language and physical reality are not so mathematically precise, Wittgenstein came to believe. He decided that his plan to devise the ultimate logical language was not only impossible but also a bad idea. For years, Wittgenstein wrote nothing–what was the point since it's meaningless anyway?–but his students took copious notes as the philosopher forged a new philosophy.

Eventually, Wittgenstein wrote *Philosophical Investigations,* in which he broadened his view of language to regard words not as the basis of propositions, but as tools that are designed to perform different tasks in communicating. He also came to see language as a game where its many players develop their own rules. Rather than create a logical (and inevitably sterile) language, Wittgenstein now began to celebrate linguistic diversity.

Michel Foucault

A postmodernist, the recent French philosopher Michel Foucault (1926–1984) is one of the most influential philosophers of modern times. Foucault was, among many things, a philosophical relativist. Much of his work reveals how "truths" have changed over the centuries, from age to age and culture to culture. Black is white and wrong is right depending on the powers that be of the belief system du jour. He made the claim, through study and research, that there has been very little in the way of Big Picture Truth over the millennia. Foucault was no fan of Sigmund Freud and Karl Marx, and his great influences were Martin Heidegger and Nietzsche.

On Madness

Foucault's first influential book was *Madness and Civilization,* in which he chronicled Western society's changing views toward mental illness over the centuries. Madness was, at one time, given mystical connotations. People were thought to be blessed by the gods, or at least in direct contact with the divine. Foucault argued that with the so-called Age of Enlightenment (which he thought was highly overrated) came the advent of what were then called lunatic asylums or madhouses. He believed that the purpose of these "bedlams" was not to "minister to a mind diseased," but actually to keep people locked up for study and scrutiny. Foucault also maintained that the creative spirit and the lunatic fringe were not so far apart, and many of the "lunatics" were actually visionaries and societal dissidents, whether active rebels, or simply souls who marched to the beat of a different drum.

On Human Sciences

Foucault's second major work is *The Order of Things.* This is no less than what its subtitle suggests, "An archaeology of the human sciences." Human sciences are defined by Foucault as history, sociology, and psychology. Again, he makes the case that "knowledge" means an entirely different thing from culture to culture and epoch to epoch. He pays special attention to the symbols and language of past cultures.

On the Penal System

Foucault's other major work is called *Discipline and Punish.* Just as he took the psychological institutions to task in *Madness and Civilization,* he critiques the various penal systems through the ages in this influential book. He makes the case that, in the Western world at least, the employment of torture and physical abuse in modern prison systems has merely switched the destructive emphasis from body to soul. Torture as a means of punishment is still widely practiced in much of the world, but in "civilized" Europe and America, it has been largely eliminated, at least as a state-approved practice.

Nevertheless, it is also generally accepted that prisons do not "rehabilitate" criminals. Incarceration actually throws people into a milieu where the criminal life is reinforced. People emerge from prison more adept criminals rather than converted citizens who have "paid their debt to society" and are ready, willing, and able to begin anew.

On Othering

Another important idea of Foucault's is his notion of what he called *othering*. This is something people have always done, and it is something that people will continue to do as part of human nature. Othering means simply making note and being aware of different people, whether they be racially, politically, socially, sexually, or in any other way different from you. For the most part, the person doing the othering considers themselves normal and the other person to be abnormal. But always be aware that someone else is over there othering you.

On Sexuality

Foucault's last phase of philosophizing involved a mammoth study of human sexuality. He completed three books in the proposed series: *History of Sexuality, Volume I: An Introduction; The Use of Pleasure;* and *The Care of the Self.* Tragically and ironically, this study of sexuality remains incomplete because Foucault's life was cut short by Acquired Immune Deficiency Syndrome (AIDS).

Jacques Derrida

Jacques Derrida (1930–) is another contemporary French philosopher who started the philosophical school called *deconstruction.* Deconstruction is the process of breaking down of a thing (in Derrida's case, language) to show that what is being stated is in fact inherently false.

Linguistics, the study of language, is Derrida's area of expertise. He sees language as a flawed means of communication, arguing that the reader can not really know the author's true intent, and for that matter, neither can the author. The text you are reading may have an entirely different meaning to you than the author intends, and the author may not even have a clue about what the meaning of his words are.

There are an infinite number of interpretations to any finite body of text, according to Derrida. To him, language is a fluid concept and often a stormy sea of contradictory meanings and multiple interpretations. And the ever-impish Derrida did not suggest that he was immune to all this. His voluminous writings, if deconstructed, would be as flawed and bogus as anyone else's.

Logocentricism is Derrida's derisive phrase for philosophy. *Logos* is the Greek word for "word," and *logocentric* means that philosophers see their writings as superior to other forms of writing, including fiction, poetry, or other manners of linguistic expression.

Derrida is considered by many to be a twentieth-century Sophist. He is playing language games to provoke and, in some cases, annoy. He thumbs his nose at traditional philosophy by saying that philosophy is logocentric.

CHAPTER 17

Sociology and Anthropology

As philosophy headed into the twentieth century, it branched off into sociology, anthropology, and psychology. These philosophical offshoots began to more aggressively employ the scientific method and apply the practices used to study the natural world to the study of societies, cultures, and the mysterious workings of the human mind.

Sociology

Sociology is the study of the human animal as he relates and interacts with his fellows—in families, communities, economic groups, and all other aspects of the human experience. Sociology originally cast its scientific glance primarily on the Western world of the Industrial Age in the mid-nineteenth century. The discipline of anthropology was directed toward those so-called primitive cultures that the Europeans were interacting with, usually to the disadvantage of the primitives.

Humans are social by nature, be they living and dying in the misty rainforests or writing a philosophy book on their laptop in the Bronx, New York (though those folks are often decidedly antisocial). Humanity, as a general rule and barring the requisite exceptions, seeks out others of their kind for business and pleasure, friendship and romance. We comprise families, social circles, religious institutions, and bodies politic under the umbrella we call a society. And how we interact with each other is a never-ending source of fascination. From the Sophists who pronounced, "Man is the measure of all things," to those who simply sit on a park bench and "people watch," to the more scientific-minded who devised an elaborate and systematic discipline around people watching, sociology has emerged as a valuable and wide-ranging field of study.

Though many philosophers made the study of mankind and his social situations an object of scrutiny, the word sociology was first coined by a French philosopher named Auguste Comte in 1838. Generally regarded as the Father of Modern Sociology, Comte sought to employ the same methods that scientists had used in the investigation and exploration of the physical world and apply them to the study of human affairs.

The three major figures in sociology are Karl Marx, Emile Durkheim, and Max Weber. Their insight and influence changed the world and is still felt today.

Karl Marx

Karl Marx (1818–1883) is the architect of what became modern socialism and communism, ideologies that went on to change the face of the globe and the state of the world in ways that Marx himself may never have imagined. A student of philosophy, he, along with Friedrich Engels, is the author of the world-altering tome, *The Communist Manifesto*. He sought social reform to combat the injustices of the Industrial Revolution. Needless to say, this made him an unpopular figure with the European powers-that-were, and he was exiled to London where he wrote another equally influential polemic, *Das Kapital*.

Certainly, Karl Marx is one of the most controversial figures in history. He and his legacy are both revered and reviled. Though Marx never lived to see it, and believed that world revolution would begin in England, avowed Marxists were responsible for the Russian Revolution of 1917 and the subsequent rise of the Soviet Union.

FACTS

Max Weber was a German thinker who, like Marx, was no fan of capitalism. He linked the rise of capitalism with the Protestant Work Ethic, a byproduct of the Protestant sect called Calvinism, which stressed frugality along with spirituality.

Marx believed that economic relationships were of primary importance, and the conflict between the classes was an inevitability, due to the chasm between the haves and have-nots. This is called the *Social Conflict theory*.

He is also famous for saying that religion was the opiate of the masses. In other words, he was not what you would call a religious man. In fact, he felt that the focus on being good little boys and girls in this life in order to be rewarded in the next led to a population of passive sheep. And this passivity was exploited by the ruling class to further their capitalist goals and keep the masses docile, yet of service.

Though a communist, Marx put a lot of stock in materialism. He believed that the major force in world affairs is production: the making and accumulation of stuff. Workers hired to produce the goods that make the world go round feel no great pride in their labors. This only leads to alienation, unrest, and ultimately, revolution.

In Marx's worldview, the majority of people toiled with little reward while the upper classes reaped the fruits of their labor. He saw an inherent inequality in capitalism. Marx believed that situation could not go on forever, and it would eventually reach critical mass and result in a revolution of the working classes against their capitalist masters. He believed the results of this rebellion would lead to a paradisiacal communist form of government with freedom for all.

Marx did not foresee the fact that the communist governments that emerged in the twentieth century have been among the most cruel dictatorships and wanton human rights violators the world has ever known. The injustices of his age were real and needed repair, but the legacy he bequeathed the twentieth century brought only more terror and totalitarianism into the world.

Max Weber

Another influential sociologist of the era was Max Weber (1864–1920). He was a German thinker who also took a jaundiced view of capitalism and sought to understand its emergence in the Western world rather than in another culture in another part of the world. He linked the rise of capitalism with the Protestant Work Ethic.

The Protestant sect called Calvinism (named for its founder, theologian John Calvin) championed the theory of predestination. In essence, predestination is a belief that God has already decided who goes to heaven and who goes to hell, and nothing you do in this life, for good or evil, will impact this divine decision. Yet rather than indulge their darkest impulses, since the die was cast long before they were born, Calvinists opted to try to please God in their lifetime. They decided that this entailed embracing the values of good old-fashioned hard work and the accumulation of money. Not, however, for the things they can provide or the good works that these attributes can accomplish for the benefits of their fellow man, but hard work and frugality for its own sake.

Whereas Marx believed that economics motivated human thought, Weber believed the opposite, that human ideas brought about particular economic systems. And while Marx spoke of class struggles and ultimately class warfare, the word Weber used to describe the division of societies was *stratification.*

ALERT

In *Star Trek IV: The Voyage Home,* Dr. McCoy said, "The bureaucratic mentality is the only constant in the universe." He believed this was bad. Sociologist Max Weber would agree with this assessment by the good doctor, but would laud it as a good thing. He loved bureaucracies.

Weber also addressed the rise of bureaucracies in Europe. He actually liked them! He thought they were the ideal organizing principle in the new industrial societies of Europe in the nineteenth century. He approved of the predictability of a routine, the structural hierarchy, believing that bureaucracies would ultimately level the playing field between the classes. Rising within the bureaucracy was theoretically based on merit and talent. A disadvantaged person could rise within the ranks based on his ability, not his connections. Weber did not believe in the theory that it is not what you know, but who you know, though time and again this proves to be a more accurate assessment of the way of the world. On a more ominous note, he noted that once entrenched in the society, a bureaucracy was difficult, if not impossible to destroy.

Emile Durkheim

Emile Durkheim (1858–1917) bridged the disciplines of sociology and the equally new notion of anthropology. He also founded the school of thought called *Functionalism.* Functionalism maintains that a society, in essence, took on a personality of its own and could be objectively viewed the way a scientist or physician may regard a living organism.

He proposed that cultures have a *collective consciousness.* The values and beliefs held by a culture direct the behavior of its members without their even knowing it. Modern Americans don't need to be told that cannibalism is wrong. This is hardwired and second nature. Yet there are cultures where cannibalism was and is not only practiced, but also considered a perfectly appropriate culinary option. Those that do not conform are deviants, and as a result, criminology and the study of deviance are offshoot sociological schools that study society's miscreants. For the most part, however, the majority of citizens fall within the parameters of their particular collective consciousness.

Durkheim and his followers also engaged in extensive *fieldwork,* the term used to describe venturing out of the confines of the classroom or the laboratory and indulging in some hands-on investigations. This fieldwork led them to the study of many primitive societies, which is a mainstay of the modern discipline of anthropology.

Anthropology

Anthropology as a science is a fairly recent discipline in the scheme of world history, but ever since mankind has formed societies and cultures, there have been people observing and commenting upon their societies as well as those of their neighbors.

Explorers, crusaders, and others who were boldly going where no one had gone before were regularly finding strange new worlds and new civilizations in their travels. From the ancient seafaring peoples to Marco Polo to Christopher Columbus and those that followed him to the New World, any explorer who made observations and wrote about their travels was an anthropologist of sorts.

FACTS

Anthropology can be broken down into the study of three main areas: society, culture, and evolution. A roving pack of baboons can be called a society, but the social intercourse among the denizens of New York City would be called a culture. There is much commonality in both groups.

Modern *anthropology* is, of course, a more systematic science with a tested and trustworthy methodology that examines humanity in all its glorious diversity of cultures and beliefs. Anthropology seeks to gain an understanding of the differences in civilizations as well as discovering many surprising similarities, thus enriching our understanding of ourselves.

Anthropology can be broken down into the study of three main areas: society, culture, and evolution. *Society* and *culture* are often interchangeable expressions, though in the strict sense, culture would be the interactions and behavior patterns of a more complex society.

Ethnocentrism

Charles Darwin is the most famous proponent of the theory of evolution. His book, *On the Origin of Species,* published in 1859, proposed the theory of natural selection. British philosopher Herbert Spencer put his spin on the evolutionary theory, applying it to humanity and calling it *survival of the fittest.* This form of *social Darwinism* was often used to justify colonialism and the xenophobic European feelings of superiority.

Anthropologists often study our primate cousins (man is a primate, and our hairy brethren include apes and monkeys) to get a glimpse into what very early man may have been like. Certain similarities can be found, and the differences chart the many ways in which mankind branched off from the rest of the primates to evolve into what we are today.

This flaw in past anthropological studies is called *ethnocentrism.* This is the belief that your society is better than the one you are studying. A nineteenth-century European anthropologist confronting a primitive Polynesian tribe often found them inferior to himself and the world from which he came, thus his findings were replete with cultural biases. Civilization was associated with the trappings of the Industrial Age, and it was inconceivable that these laid-back beachcombers may be on to something.

Ethnocentrism was the prevailing anthropological view for many years and it justified an inflated sense of European pre-eminence and rationalized a multitude of sins.

Cultural Relativism

An influential anthropologist who sought to make anthropology more respectable was Franz Boas. He believed in fieldwork, living among the civilization you were studying for an extended period of time. He also rejected the ethnocentric and racist views of many of his predecessors. He trained a whole generation of anthropologists, and his work was the basis for the practice of *cultural relativism*.

The contemporary anthropologist, now keenly aware of the analytic flaws and prejudices of previous anthropologists, strives not to judge the foreign civilizations they study. What works in Des Moines may not work in the Amazon, but that does not make one inferior to the other. Celebrating diversity is the watchword of modern anthropology. Comparisons can certainly be made, but judgments are to be avoided.

CHAPTER 18

Psychology

P *sychology* is the study of the mind and the role it plays in human behavior. The Greek roots of psychology are *psyche,* meaning *soul,* and *logos, word.* In ancient times, soul and mind were more or less interchangeable.

The Roots of Psychology

Though psychology is a relatively modern discipline, we can look back to our old friends the Greek philosophers and see that the genesis of psychological thinking began back then. Plato's myth of the cave, wherein we the cave dwellers only see shadows of reality while the Truth is forever obscured to all save brave inquiring minds, can also be a metaphor for the unconscious. Our conscious selves are only the tip of the iceberg, a mere fraction of the totality that makes us tick.

The ancient philosophers and medical men also tried to come to terms with the problems of insanity. In the earliest speculations, demonic possession and other supernatural forces took the blame. Later thinkers sought to find physical causes for mental illness. Plato and Socrates believed that insanity arose when man's animal nature overwhelmed his logical mind. This is a precursor to the twentieth-century concepts of the Id and the shadow. An early physician named Galen came up with the idea that bodily fluids, or humours, regulated the emotions. If the four humours were out of balance, mental illness occurred. The four humours identified by Galen are blood and the unappetizing sounding black bile, yellow bile, and phlegm.

It wasn't until the late nineteenth century that psychology came into its own as a separate discipline. And perhaps the most famous of the fledgling psychiatrists was Sigmund Freud.

Sigmund Freud

Sigmund Freud (1856–1939) is one of the most famous and influential psychologists of the twentieth century. Even those who don't know much about psychology or give much thought to the workings of the unconscious have some awareness of Freud. They have heard the term *Freudian slip*. They might have a vague notion of what the Oedipus Complex is, and the words *ego* and *id* have entered the vernacular. Most people have heard the expression "Sometimes a cigar is just a cigar," though not everyone takes that adage to heart. The pop culture representation of a psychologist is often a bearded, bespectacled egghead pompously intoning psychobabble in a German accent. Freud has as many detractors as advocates, and

Freudian psychology falls in and out of favor, but there is no doubt that he is a pioneer in the exploration of the mind and its motivating forces.

Psychoanalysis

Freud practiced medicine in Vienna, Austria, in the latter half of the nineteenth and early twentieth centuries. He was a neurologist by formal training. He encountered many patients who complained of ailments, but upon thorough examination, had nothing physically wrong with them. Freud deduced that their conditions were *psychosomatic* in nature. In other words, they were caused by a mental condition or disorder. If he got to the root of what was really bothering them, the physical manifestation of their psychic distress would alleviate. This was done through hypnosis, or sometimes by simply talking about it. Thus, *psychoanalysis* was born, the most influential psychological school of the twentieth century.

The next time your friend complains about her boss, saying, "He's, like, *so* anal!" ask her whether she really thinks he is stuck in one of Freud's stages of psychosexual development: They are, in order, the Oral, Anal, Phallic, Latent, and Genital Stages.

Freud was intrigued by the concept of the unconscious. He used the popular iceberg analogy to explain the workings of the mind. Our consciousness was a mere tip of the iceberg, and the unconscious was looming below the surface of our waking hours, a formidable force that was directing our thoughts and our actions in ways in which we were completely unaware. Why does a woman constantly sabotage relationships? Why does a hack writer lay fallow with writer's block as his deadline fast approaches? Why does a man get laryngitis the night before he must deliver a speech to a large audience? Why do people do things that seemingly make no sense and create unnecessary problems for themselves? Freud posited that this was the unconscious at work.

The unconscious forces that clandestinely drive us are largely sexual and aggressive in nature, according to Freud. They are thoughts and impulses that are best kept under wraps. But the unconscious must find expression in some form. Just as matter is neither created nor destroyed, buried emotions do not go away. They lay dormant, and if not owned and faced, they will surface unsummoned with, at best, embarrassing results. They must find expression in a socially acceptable form in order for the individual to stay psychologically fit.

Two of the techniques of Freudian psychoanalysis are the interpretation of dreams and free association. Even while sleeping, the mind is busily processing data. Dreams are the mind's method of dealing with unresolved issues and baggage. Dreams speak to us in symbols, some obvious, others obscure. According to Freud, dreams are like one act plays and surreal videos that give us clues to what is *really* on our minds. The patient discusses his dreams with the doctor, who tries to interpret what the dream is really revealing. Freud once said, "Every dream is a wish," which means most of us have some very bizarre wishes indeed.

Via free association, the psychiatrist also tries to unlock the mysteries of the unconscious. The patient reclines on a couch and chatters away about whatever comes to mind: memories, fantasies, issues of the day, resentments. Anything and everything is grist for the analyst's mill, who tries to find rhyme and reason amid the patient's rambling.

The Oedipus Complex

Freud also came up with the infamous theory of the *Oedipus Complex*. Oedipus was a character in a play by the Greek playwright Sophocles. It tells the story of Oedipus, a king who, through a series of coincidences, happens to murder his father and then marry his mother. Upon discovering the truth, the horrified Oedipus gouges out his own eyes in penance.

Freud felt that every young man goes through his internal Oedipus Complex, a rivalry with the father for the attentions of the mother. He suggests that young boys unconsciously want to get the father out of the picture and possess the mother, to put it politely. They are in a maelstrom of love and hate, torn with jealousy, desire, confusion, and rage. Healthy young men outgrow the Oedipus Complex, but pity the poor souls who do not. They are walking wounded, and their dysfunction will continue to hound and cripple them unless they seek treatment.

Sigmund Freud is one of the founding fathers of modern psychology. Though he falls in and out of favor, his theories on the unconscious, the Oedipus Complex, and the interpretation of dreams continue to intrigue both professional and armchair psychologists.

Freud, a product of Europe of the nineteenth century, believed that the Oedipus Complex was a universal phenomenon. Other researchers believe that this is not an archetypal condition that spans all cultures. Freud assumed girls had a corresponding love-hate relationship with their mothers. He didn't assign it with its own name, but the distaff version was later called the *Electra Complex,* named after a character from Greek drama who murdered her mother.

The Personality

Freud divided the personality into three components:

- The Ego is the part of a person that he or she is most aware of and that the rest of the world sees. It is the conscious, rational part of the personality.
- The Id: The Id remains largely unconscious. It is the sensual, primal side of ourselves, pure instinct and libido. When the Id is allowed to run rampant, all manner of havoc ensues.
- The Superego is the "conscience." It contains the ethics and values that have been instilled by parents and society.

The Stages of Development

Freud also categorizes the stages of psychosexual development. The Oral Stage is from birth to eighteen months. During this stage, the baby discovers the world via oral sensations.

The Anal Stage, from eighteen to thirty-six months, coincides with the toilet training period. Adults who get psychologically stuck in this stage are either fastidious and fussy or a total slob.

The Phallic Stage lasts from three to six years. The child becomes fascinated with their genitals, and the Oedipus Complex kicks in.

Sexual feelings are suppressed in the Latency Stage, according to Freud. It lasts from age six to puberty. It is the period for boys when girls are "icky," and vice versa.

The final stage is the Genital Stage, which starts at puberty and continues throughout life. The normal person begins what will hopefully be a happy and gratifying sexual life.

Freud's Legacy

Freudian psychoanalysis became enormously popular in medical and scientific circles, and Freud found himself a mentor with many protégés. As is always the case, the pupil rebels against his teacher, and these men of science and medicine adapted and built upon Freud's work. They all embraced the belief in the major role the unconscious plays, but many disagreed with Freud's emphasis on sex.

Carl Gustav Jung

Carl Gustav Jung (1875–1961) is the most famous follower of Sigmund Freud. Jung used Freud's psychoanalytic techniques in his medical practice, and both men agreed on the significant role played by the unconscious. Freud was fond of Jung and began to see him as his heir apparent, the successor who would carry on the Freudian school of thought.

A Parting of Ways

Eventually, Jung and Freud had an acrimonious split about the nature of the unconscious. Jung veered away from the emphasis of sexual forces being the driving factors that could explain every action and motivation. Not thinking and acting as objective men of science, each felt betrayed, and the split led not only to the end of a friendship and professional rapport, but it was instrumental in bringing about Jung's being shunned as a pariah by his fellows.

Jung took a radical sabbatical wherein he indulged in the unheard of practice of self-analysis. He chronicled this in his memoir *Memories, Dreams, Reflections* and called it a "confrontation with the unconscious." Jungian theories and the Jungian school of thought were the result of this inward journey, and his ideas are a major contribution to psychology, transcending it to embrace the worlds of mythology, folklore, astrology, Eastern spirituality, and alchemy. It is no surprise that Jung is quite fashionable in New Age circles, given the mystical nature of his later writings. He is also deeply criticized in other circles for his failure to denounce the rise of Hitler and the Nazis in Germany in the 1930s. He ultimately did so, but many feel it was too little and too late.

The Collective Unconscious

While Freud was fond of the iceberg analogy to explain the unconscious (the unconscious part of our mind and personality being the 90 percent of the glacier that is below the surface), Jung made the comparison of a cork gently bobbing on a vast ocean. The cork is our conscious mind, and the ocean is the unconscious. The cork is tossed about at the whim of the cruel sea unless we get a handle of the nature of the true Self (of which we are only dimly aware, if at all) via the psychotherapeutic process he called *analytical psychology*.

FACTS

The best modern example of the Hero's Journey is the first *Star Wars* trilogy. George Lucas has acknowledged that Campbell was a big influence on him and his writing. One of the possible reasons for the enormous success of *Star Wars* is that it taps directly into the collective unconscious and appeals to people on an archetypal, unconscious level.

Jung's most famous theory is that of the *collective unconscious*, a shared memory of symbols, imagery, and memories that he called archetypes. These harken back to the dawn of human consciousness and are common in all cultures and civilizations. The famous mythographer Joseph Campbell supports this theory in his work *The Hero with a*

Thousand Faces. By cataloguing and cross-referencing myths from a broad spectrum of cultures and time frames, he came up with the notion of the *monomyth.* There is basically one story with the same cast of archetypes that Campbell called "The Hero's Journey."

Jung encountered a wide array of archetypes in his journey within. For many of his contemporaries, this bordered on fantasy. Men of science found the idea of mythical energies springing forth from a primordial reservoir and dwelling within every human a little too poetic a principle.

Gender Bending

Jung also proposed that within every man there is an inner woman, and within every woman there is an inner man—a feminine and masculine energy, actually, which he labeled the *anima* (inner woman) and *animus* (inner man). He felt that you had to embrace that side of your self and own it in order to have optimum mental health. If the anima or animus was too powerful or too passive, you were prone to psychological problems. This is similar to Plato's notion on love that proposes that humans were once a large androgynous bloblike creature embodying both genders. These creatures were split by the gods into men and women. And that is why each seeks out their counterpart to find balance and the other half of them that was long lost. Jung believed that this struggle goes on within each person whether we know it or not.

QUESTIONS?

Are you a different person in public than you are alone?
Of course you are. The self that you show the public is what Jung called the Persona. It is both revealing and concealing. We act differently with our boss than we do with our sweetheart; we're different with one friend than we are with another.

This theory is often criticized these days, and Jung is accused of some politically incorrect gender stereotyping. He suggested a man with a dominant anima was an overemotional whiner, and the woman with a powerful animus was overbearingly bossy and obnoxious. And the cliché of a man trying to embrace his feminine side has become fodder for standup comics and sitcom writers.

The Shadow

Jung has his own variation on Freud's theory of the Ego, Superego, and Id. Like Freud, Jung's definition of ego is the conscious part of the mind. The ego is that cork bobbing on the ocean, and its goal is to seek what Jung called *individuation,* bringing together all the myriad elements of the human psyche into one Self. Fully individuated individuals were the model of sound psychological wholeness.

Jung called his equivalent of the Id and Superego combined the Shadow. The Shadow is, in simple terms, a person's dark side, the impulses and desires and traits that remain beneath the surface after years of parental and societal pressure. Jung felt people have a tendency to project those negative shadow elements on people that we dislike.

FACTS

Do you remember the Star Trek episode where Captain Kirk was split in two because of a transporter accident? His "good" half is gentle and passive; his "bad" self is lustful and aggressive. The "evil Kirk" is a pop culture representation of Freud's theory of the "Id" and Carl Jung's "Shadow."

Think about it: Have you ever had an immediate dislike for someone for no apparent reason? And after time, if you are honest with yourself, you realize that you saw aspects of yourself in that person. Just as you can see your own soul reflected back at you through your beloved's eyes, you can see your shadow in the obnoxious neighbor or coworker.

Jung felt that the objective was to own your shadow and not try to bury it. Burying it never works. The shadow will be heard, usually when you least expect it. Everyone has aspects of himself or herself that they're not proud of. Jung believed we must own it and integrate it on the path to Wholeness.

Behaviorism

One school of psychology vigorously rejected Freud and his staunch accent on unconscious motivations, the reduction of everything to sexuality, and the reliance on the ramblings of the patient. They were the "doubting Thomases" of psychology. They favored an empirical approach that could be observed, studied, and confirmed through a scientific method. This group became known as the *Behaviorists*.

John Watson

One of the first Behaviorists was John Watson, no relation to Sherlock Holmes's sidekick. He viewed psychology as one of the natural sciences, an objective discipline to predict and even control behavior. He had no use for delving into the unconscious. He felt everything that you needed to know you could see for yourself through your own powers of observation. He was originally an animal psychologist, and he believed that the differences in behavior patterns of humans and animals were nominal.

SSENTIALS

We may have multiple personae, which is not the same as multiple personalities. Problems arise, as they always do, when one aspect of the psyche predominates. The objective is to know your persona and use it as necessary, but to also know that it is only a small piece of your *Self*.

B. F. Skinner

B. F. Skinner (1904–1990) is the most famous Behaviorist. He believed that people's behavior could be changed through the process of conditioning. The famous example of conditioning involves the rat in a box (designed by Skinner and appropriately named the Skinner Box). The rat learned that if it presses a lever, a food pellet is released. This positive reinforcement ensures that the behavior will be repeated and is called *operant conditioning*. This is similar to the famous experiment conducted by the Russian behaviorist Ivan Pavlov. He would ring a bell every time he served his dog a meal, the end result being that the dog would salivate in preparation for a snack whenever he heard a bell, even if no food was served.

Skinner and his followers felt that these techniques could be applied to people, and they conducted many experiments attempting to modify the behavior of humans. They learned that as far as conditioning was concerned, a human and a rat were not that far apart. His controversial book *Walden Two* outlines his vision for a utopia where good behavior was sustained by what he called *positive reinforcement*.

Humanistic Psychology

Carl Rogers (1902–1987) and Abraham Maslow (1908–1970) were pioneers of *humanistic psychology*. They were dissatisfied with the rigidities of psychoanalysis and behaviorism. Their theories, neither psychoanalytic nor behaviorist, came to be called the *third force*. These men saw psychology as a means to help people fulfill their maximum potential. Rogers felt that all people are instilled with an innate drive to "be all they can be," and it was the role of psychotherapy to facilitate the process.

Abraham Maslow devised a hierarchy of needs, which is the path a person takes from the basic needs of survival on the road to the achievement of their potential. The lowest levels on the scale would be food and shelter, and further up the scale would be things like security and love. The top of the list of needs is what Maslow called *self-actualization*. One of his most famous comments is, "A musician must make music, an artist must paint, a poet must write, if he is ultimately to be at peace with himself. What a man can be, he must be." Maslow was also one of the first to practice *group therapy,* a gathering of patients in a communal session with a therapist.

And the Rest . . .

Freud and Jung are the two most well-known psychologists of the twentieth century, but they're certainly not the only ones. Here, in brief, are some of the other major players in the world of psychology.

Alfred Adler

Alfred Adler (1870–1937) was another of Freud's students who learned much from the maestro, but, like many others, differed with him on the sex issue. Adler believed that feelings of inferiority rather than sexuality were the main motivating unconscious force in people. In fact, he was the guy who coined the phrase "inferiority complex." People basically felt inferior, and much of psychological energy was spent finding ways to compensate for these feelings and strive for perfection. He researched and wrote about family dynamics and the role that birth order plays in personality development. He also got people off the Freudian couch and preferred the patient and doctor to sit face to face. This created a sense of equality and made the therapist less of an imposing authority figure.

William James

The Father of American Psychology is William James (1842–1909), brother of the novelist Henry James. His two-volume *Principles of Psychology* was the bible for a generation of American psychologists. His approach was Functionalist, proposing that the important purpose of psychological study was to examine the functions of the conscious. This involved studying selected subjects over a lengthy period of time, which consisted of observation and tests and was called *longitudinal research.* James was influenced by Darwin's theory of evolution. It was James and his research that took psychology out of the philosophical realm and placed it in the laboratory. He wrote many books, one of which, *The Varieties of Religious Experience,* influenced the founders of Alcoholics Anonymous.

Jean Piaget

Jean Piaget's (1896–1980) main claim to fame is the work he did with children. After years of working in schools and interviewing thousands of children, the Swiss psychologist identified four stages of childhood development.

- The *sensorimotor stage,* from birth to age two, involves the mastering of motor controls and learning to deal with the physical world.
- In the *preoperational stage,* from ages two to seven, the child focuses on verbal skills and communication.
- In the *concrete operational stage,* children begin to deal with numbers and other complex concepts.
- Logic and reason evolve in the *formal operational stage.*

CHAPTER 19

Eastern Schools of Thought

Philosophy and religion weren't just limited to the great minds of the Western world. The Eastern world had its share of thought as well, including the well-known Hinduism and Buddhism religions. But the major schools of Eastern thought aren't limited to the popular Hindu and Buddhist beliefs. Other important philosophies emerged as well.

Hinduism

Hinduism is the main religion of India. The word *Hindu* is from the ancient Sanskrit language and means Indus, as in the Indus River. Approximately 700 million Hindus practice today, making it one of the major world religions.

Hinduism is an action religion. It is not so much what you think as what you do. The religion is replete with rituals, and the people may look like they are part of a religious monolith, but Hinduism is a diverse creed that is practiced in different ways by different sects.

Universal Themes

Hinduism, of course, has its universal themes: belief in reincarnation, vegetarianism, and the reverence for cows. Americans and Europeans are often shocked when visiting India to find people starving in the streets while cattle wander freely and unmolested.

Hindus observe a rigid caste system, wherein there is no such thing as upward mobility. You are born into a socioeconomic class, and there you shall remain. Intermarriage between castes is forbidden, and the lowest caste is called untouchable. You will not find any "yuppies" in the Hindi tradition.

The Hindu Gods

Hinduism is a polytheistic religion. *Polytheism* means the worship of many gods, as opposed to Christianity, Judaism, and Islam, which are the three main monotheistic religions. Shiva and Vishnu are the main gods, and Devi is the main goddess, though hundreds of minor gods and goddesses are in the Hindu cavalcade of deities.

Shiva is a contradictory god. He is the god of those who renounce the material world and the pleasures therein, but he is also the deity of the phallus. This is made prominently clear in the statues of Shiva. Shiva killed his father Brahma, an unsavory sort who apparently had it coming, but was forced to carry his skull around with him at all times thereafter.

This is very similar to the Greek myth of Zeus, who castrated his own father Cronus.

Beware of single goddesses! The Hindu tradition has a pantheon of gods and goddesses, some benign and others quite nasty. Among the goddesses, single ones are to be feared, because unlike the married goddesses, they are given to mood swings and hormonal rages. As goddesses go, they make the characters on Sex and The City seem like Girl Scouts.

Vishnu is the main god in the Hindu belief system. A lotus sprang from his navel and from that emerged Brahma, the hapless father of Shiva. Vishnu has gone through many incarnations since his initial appearance. These incarnations are called *avatars*.

The main goddess, Devi, is worshipped under that name and sometimes in the form of other goddesses who are believed to be incarnations of Devi. By another name, she is called Kali, an unsavory deity who kills and eats her victims and then performs a frenetic dance while wearing the skulls and the hands of her dinner. Under still another name, Devi is known as Druga the Unapproachable, a Xena-type warrior princess.

Fortunately, there are more pleasant goddesses in the Hindu pantheon: Lakshmi, the fertility goddess; Ganga, the river goddess (the Ganges river is named for her); Parvati, the goddess of the Himalayas; and many more.

Hindu Texts

The four main texts of Hinduism are called the Vedas. Rig-Veda is the oldest and has been committed to memory by devout Hindus for thousands of years. The other three are called the Yajur-Veda, the Sama-Veda, and the Atharva-Veda.

Two other important Hindu texts include the Brahmanas, which is a Sanskrit document detailing the rituals to be practiced by Hindu priests. And perhaps the most famous Hindu text to Westerners is called the Upanishads. This is the most popular text to Westerners because of its very "New Age" sounding mystical meditations on the meaning of life.

The spiritual literature of Hinduism also contains a unique view of the universe. They believe that the universe is an enclosed shell with concentric universes going round and round with India at the center. It is not surprising that almost every society and culture has regarded themselves as the chosen people and their neck of the woods as the center of the universe. Hinduism also teaches that things have been going downhill since a golden age, called the Krita Yuga, in prehistory. Things fall apart, and the center cannot hold until that universe is destroyed and another golden age begins.

QUESTIONS?

What is meant by the transmigration of souls?
This is another name for reincarnation. Hindus and Buddhists believe that we are reborn into another body after death, learning and growing (hopefully) in each subsequent lifetime. The goal is to become enlightened to the degree that you transcend your humanity and become one with all.

Reincarnation

When Sinatra sang, "Life keeps goin' in cycles," he could have been discussing Hinduism. Everything in the universe is cyclical, including human life. Hindus believe in the *transmigration of souls,* which is another name for reincarnation. Whether you return as a supermodel or a giant tree sloth depends on your karma.

Karma is the principle that maintains there is an inherent balance to the cosmos. In the Bible, it says, "What you sow, so shall ye reap." In Hindu terms, this means that what you do in your life, good or bad, will come back and bite you in the next, either in the form of rewards or punishments. A murderer will be a victim; an insensitive super-stud will be a monk in the next life. You acquire karma through your multiple incarnations over the millennia. The goal is to become more and more enlightened until finally you do not have to return to the physical realm. Then you can enjoy eternity as fully awakened spiritual being.

SSENTIALS

You had better be good for goodness sake, because if the Buddhists are right, your actions in this life will affect your karma. Karma is the force of cosmic justice in the universe. If you are an evil person in this life, you can expect payback in the next.

Hindus typically take one of two paths in life. Many work, have families, and live normal lives within the framework of the real world; others take their ancient scriptures more to heart and live lives of ascetic self-denial, seeking to jumpstart the process of karma and reincarnation and grow closer to enlightenment in this lifetime.

Buddhism

Buddhism came into being from the life and teachings of an Indian prince called Siddhartha Gautama (ca 563–ca 483 B.C.), later more famously known as Buddha, which means the Enlightened One. Siddhartha was a Hindu, but the faith he instituted and that evolved around him discarded many Hindu traditions, including the notorious caste system, the power and influence of the Braham priesthood, and many of the holy Hindu writings.

Buddha was a prince who spent his youth in luxury, sequestered from life outside the palace walls. He had a very strong reaction of horror when he was confronted with the rampant pain and suffering endured by the majority of the people. As a member of the ruling class, he had been spared this exposure to the real world. Upon being confronted with the cold, cruel world, he gave up the lifestyle of the rich and famous, finding no joy and no meaning therein, and left his not-so-humble abode to live an austere and monastic life.

The Middle Way

He eventually found what came to be called the "middle way." Neither self-indulgence nor self-denial was the key to happiness and enlightenment. Legend tells us that he sat under a tree for days without moving, and gradually his consciousness evolved until he achieved the long sought after and highly elusive Enlightenment. This wisdom did not come easily, however. Buddha, like Jesus in the desert, was tempted three times. In Buddha's case, the temptations were lust, fear, and social duty. Surmounting these temptations that would have compelled him to stray from his path, he achieved Enlightenment. Buddha then spent the rest of his life preaching, teaching, accumulating loyal followers, and establishing a monastery.

The Four Noble Truths

Like Jesus, Buddha never committed anything to paper. As a result, it was his followers who chronicled his life and philosophy. The core of Buddhism centers on what are called The Four Noble Truths.

The truth is not always what you want to hear, but the truth shall set ye free. The first Noble Truth is that life is inherently sad and full of suffering. Birth is a painful process and so is death, and in between is affliction, heartbreak, the death of loved ones, and your own inexorable trot toward your inevitable demise. Nobody gets out of here alive. And because Buddhists believe in reincarnation, you don't even get your wings when it's over. You get to do it all over again in another life.

The second Noble Truth explains why we suffer. It is because people are unenlightened and unaware of the true nature of the universe. This and our obsession with earthly desires and material things add to life's endemic melancholy. Most people are mired in the world of sensual pleasures and creature comforts, yet while such things may provide transient gratification, they thwart true enlightenment.

The third Noble Truth is an optimistic one. You can transcend your earthly woes by shaking off the shackles of materialism and other sensual indulgences and seek enlightenment. Meditation is the path for most Buddhists. In this age of decreasing attention spans, meditation is a tall order. You cannot fiddle with your Sony PlayStation while waiting for the Great Awakening. Meditation is difficult work—most people get antsy waiting in line for a movie or at the bank, let alone sitting with legs crossed, concentrating on their breathing and waiting for something to happen.

Hinduism and Buddhism believe that you can regress in reincarnation, going from human to pigeon because of your karma. Modern New Age spins on reincarnation suggest that once you are a human, you do not go back to the animal kingdom.

The fourth and final Noble Truth is that by following the Eightfold Path of Enlightenment, you can find the bliss that we all seek. The Eightfold Path is as follows:

- Right Understanding is awareness of the Four Noble Truths and seeing yourself and life as it really is.
- Right Thoughts involve renouncing earthly pleasures, keeping positive thoughts, avoiding negative emotions, and maintaining peaceful, nonhostile thoughts.
- Right Speech means not lying, verbally attacking, maliciously gossiping, and so on.
- Right Action means not committing murder or other wrongs and exercising self-control in all your affairs.
- Right Livelihood, now taught as a New Age school of thought, teaches ethics in the workplace; in ancient times, it was more specific. Right Livelihood said the following businesses and practices should be avoided: munitions; livestock slaughterhouses; the slave trade; wine, spirits, and other mood-altering substances; and poisons.
- Right Effort entails avoiding evil in the world, not contributing to generating new evil, encouraging the good that already exists, and promoting new goodness. The old cliché that nothing is achieved without effort is no mere bromide. It is a universal truth. If you want something badly you have to work at it, and if that something is Enlightenment, the effort required is great indeed.
- Right Mindfulness means to maintain awareness at all times—awareness of your body, your feelings, your mind, and your thoughts.
- Right Meditation involves learning to meditate in order to achieve peace at the center and follow the path to Enlightenment.

Buddhism, like Hinduism, also posits karma as a universal force of balance and justice. The next time you wonder why your life is unfolding in its singular path, think about the theory of karma. It states that you chose this life, your parents, and your gender. The life you are living is designed to provide you with lessons, blessings for injustices, and payback for injustices that you are guilty of in a past life.

Nirvana

The historical Buddha did not deny the existence of the Hindu gods, but he paid them no attention. They are off doing their own thing and need not be feared or worshipped. In fact, he believed that Enlightenment was not possible for them. Only humanity had the potential for a great Awakening. And, like Hinduism, the Buddhist goal is to be relieved of the burdens of physical existence, the limitations and the obstacles of the earthbound prison, and the achievement of what they call Nirvana.

FACTS

Asian culture has given the world great spiritual and philosophical principles over the millennia, yet in the modern era, China has tried to destroy this rich tradition. China invaded Tibet in 1959 and forced the Dalai Lama into exile, and today Buddhists in Communist China are subject to persecution for their beliefs.

The path to Nirvana involves living a life of kindness, compassion, and composure. That also means adhering to the moral code of Buddhism, which is a five-pronged code that prohibits murder, theft, bad language, sexual misconduct, and the use of mood-altering substances. This lifestyle leads to a better life the next time around and subsequent lives on the road to Enlightenment. This lifestyle also helps you avoid the three main causes of evil in the world, according to Buddhists: delusion, hatred, and lust.

Nirvana can be achieved by anyone willing to work for it, but your chances are greater if you sequester yourself in a monastery. For those who are nowhere near achieving Nirvana, they can hope to lead progressively better lives until they are finally spiritually evolved enough to arrive at that exalted state.

Buddhism Today

Buddhism continues to be a popular belief because of its flexibility, adaptability, and absence of rigid dogma. It is thriving in Japan and has been growing in popularity in the Western world, but it has not been faring too well in Communist China in recent decades. In 1959, Red China invaded neighboring Tibet, homeland of the most famous Buddhist, the Dalai Lama, and forced him into exile. The repressive totalitarian Chinese regime routinely represses practitioners of Buddhism to this day.

Zen Buddhism

Buddhism has branched off and evolved over the millennia. One of the most popular offshoots is Zen Buddhism. Zen, a form of Buddhism, began in China and spread to Japan and is a combination of Indian Buddhism and Taoism.

Zen Buddhism influenced many aspects of culture from the aforementioned haiku to the Zen rock garden. Do you know someone who has one of these miniature sand and rock gardens on their desk that they gently landscape with a tiny rake? They are trying to reduce their stress level and find a little peace, Zen-style.

Zen suggests that you strive to see the world exactly as it is without clouding reality with your preconceptions. It is the Buddhist principle of "no mind." Zen stresses meditation as a key to gaining the necessary insight required attaining enlightenment. Zen Buddhism is also responsible for the poetic form of haiku, a poem that must be seventeen syllables—no more, no less. Zen Buddhism emphasizes meditation as the path to discover your own "Buddha nature" and thus the keys to an Awakening. This speed-reading equivalent of achieving enlightenment is called *satori* in Japanese. It places less value on the study of Buddhist scriptures.

Taoism

Taoism is a Chinese philosophy that is one of the major forces in Eastern thought, and it also has fascinated and intrigued the Western world. The word *Tao* is translated as "The Way." The Taoist "bible" is the *Tao Te Ching* (The Way and Its Power), a slim volume of aphorisms and maxims attributed to a philosopher called Lao-Tzu, though, like the gospels of the New Testament, it was compiled by Lao-Tzu's followers after his death.

Lao-Tzu

Lao-Tzu apparently was suspicious of the written word and had seen how, once things were set in stone or on papyrus, they were treated as rigid dogma. And Taoism is anything but rigid. It is a fluid, formless, maddeningly elusive philosophy. But apparently, once you get it, the scales fall off your eyes big time. You were blind, and now you can see.

Little is known about the historical Lao-Tzu, but many legends surround him. One says that he was born of a union between a woman and a shooting star. He gestated in his mother's womb for sixty-two years and sprang to life as a white-haired, wise old-timer. This tells more about the ancient Chinese people's reverence for him than anything else. Lao-Tzu is forever in their minds and hearts as an amiable and insightful old philosopher, wandering down the paths in robes, carrying a staff, and dispensing deep and commonsensical maxims to all who would listen.

Another legend has Lao-Tzu at the end of his life, saddened at how little men have changed despite his years of teaching, hopping upon a water buffalo and heading beyond the Great Wall of China into destiny. Even Lao-Tzu's name is the legendary. It can be translated into English as "the Old Fellow," or "the Old Boy." This conveys the lightness of the Tao.

The Tenets of Taoism

Taoists believe that there is an unseen and omnipresent design to the universe that is incomprehensible to the human mind. Only a dim awareness of its existence taunts our psyches. We know it is there, but it is ephemeral and beyond our grasp. The Tao is a timeless and formless unknowable force that governs the cosmos.

The basic tenet of Taoism is the principle of *nondoing,* which should not be interpreted as a license to procrastinate. Couch potatoes do not rejoice—the Tao is not with you. The Taoist version of doing nothing entails ridding yourself of preconceptions and beliefs that were, if you examine them closely, imposed on you by a counterproductive societal structure and an essential bogus reality. "Be still and know" is a popular Buddhist axiom. "Listen to your heart" would be another way of describing it. Through meditation and other forms of "quiet time," we can access the Tao. In the unhealthy hustle of the maddening rat race, the Tao cannot be intuited.

QUESTIONS?

Have you ever felt a connection with the world?
Perhaps you experienced an inner peace while you were on a solitary stroll on a windswept beach or on a hike in a forest primeval. If so, you have tasted the elusive Tao.

Tao Te Ching

The *Tao Te Ching,* the Taoist bible, is written as a series of verses. Eighty-one sayings comprise about 5,000 words, yet its impact on the world of philosophy is tremendous. It employs numerous paradoxes to explain The Way and the inherent harmony of the universe. Being and nonbeing, difficulty and ease, high and low, long and short are all complementary. The *Tao Te Ching* rejects materialism as a hindrance to enlightenment and advocates acceptance as the path to inner peace.

The *Tao Te Ching* includes the famous line, "A journey of thousands starts with a single step." In other words, keep it simple. Do not be overwhelmed by the demands of your harried modern life. Certainly, these things must be tended to in order to survive, but if you endeavor to rid yourself of stress and strain and simply go with the flow, you can make your life much easier and possibly even gain insight and maybe even a spiritual awakening.

The Art of War

The Art of War is an influential Taoist primer for fighting and winning wars. It is attributed to the enigmatic Sun-Tzu, about whom little is known. It is believed to have been composed sometime between the fifth and third centuries B.C., during a time of tumultuous civil war in ancient China.

This work is as popular today as when it was written. Western minds have embraced it as well. In the hit movie *The Rock*, Sean Connery plays a British spy (not unlike an old Bond, James Bond) who is illegally imprisoned by the America government. When prison officials come into his cell to compel him to undertake a dangerous mission, the two books we see on his shelf are the complete works of Shakespeare and *The Art of War*. It is an extremely brief shot, almost subliminal, but it says much about the character, who, as the movie progresses, employs the precepts espoused by Sun-Tzu to survive.

Nowadays, businessmen as well as military types study it. In fact, Asian corporate structure, which resembles the feudal clans of old Japan, and the Japanese motto, "Business is war," indicate that they take their multinational machinations quite seriously. The Japanese took the principles presented in *The Art of War* and ran with it.

The Chinese are also entrenched in the philosophy of *The Art of War*. To them, this is a living document. They are applying its principles twenty-four/seven, and it would behoove both American businesses and military personnel to remain keenly aware of this. In the 1920s, one of the few politicians to read Adolf Hitler's *Mein Kampf* was Britain's Winston Churchill. Churchill warned, like a mystic predicting the impending apocalypse, of the dangerous nature of this little corporal with the funny mustache and penchant for guttural, gesticulating speechifying. Hitler announced his intentions to the world years before he came to power. And the world did not listen until it was almost too late.

In the movie *Mystery Men*, a superhero called the Sphinx trains a ragtag group of nerdish superhero wannabes. He imparts wisdom in the form of cryptic bromides and other forms of paradox, such as "Until you learn to master your rage, your rage will become your master." One of his students, the volatile Mr. Furious, continually mocks the Sphinx's never-ending collection of clichés. The use of paradoxes is used to comedic effect in the movie, but the Wisdom of the East is replete with paradoxes.

The Art of War is no exception. They may seem as obvious and simple to you as they do to Mr. Furious, but there is an inherent truth in these ancient Chinese secrets, and they are not always apparent until you take the time to mull them over.

ESSENTIALS

The word Tao is translated as "The Way." The Taoist "bible" is the *Tao Te Ching* (The Way and Its Power), a slim volume of aphorisms and maxims attributed to a philosopher called Lao-Tzu. Taoists believe that there is an unseen and omnipresent design to the universe. The Tao is a timeless and formless unknowable force that governs the cosmos.

The first and most important paradox is that the best way to win a battle is not to fight one. In other words, the most accomplished warrior is a skilled strategist who can use other means to defeat his opponent. In fact, armed conflict is the last resort and an indication that the warrior is not especially skilled. According to Sun-Tzu, to win without firing a shot, or hacking with a saber, as was the method in those days, is the sign of a warrior of genius.

It is no secret why, despite the multitudinous management and business books on the market, the wisdom of *The Art of War* is still widely regarded and studied. If you take the notions of "warfare" and "enemy" as metaphors, it reads like a "How to Succeed in Business" manual. Here are a few paraphrased insights that are equally applicable to the contemporary business world as they are to an ancient battlefield.

The true warrior (or CEO):

- Makes the opponent angry while remaining calm themselves. Anger clouds the judgment of the adversary.
- Plays dumb to create a false sense of superiority on the part of the opponent.
- Uses rhetorical "fast talk" to confuse the enemy.

- Wins through intimidation.
- Is prepared, just like a Boy Scout.
- Knows thyself.
- Never lets the enemy know what he's thinking.
- Enacts a system of rewards and penalties for his staff.
- Knows that if he treats his solders (employees) like family, they will follow him anywhere.
- When delegating responsibility, ascertains the strengths and weaknesses of his staff and finds the right person for the right job.
- Is always adaptable to any situation.
- Knows everything he can about the competition, even going as far as to employ spies and seduce disgruntled members of the opposition with bribes to create double agents.
- Exploits the character defects of the opponent.
- Knows that when there is grumbling among the troops (negative office gossip), he's in trouble.
- Is consistent. He means what he says and says what he means.
- Thinks outside the box.
- Is proactive.

ESSENTIALS *The Art of War,* an ancient text that teaches strategy and tactics for military men and political leaders, is still studied today by businessmen. The rules can easily be adapted to apply to corporate wheeling and dealing. After all, the Japanese corporate world still adheres to the martial motto, "Business is war."

Sound familiar? You have heard these points if you have taken business courses, yet these philosophies were proposed thousands of years ago. *The Art of War* should be read whether you are negotiating a business deal or a domestic arrangement. It is a practical application of Taoist principles that, rather than scratching your head, baffled by inscrutable Asian mysticism, can serve you well in the real world.

Confucianism

Confucianism is more complex than the typical Westerner's notion of bromides in fortune cookies and Asian stereotypes that were once ubiquitous on old TV shows, who would intone in broken English, "Confucius say <insert inscrutable cliché>."

About Confucius

Confucius (551–479 B.C.) was born into a well-to-do family, but a series of tragedies thrust him into poverty. He was a traveling philosopher, around whom disciples would form and imbibe of his insights and wisdom. He lived in a time of chaos and corruption in ancient China, and his philosophy stressed the ethical in interpersonal and political relations and family values, emphasizing a deep respect for parents. His centerpiece of this belief was setting a good example. The leader should be of exemplary moral fiber, and in an ethical trickle-down theory, the citizenry would toe the virtuous line. Confucius had a brief tenure in political office and put his beliefs into practice with remarkable results. He was so successful that less noble politicos had him removed from office. He spent the rest of his life trying, through his writings and teachings, to convert the wicked to his philosophy of truth, justice, and the Chinese way.

FACTS

Ren is defined in English as "love" or "virtue" and is the focal point of Confucian philosophy. It is expressed in another way, a phrase very familiar to Western ears: "Do unto others as you would have them do unto you." That's right, the famous "Golden Rule" is also a mainstay of ancient Chinese thought.

Confucius, like Jesus and Buddha, did not put anything in writing, which seems to be a trend among the great spiritual leaders. They leave the transcribing to their disciples. The best distillation of Confucius's life and his teachings is called *The Lunyu*, which is also known as *The Analects*. Confucius is not a religious leader, though there are those who have worshipped him as a divine messenger over the centuries. His is an ethical teaching that valued deep respect for parents, including ancestor worship, loyalty to the state and its leaders. He also concluded that five virtues were what one need to lead a good life: compassion, decency, good manners, insight, and fidelity.

Confucius and his followers created a philosophy that changed Asian culture on social, political, and spiritual levels. Starting in China, it spread across the world and is of continuing fascination to the Western mind.

A Secular Philosophy

Confucianism is not an organized religion. It is a secular philosophy. There are no monks or priests or a dogma. Confucius is revered as a great man, not a divinity or an emissary of any Deity. There are Confucian "temples," but they have functioned more as community centers. Confucius sensed that it was human nature to turn great leaders into superheroes and gods, and he expressly forbade any attempts to worship him as a god either during his life or afterward.

The Two Schools

Two schools of Confucianism vied for predominance in Chinese history: the philosophy of Mencius and the teachings of Xunzi. Mencius, like his mentor, believed in the inherent decency of mankind, but his teachings addressed the possible dark side. Speaking of heredity and environmental factors, Mencius felt that people were born pure of heart, but could be corrupted by their own natures and the world around them. This belief is the opposite of the Christian notion of Original Sin, which proposes that people are inherently sinful, but can be redeemed through the Christian faith.

The other main school of Confucianism, espoused by Xunzi, mirrors the Original Sin theory. He believed that people were inherently evil but could be redeemed through exposure to a moral upbringing and life in a just society.

Confucianism Versus Taoism

Confucianism, with its emphasis on proper behavior, and proto -cols and etiquette for every occasion, is the opposite of the footloose, fancy-free, and formless Tao. There is a legend that the young Confucius met the elder Lao-Tzu and left saying, "I have met a dragon." By this statement, he did not mean that he had met a cranky, fire-breathing old coot. In Chinese legend, the dragon is not earthbound; it soars through the clouds and is not confined by mundane matters. Confucianism is a philosophy concerned with the concrete; Taoism is not concrete in the least.

 SSENTIALS

Confucianism was eclipsed by Buddhism and Taoism, but never faded away as an influence on Chinese social and political life. Eventually, a new school of Confucianism, which was an amalgam of Buddhism and Taoism called Neo-Confucianism, developed.

Its Legacy

Confucianism was always, in one form or another and in and out of favor, a significant Chinese school of thought until the Chinese Communist revolution of 1949. Wanting a monopoly on dogma, the Communists aggressively discouraged the study of Confucius, and new philosophical writings were not well received. However, the main books of Confucian philosophy are still around for any and all to read, despite the best efforts of their detractors. The most famous of these ancient texts is the *I Ching*, meaning "Book of Changes." The *I Ching* is often used as a fortune-telling parlor game by contemporary Westerners, but it is an ancient and sacred text. Lots are cast and then you refer to the book to get the appropriate quotation (based on the number in your casting of the lots), and it is more often than not appropriate to the question you asked!

Shinto

Shinto is an ancient Japanese religion that has undergone many transformations over the centuries. Shinto can be translated as "the way of the gods" and began as a somewhat vague form of spirit worship. Like the ancient Greek myths, these spirits personified elements of nature—the sun, moon, the weather, and other facets of the environment that had an impact on the lives of the primitive Japanese. This is a common element of primitive religions, an attempt to explain the world around them by anthropomorphizing it. To *anthropomorphize* something means the application of human personality character traits to inanimate objects, animals, and forces of nature. Shinto is a faith that has no sacred text, no commandments, and no dogma.

Shinto Versus Buddhism

Shinto did not even have a name until the sixth century. Around this time, it encountered competition from the emerging doctrines of Buddhism and Confucianism that came from China and began impacting upon Japanese culture. Buddhism burst onto the scene and largely usurped Shinto. Buddhist monks even took over Shinto shrines and Buddha-fied them. The religion that emerged from this synthesis was called *Ryobu Shinto* and was an amalgam of Buddhism, Confucianism, and Shinto, with Buddhism being the predominant influence.

Shinto Returns

The revival of Shinto in the eighteenth century was largely a nationalist movement, inspired by the insular nature of the Japanese and their distaste and distrust of all things foreign. In this neo-Shinto faith, the emperor was said to be there by divine right, a familiar tactic employed by almost every monarch from East to West and all points in between. And, of course, the Japanese were the "chosen people." They also felt that it was the manifest destiny of Japan to rule the world, which prompted military aggression that culminated in World War II.

Their dreams of world domination shattered after their defeat, Shinto was reshaped yet again by an American. General Douglas MacArthur of "I shall return" and "Old soldiers never die, they just fade away" fame imposed a dose of separation of Church and State while occupying as governor of the defeated Japan. There had been two forms of Shinto, State Shinto and Sectarian Shinto. The State faction was the nationalist wing, and American occupational forces saw to it that it was no longer government sponsored and taught in the schools, lest its less than spiritual impulses inflame the populace and create more problems. The emperor was also compelled to renounce his claims to divinity. Sectarian Shinto was left alone and continues to thrive in modern Japan, in the form of many sects large and small.

Sufism

Sufism is the form of Islamic mysticism that emerged as an offshoot of traditional Islamic religion shortly after its inception in the seventh century. The word *Sufi* literally means "man of wool." The wandering Sufi mystics were into ascetic self-denial and suffering for their faith and deliberately wore uncomfortable woolen clothes as part of their mortification of the flesh. Both Judaism and Christianity have had their share of mystics and mad monks whose seemingly bizarre and nonconformist lifestyles were designed to bring them closer to God.

Sufi Techniques

The techniques that the Sufis believed would bring them in direct communion with Allah included atonement for their sins, self-denial, vows of poverty, and a dedication to following the will of God, as they understood it. The end result would be the attainment of a higher level of consciousness always sought by mystics of all faiths.

This claim to a direct pipeline to the divine made the Sufis unpopular, to say the least, with mainstream Muslims. Many Sufis also conveyed contempt for the many rules and regulations associated with Islam and also expressed belief in a form of pantheism, claiming that Allah and nature are one. This was anathema to traditional Muslims. Eventually, a rapprochement was reached between the Sufis and the rest of the Islamic community.

QUESTIONS?

Did you know some circuslike practices have Sufism roots? Practices like swallowing swords and walking on hot coals have been seen and stereotyped in movies and television. These "snake charmers" and their amazing feats are really living testaments to the amazing things that the human body can do when the mind is focused, intense, and driven.

Rumi

Perhaps the most famous Sufi is the poet Rumi (1207–1273). His poetry is quite fashionable these days. Not many a Muslim mystic is frequently recited, to the accompaniment of a lute, in Greenwich Village coffeehouses. Rumi met a Sufi master who became a great influence and inspiration for his poetry, especially after his mysterious disappearance. Rumi's poetry is entrenched with the Sufi philosophy and is also romantic, even erotic. After his death, a sect was formed around his memory.

Sufi Practices

After Rumi's death, a sect was formed around his memory, and its members became known as the "whirling dervishes." The distinctive practice of these Sufi mystics was to dance themselves into an ecstatic frenzy, often collapsing into convulsions afterward. Many of the descriptions of these men and their rituals come from European observers, hence the language is biased. Howling dervishes is one such description, but the "howling" was a religious chant, not just shrieking.

CHAPTER 20

The Big Three Religions

T hree religions, forged in the fiery furnace of the ancient Middle Eastern deserts, have done more to reshape the face of the world than any Socratic dialogue or ontological conundrum. These religions are Judaism, Christianity, and Islam.

For Better and for Worse

For good and sometimes for ill, the influence of Judaism, Christianity, and Islam continues to shape the world at the personal, sociocultural, and political levels. Though these faiths have inflamed the souls of their followers with the ecstasies of illumination, atrocious acts of bigotry have sometimes resulted when one of the three sought prominence in world affairs and the hearts of men and women. When somebody steadfastly believes himself or herself to be a member of the one true faith, then the other fellow is clearly, in their mind, in need of either conversion or killing.

ESSENTIALS

Monotheism is a form of religion where one God is worshipped. Judaism, Christianity, and Islam are the three main religions that practice monotheism. The philosophy of monotheism shapes our contemporary world at almost every level, both secular and spiritual.

Just as *All in the Family* led to *Maude,* which led to *Good Times,* so Christianity and Islam are spinoffs of Judaism. Yet despite their common origins, there has been little in the way of peaceful coexistence over the millennia. Many a crusade, pogrom, and jihad have been in the name of Yahweh, God, and Allah, which enhances the tragedy since these are really three names for the same Deity. Judaism, Christianity, and Islam are the three main religions that are *monotheistic,* meaning that the faithful believe in one God who has dominion over Heaven and Earth. Even in this age of secular Humanism, the impact of these big three monotheistic religions is ingrained in our culture and our mindset.

Judaism

The first Israelites were not monotheists. They are what is called *henotheistic,* meaning that they had their God, but they accepted the deities of their neighbors as equally valid for them—a theological live and let live, as it were. They shaped their belief that there was one God, whom they called Yahweh, during their trials and tribulations as slaves in

Egypt, their subsequent liberation and wandering in the desert, and according to the Old Testament, being presented with the Ten Commandments. During a later period of domination by the Babylonians, the monotheism of the Israelites was reinforced and the belief that a messiah would eventually come and save the day was established. This set the stage for the emergence of Christianity.

The Israelites were always beset by conquerors. Eventually, the Romans arrived on the scene. The Romans occupied Judea for many years. Jesus Christ lived during the Roman occupation. Jerusalem was destroyed in A.D. 70 in one episode in a culture history that is called the Diaspora, the Greek word for "dispersion." The foundation of the state of Israel in 1948 was the first Jewish homeland in almost two millennia. The generations of being a culture without a home, wandering and living in other lands where they were treated with prejudice that often exploded into violent persecution, did much to shape Judaism and the Jewish philosophy.

The Torah and Talmud

The Torah is the foundation of Jewish religion, tradition, and law and is Hebrew for "doctrine." Part of the Torah is the Pentateuch that comprises the first five books of what Christians call the Old Testament. Because Jews do not embrace the teaching of the New Testament, they do not call their spiritual scriptures "old." The term Torah is also used to cover the whole body of Jewish scriptures and the various commentaries written by scholars and rabbis over the centuries.

Talmud is another phrase that includes the entire body of Jewish religious and civil law—the Pentateuch, the Torah, and the commentaries on the Torah. There are two versions of the Talmud: the Jerusalem Talmud and the Palestinian Talmud.

The Chosen People

The Jewish tradition maintains that they are the "chosen people." This was revealed to Moses by Yahweh. The irony is not lost on them that they have had to endure a great deal of hardship for those "chosen" by God. The Book of Job in the Old Testament tells the story of the hapless Job who endures one trial after another as tests from God because he is God's favorite.

Jewish tradition espouses the belief in one God who created and presides over the universe. God's design for living is presented through the Ten Commandments, which were given to Moses on Mount Sinai. Judaism is based on a contract, or covenant, made between God and the Jewish people. The people acknowledge God as their ultimate king and lawgiver, and God singles out the Jews as his chosen people. The fates that befell the Israelis were often interpreted as signs of God's displeasure, which would indicate that, in Yahweh's estimation, the Jewish people did not always live up to their end of the covenant, given the trials and tribulations they have had to endure over the centuries.

The God of the Old Testament is, in His own words, an angry and a jealous God, quick to punish, and demanding in his devotion. Hence, Judaism is replete with rituals that must be performed and laws that must be obeyed. The Book of Leviticus is a lengthy list of laws, some of which are quite sound (a man should not have sexual relations with his daughter) while others (a man should kick his wife out of their tent for the duration of her period) simply will not be tolerated in this day and age.

The suffering of the Jewish people at the hands of oppressors over the generations gave birth to a belief that a Messiah would come to save the day. Contemporary Jews believe this day has yet to come. However, many people believe that he arrived on the scene some 2,000 years ago and a religion was formed about his birth, teachings, death, and for believers, resurrection. The new religion is, of course, Christianity.

Christianity

In the history of Judaism, many have claimed the mantle of Messiah over the centuries. Many preached their message to the masses, inspired disciples to follow them, and died for their efforts. Most of them are forgotten, their names and their ministries swept away with centuries of desert sand.

One of these men and his message caught on, and the world has never been the same. In fact, the largest and most influential of the Big

Three monotheistic religions was inspired by the teachings of a humble Jewish carpenter who preached of love and forgiveness. He lived and died in thirty-three brief years, but according to his followers, that is just the beginning of the story.

Jesus of Nazareth

Christianity is the religion that formed around the preaching and teaching of Jesus of Nazareth. We know that the historical Jesus taught and had a following, was perceived as a political and social threat to the status quo, and was ultimately executed by the Romans in the grisly manner of crucifixion. There have always been skeptics who doubt that the historical Jesus existed, but secular Roman writings confirm that he did indeed walk the earth. But was he the Son of God, as Christians throughout the world firmly believe?

In the year 999, there was mass hysteria about the forthcoming Apocalypse, the return of Jesus Christ, and the ultimate battle between Good and Evil. Nothing happened. In 1999, the same fears were rampant, along with equal hysteria about Y2K. Silence ensued. Are we safe for another thousand years?

Little is known about the historical Jesus that does not come from the four gospels, which comprise the first part of the New Testament. These are the "authorized" biographies, authorized some 400 years after the fact. The Church fathers had dozens of chronicles of Jesus from which to choose, and they elected to pick gospels that stressed the divinity of Jesus. There are others that give equal consideration to the humanity of Jesus, but these have been relegated to controversial asterisks in Christian history.

Christians believe that Old Testament prophecy was realized in the person of Jesus, and that in his death on the cross he took on the sins of humanity and offered salvation to all those who believe. The early Christians were all "Jews for Jesus," thus Christianity is an offshoot of Judaism. Christianity eventually eclipsed Judaism in sheer numbers when, largely though the efforts of St. Paul and other missionaries, the Christian message spread across the ancient world, available to any and all whose minds and hearts were swayed by the Christian philosophy.

Christian Rituals

The key element of faith of the Christians is the belief that Jesus Christ rose from the dead after being crucified and entombed for three days. Many accept that Jesus was a wise sage; the Muslims revere him as a very human prophet, but the crux of the Christian faith is belief in the resurrection of Jesus and their own eternal life with him in heaven.

Christianity, like the other two monotheistic religions, has numerous rituals, also known as *sacraments*. *Baptism* is an immersion in water and is considered the official initiation into the faith. Some Christians practice the total immersion in a river and wait until the convert is an adult or of the age of reason. Other Christian denominations baptize infants shortly after birth and have two representatives (godparents) who answer the priest's questions on behalf of the child. The other main ritual, or sacrament, is the *Eucharist*. This is a recreation of the Last Supper, where Jesus shared bread and wine with his apostles and exhorted them to carry on in his name. Catholics believe that there is transubstantiation, that the bread and wine is literally transformed into the body and blood of Christ by the priest during Mass. Many Protestant denominations believe it is a symbolic ritual, and others do not incorporate it into their services.

FACTS

The quarreling and tension that has occurred among Judaism, Christianity, and Islam over the millennia is tragic on many levels and absurd in this key point: Yahweh, God, and Allah are all names for the same deity that is worshipped in different fashions by all three religions.

This is indicative that Christianity is clearly not a monolith. From the death of Jesus through the Renaissance, there was one Church that evolved over time into the Roman Catholic Church in the Western world. In the East, Greek and Russian Orthodox Christianity grew and thrived without any input from the papacy in Rome, and many other smaller sects have always existed through the millennia.

Numerous Denominations

During the Renaissance, the Protestant Reformation created numerous Protestant denominations. Jesus Christ and the teachings of the New Testament remain at the core of all, but their differences are legion, and rivalry, bad feeling, and outright hostility have sometimes blemished the relations between these sects that worship the same God.

All preach of the promise of everlasting life through accepting Jesus as your savior. Some are tolerant of other creeds, while other insular Christians seem more obsessed with who else is going to Hell than tending to their own house.

Most Christians believe that Jesus will come again, and there will be quite an upheaval when he does. Mystics and madmen have been telling us the end is nigh almost since Day One. So far so good.

If we keep things simple and reduce all the dogma to the basic Christian belief that "God is Love," then Christianity is a beautiful faith that gives spiritual succor to millions and does good deeds and charitable works throughout the world.

Islam

The word *Islam* means "surrender." It implies total submission to Allah. Allah is the Islamic name for God, but it is the same God of the Judeo-Christian tradition. Devotees of Islam are called Muslims, which means "one who surrenders to God." The third of the great monotheistic religions in the order of origin, Islam also preaches unwavering loyalty to the one true God, and that all men are equal in God's stern but loving downward glance. Unlike more insular religions, Islamic tradition teaches that you can convert to Islam with a simple personal decision. You are a Muslim if you say you are and, of course, agree to abide by its precepts. And all Muslims belong to one community called an *umma,* whether they are in Arabia or Indonesia or Omaha.

The founder of Islam was Muhammad, who was born circa 570. He was given a divine revelation that prompted the formation of the Islamic faith. He was the latest in a long line of prophets who were beloved by God. In Islamic tradition, Moses and Jesus were holy messengers of God and the Old and New Testaments are valid spiritual documents, but the ultimate expression of God's mysterious plan for mankind, according to Muslims, found its voice in Muhammad and their holy book, the Koran.

Rituals are extremely important in the Muslim culture and must be rigorously observed. Included in these multitudinous series of standards and practices are the Five Pillars of Islam. They are the profession of faith, prayer, almsgiving, fasting, and at least one trip to Mecca (Muhammad's birthplace) during one's life.

Profession of Faith

The profession of faith, sometimes called giving witness, is common in other creeds. Muslims orally reaffirm that Allah is the only God and that Muhammad is his true prophet several times a day, during daily prayers or whenever the mood strikes them. This profession is the major requirement for membership and can be taken by anyone at any time. And no other Muslim can challenge another's veracity. It is a sacred contract between the individual and God.

Prayer

Muslims must also pray five times a day. This is the second pillar of Islam. They must first engage in a ritual cleansing and then face Mecca, no matter where they are on the planet. The prayers are typically performed approximately at sunrise, noon, midafternoon, sunset, and at night. In countries where there is a large Islamic population, it is customary for a crier to ascend the tower of the local mosque (the Islamic place of worship) and vociferously remind the populace that it is prayer time. Group praying in the mosque occurs at noon on Fridays.

Almsgiving

Charitable donations, also known as *almsgiving,* is the third pillar of Islam. Islam exhorts its followers to give generously to the poor. Just as the other monotheistic religions endorse helping those less fortunate, the Islamic tradition considers it a duty.

Fasting

Fasting is the fourth pillar. The main time of fasting is during the month of Ramadan, which is the ninth month in the Islamic twelve-month calendar. From dawn until dusk, devout Muslims refrain from food, drink, and l'amour. Fasting is practiced at certain times in all major religions. The ascetic denial and discomfort provides a cleansing sense of atonement. This is similar to the Christian tradition of Lent, where the faithful temporarily deny themselves the pleasures of life. And just as Lent ends with Easter Sunday, Ramadan ends with a three-day holiday.

Mecca Pilgrimage

The fifth pillar of Islam is a trip to the holy city of Mecca once in your life. Mecca is the center of the Islamic faith, the home of Muhammad, and Muslims who are physically and financially able should make the trip to show their devotion. Muslims dress in plain, nonflashy clothes. Jewelry, perfume, and l'amour are prohibited during the pilgrimage. Some men shave their heads, and the men and women wear simple white sheets, symbolizing the equality of all in the eyes of Allah.

Some Muslims also make pilgrimages to Jerusalem. Jerusalem has the distinction of being a holy place in the traditions of Judaism, Christianity, and Islam.

Jihad

Some Muslims consider the concept of the *jihad* to be the sixth pillar of Islam. The word jihad conjures images of terrorism to many non-Muslims, because some militant Muslims use it as a rallying cry for a holy war against their enemies. The actual definition of the word in

Arabic is more accurately translated as "to struggle" in order to please God and can be interpreted by Muslims as anything from preaching and performing charitable deeds, to fighting in defense of Islam.

The Koran

Just as Judaism and Christianity have the Old and New Testaments, so Islam has its good book, the Koran. Muslims believe that the ultimate Word of God is represented in the Koran. These are believed to be the actual words, in essence dictated verbatim to Muhammad. As a result, translations into other languages are suspect, because everything loses something in translation.

QUESTIONS?

What are the five pillars of Islam?
The five pillars of Islam are mandatory duties to be performed by all devout Muslims. They are the profession of faith (shahada), prayer (salat), almsgiving (zakat), fasting (sawm), and a pilgrimage to the holy city of Mecca (hajj).

The Koran gives honorable mention to Moses, Jesus, and other figures from Judaic and Christian tradition. They are respected as holy men, but Muslims believe that the final word on the subject rests with the Koran, Allah's message as told to Muhammad. For example, Jesus is portrayed as a mortal man, not the Son of God. As a prophet and beloved by God, the Koran also teaches that Allah would not allow one of his prophets to suffer something as horrible as death by crucifixion. The Koran tells Muslims that, at the last minute, Jesus was rescued by God and replaced by an identical impostor. In telling the story of Abraham and his son, the Koran switches sons. In the Old Testament, God exhorts Abraham to offer his son Isaac as a human sacrifice to prove his devotion, only to stop him at the last minute and tell him that it was only a test of his love. In the Koran, the son is identified as Ishmael, from whom it is believed that the Arab offshoot of the Semitic people descended.

Final Thought

It is a basic truth that if people focused on the things that united them rather than the differences that divided them, the world would be a better place. It is unfortunate that the Big Three did not do that during their two millennia, give or take a century, of not always peaceful coexistence. Not only are all three monotheistic, all three worship the same God.

The Jewish scriptures include the Old Testament, the Christians have both the Old and the New Testaments, and the Muslims honor both those books as spiritual documents and have added what they feel is the last word on the subject, the Koran. There is much in common among these three religions.

Faith is a beautiful thing, and so is tolerance. Can't we all just get along? Isn't that what God would really prefer from his beloved creation?

CHAPTER 21

Objectivism and the Right Livelihood

O ver the years, other philosophies have developed, including the philosophy of Objectivism and the Right Livelihood. While objectivism lauds reason, individualism, and egotism, the Right Livelihood has its roots in Buddhism.

Objectivism: Looking Out for No. 1

Ayn Rand (1905–1982) was an American novelist and philosopher. She is famous for the novels *The Fountainhead* and *Atlas Shrugged,* and her philosophy is called objectivism. She put reason before emotion and individualism over groupthink and thought egotism was a good thing and altruism was a negative character trait. Needless to say, she was no stranger to controversy.

Perhaps the reason Rand developed her philosophy was the circumstances of her youth. She was a child in Russia in the tumultuous days of the Communist Revolution of 1917. She came to the United States in 1926 to seek her fortune and to be able to express her thoughts and beliefs freely and without fear of persecution. Such freedoms that we take for granted were not to be found in the former Soviet Union. In fact, her first novels, *Anthem* and *We the Living,* are cautionary tales set in what are called *dystopias.* Just as the word utopia means a perfect paradise, a dystopia is the reverse, a repressive totalitarian state. George Orwell's *1984* is the most famous example of this literary device.

 **SSENTIALS**

Objectivism is Ayn Rand's philosophy that values and extols the virtues of rugged individualism and the free market economy. Ruthlessness, though not cruelty, is accepted as a means to achieve your fullest human potential. The four pillars of objectivism are the belief in objective reality, reason, self-interest, and capitalism.

Rand believed in the ultimate heroism of man, and that mankind's goal is to achieve great success, fulfill his and her human potential to the max, and that self-interest supercedes the needs of the needy collective. Individual accomplishment is what makes society great. Food stamps and the welfare state are not in the Objectivist playbook.

Mankind is the ultimate in the cosmos, so say the Objectivists. No gods, angels, or demons. There is no Prime Mover in the Aristotelian tradition. Man is the Prime Mover and is the end, not the means to anything or anyone else.

The Four Pillars

The four pillars of objectivism are the beliefs in objective reality, reason, self-interest, and capitalism. *Objective reality* simply means that reality is reality, and it exists whether you are there or not. No philosophical speculations on the questionability of the senses apply here. We do not create our own reality, and reality is not an illusion. There is no spiritual realm for the Objectivists. It is atheistic, and they believe that when you're dead, you're dead. Case closed.

Objectivism states that we can perceive the world through reason alone. No psychic hotlines, no women's intuition. Reason rules. You do not have a soul. That is merely your conscious mind. People are not victims of forces beyond their control. If you are an Objectivist, you cannot blame your parents, your teachers, your congressman, improper toilet training, or anything else.

FACTS

One of the reasons why Ayn Rand may have developed such an extreme philosophy is because her childhood was spent in Russia during the Communist revolution. Having seen her world come crashing down around her courtesy of the Communists, it is no surprise that her philosophy has a strong antitotalitarian bent.

Reason, purpose, and self-esteem are the three prime values of mankind. The main ethical standard is simply this: survival. Survival and success for your own sake, not to enrich the world or to serve others less fortunate. Your own self-interest and your own happiness are the purest pursuits. The Objectivist ignores the bell-ringing Santas on wintry city streets. They do not believe in "giving something back."

If this sounds pretty harsh, Objectivists do not take it to the militaristic degree. No one has the right to impose his or her beliefs on others through force or violence. Force is only to be used in self-defense. Men and nations should interact as free market traders and entrepreneurs. The ideal political expression of objectivism is capitalism. Individual rights and property rights are what it's all about. Government interference is anathema to the Objectivist.

The Romantic Realist

Can such a philosophy celebrate art? Yes. Ayn Rand called herself a Romantic Realist. Her Romantic streak creates characters that are her Ideal and puts them in then-contemporary situations. She claimed her novels were not intended to be didactic, but rather artistic. Her success on this score is debatable.

The Fountainhead is the story of Howard Roark, an uncompromising architect who will not budge one iota in his artistic vision. He does not sacrifice his integrity or make any accommodations for anyone or anything. He suffers much for his art, but does so stoically with the endurance of Prometheus. He blows up the building he designed because other people have meddled with it and are corrupting his vision. He goes to trial, defends himself, and delivers a summation speech to the jury that, a little too melodramatically, acquits him. This speech is a distillation of the Objectivist viewpoint. One can appreciate the rugged individualism in *The Fountainhead* and the pull-yourself-up-by-your-own-bootstraps approach of objectivism. It may go a little too far, however, in a speech by one of the major characters, who bombastically intones that some may see a mountain and appreciate its beauty, but he only sees stone to be forged and fashioned into a skyscraper. Some may see a lush forest and be awestruck by nature's majesty, while he sees lumber to build things and turn into newspaper. This is delivered as the right and proper way to view the Grand Tetons, Yellowstone National Park, or the rainforests. There are no contributors to the Sierra Club among the Objectivists.

Ayn Rand's *Atlas Shrugged* is her bestselling novel that presents, through the vehicle of a fictional story, a complete exposition of the Objectivist philosophy. But be forewarned: The book is weighty in more way, than one. It is over 1,000 pages long. You will need a mega amount of sunscreen if you make this your "beach book."

Atlas Shrugged is Ayn Rand's other major work of fiction. Its female protagonist struggles to run a railroad in a man's world. She encounters all manner of mealy-mouthed politically correct types who are out to thwart her capitalist ambitions. Throughout the novel, many characters ask the cryptic question, "Who is John Galt?" for no apparent reason. It is kind of used the way a singsong "Whatever" is today. Dagny Taggart learns the meaning when she ends up in Galt's Gulch, an Objectivist commune where the ideals of Rand are put into practical application.

Both novels were bestsellers and are still widely read today. As works of literature, they leave something to be desired. Subtlety is not Rand's strong suit, and the narrative and dialogue is on the stilted side. Nevertheless their impact on twentieth-century philosophy is not diminished by their purple prose. Fans of the free market economy, capitalism, libertarianism, individualism, self-responsibility, laissez-faire government, and the American dream will continue to savor these weighty tomes.

Ayn Rand never wrote another novel after *Atlas Shrugged,* but she continued to philosophize. She published a newsletter and wrote nonfiction works, including *The Virtue of Selfishness: A Concept of New Egoism* and *Introduction to Objectivist Epistemology.*

Right Livelihood: Doing the Right Thing

Is the phrase "business ethics" an oxymoron? Are these two concepts mutually exclusive? If you have had any experience navigating the dog-eat-dog rat race, you would find this to be the case. The ruthlessness and duplicity of your corporate masters have no doubt filled you with profound revulsion. Or perhaps you are a premiere player in the game, and have risen to the top by any means necessary?

For those who seek some civility in the workplace and who strive to live a moral and ethical life and still make a decent living, there is the contemporary philosophy called Right Livelihood. However, it's contemporary only in how it is applied to modern life. Like almost every modern philosophy and/or fad, it has its roots in antiquity.

Its Roots

The first appearance of the phrase Right Livelihood appears in the Buddhist Eightfold Path, an early Eastern guide for living. The Buddhist goal is to grow closer and closer to enlightenment and an awakening in this incarnation, or lifetime. And the business world is not a world rife with spiritually enlightened Buddhas-in-training. Even the popular coaching and mentoring programs in the corporate world that are designed to emulate the age-old master-and-pupil relationships through popular bromides and self-evident clichés have the profit motive first and foremost. If said pupil does not increase the bottom line by the end of the fiscal year, the coach may employ a little tough love by sending him or her to the unemployment line.

SSENTIALS

Right Livelihood is a contemporary philosophy derived from the teachings of Buddhism that espouses the belief that the best work situation is one that does not involve lying, dishonesty, or harming other people or the planet. Though a noble ideal, it is a tall order to put into practice in this day and age.

Needless to say, Ayn Rand's Objectivists would consider followers of the Right Livelihood to be wimps. "Business is business, business is war. May the best man win and if you lose, you're a loser and so long sucker" is the Objectivist approach to the business world. Right Livelihood is a workhorse of a different color.

What's It All About?

Right Livelihood can mean many things. For some, it can mean simply trying to be ethical and moral in a world where such virtues, though loudly touted, are not practiced in abundance. While this is difficult, it is not impossible. For Right Livelihood purists, it means adherence to a more rigorous set of principles that would be almost impossible to follow to the letter in modern multinational corporations.

The principle is called *Sila,* from the Buddhist Eightfold Path. Sila is a three-tiered philosophy and includes Right Speech, Right Action, and Right Livelihood. The precepts involved are good rules to live by, if possible.

Have a Nonharming Job

There are five aspects to Right Livelihood. The first principle is nonharming. Do not have any job that will cause harm to others. Easily done, right? Well, both the tobacco magnate and the convenience store clerk sell cigarettes. That minimum wage clerk also sells beer, sugar, lottery tickets, and haute couture fashion magazines wherein anorexic supermodels are displayed as Platonic Forms of femininity. All these things have been proven to have deleterious effects on people. If the teenage cashier cannot get through the day without a nonharming ethic, what about you and your job? Think about it.

Nonharming also includes, of course, not harming the planet. This eliminates a whole battery of jobs, from big oil all the way down to the silkscreen printer who illegally dumps his toxic inks rather than pay to have them disposed of by a professional. And, of course, you should not choose a job that will compel you to lie. That eliminates a career in advertising.

Find Appropriate Happinesss

The second aspect of Right Livelihood is finding "appropriate happiness." You have to feel good about what you do, or you will suffer and all those around you will suffer. How many miserable cubicle neighbors have you had? How many disgruntled bureaucrats have victimized you, taking out their frustrations on the next person in line? People who settle for a bland job that pays the bills or join the fast track to big bucks despite the stress and unpleasantness that is attendant to the job are not finding appropriate happiness. The ideal would be to find a job that suits you perfectly—a job where you feel fulfilled, a job that you believe is helping you contribute to making the world a better place. Part of your spiritual path is to find it. No matter how long it takes, destiny dictates that the right fit is out there somewhere for the taking.

Additional "appropriate happiness" comes from producing goods and services that help the community at large. Another is using your job to become and remain free of debt. Statistics tell us that the average American family has, during any given month, $1,000 in their savings account and $8,000 in credit-card debt. The fear of financial security that hangs over so many heads like the Sword of Damocles is a hindrance to peace of mind, and hence the path to enlightenment. You cannot be as free spirited as the Buddha with the Four Horsemen of the Apocalypse (MasterCard, Visa, Discover, and American Express) chasing you down the path.

QUESTIONS?

Are you "following your bliss?"
This should be the goal of one and all, according to Right Livelihood. The theory is that if you do what you love, what inflames your soul and fires your passion, eventually the money will follow. In a climate where surveys tell us that the overwhelming majority of us hate our jobs, bliss is apparently not in abundance.

Another happiness to be achieved is being above reproach in your job. Your choices and your actions will not adversely impact others, and you can conduct your business with a clear conscience.

Grow Spiritually

The third aspect of Right Livelihood is the ability to use your job as a vehicle for spiritual growth. In this day and age, people are identified with their job. One of the first questions asked when meeting someone new is "What do you do?" Many people, unless they are a big shot or high-powered person, do not want to be identified with what they do. It is only a small part of what they are, and for too many, their job is a necessary evil, not a source of satisfaction. This aspect of Right Livelihood suggests that you can make your job, any job, an exercise in meditation.

Meditation often involves repetitive acts. Their very repetition is conducive to entering a meditative state. Have you ever found yourself in your car halfway to work before you are really aware of it? You had a quick breakfast, kissed someone goodbye if you're blessed, started your car, and were on the road before you knew what hit you. That's a form of a meditative state. You were perfectly functional, and yet you were elsewhere. It is likely that your job entails a lot of repetitive tasks. It is possible to turn that monotony into a discipline. Turn repetitive motion syndrome into repetitive motion enlightenment. Whistle while you work and find inner peace.

Keep It Simple

The fourth aspect is simplicity. This is a universal spiritual principle. Keep it simple in all your affairs. Do not overcomplicate your work life with extraneous dalliances such as office gossip or office politics. Doing your job to the best of your ability and being able to sleep at night is its own profound spiritual reward.

Help Others

The fifth aspect is Service. This would create an uproar among the Objectivists, who see altruism as counterproductive, destructive, and a sign of weakness. Right Livelihood teaches that the best jobs are those that do good works for your fellow men and women, and the planet.

Follow Your Bliss

Right Livelihood is also about knowing how to "follow your bliss." This phrase was made popular by the scholar and mythographer Joseph Campbell. He maintained that if you truly do what you love and pursue your dreams, you will be rewarded on many levels, including financially. *Do What You Love and the Money Will Follow* is the title of a bestseller espousing the same theme. The next time you visit your local bookstore, make a note of the numerous books claiming to teach similar tips, tools, and techniques to financial and spiritual happiness. It is safe to say that at least these authors are following their bliss and reaping the rewards.

A Dot.Comedy of Errors 1.0

Right Livelihood is easier theorized than implemented. Consider the following case study. A company that no longer exists fancied itself a new and improved business model for the new millennium.

Once upon a time, there was a company that claimed to practice a form of Right Livelihood. This was a dot.com company, and dot.com companies often believed that they were hip, cutting edge, and vastly superior in methodology and ethics than those stodgy "old economy" businesses.

The partners spent a lot of money to make it a fun and friendly atmosphere. The "hip" interior design and furniture were contracted and implemented at considerable expense. The goal was to create what the creative people called a "funky" look. Given that this was a company that designed, built, and maintained Web sites for *Fortune 500* clients, it was surprising that functionality was not a consideration.

The ultra-cool metal stools in the cafeteria, the seats of which seemed to be metallic imprints of an anorexic supermodel's behind, were about five feet high. The dining table they were clustered around was approximately three feet high. The designers pronounced it too chic for words, but there was one minor glitch. A person cannot sit and eat at a dining ensemble that has five-foot high chairs and a three-foot high table unless they are an orangutan. Hence, the cafeteria was unfrequented, with the exception of trips to the refrigerator for designer water and free Coca-Cola.

Selected conference rooms were supplied with crayons, and the staff was encouraged to write on the walls in an effort to encourage their Inner Children to come out and play.

Staff traversed the aisles between the rows of cubicles on goofy silver scooters that were all the rage at the time. People also played soccer with beach balls up and down the aisles, and the cafeteria had a pool table.

There was no dress code because that was simply too Old World. Freedom of expression was encouraged because they were "artists." Free yoga classes were offered, but you had to get to the office at 7 A.M. to take advantage of them. Free lunch was provided, and fruits and other delectables were placed in communal areas throughout the day.

After-hours social activities were encouraged. In fact, attendance was taken. Because the extracurricular activities invariably involved boozing, those of a temperate disposition were regarded as pariahs. A partner actually told several staffers that they were "not cool" when they refused to "do shots"—at a 10 A.M. meeting!

The company was a leviathan that gobbled up numerous start-ups from coast to coast. People from the Des Moines office were surprised to find employees of this New Economy company reviving the tradition of the three-martini lunch and announcing in a conference room that everyone must expose the waistband of their underpants in the "getting to know you" portion of the meeting.

FACTS

In the new economy, many companies are offering perks to make the working life a more positive and even a spiritual experience. What would the robber barons of the Industrial Age make of ergonomic workstations, yoga and mediation classes, and even on-site masseuses? Nevertheless, business is still business as millions of dot.com employees learned the hard way.

These and many other "quality of working life" issues were enacted to create a family atmosphere and an environment where people could not wait to get to the office and go the extra mile, the whole nine yards, and all that jazz. The message was that they were one big happy family making the workplace better through advertising.

Paradise was punctured with the failing economy. Layoffs began, and the former extravagance led to nickel-and-diming. Employees, listening to Napster on their laptops, received a tap on the shoulder. Removing their headphones, they swiveled their ergonomic chair around to see their manager/mentor/drinking buddy and a large, blue-blazered security guard by his or her side. They were told to step away from their workstation. Their computers were seized; they surrendered their cell phones and Palm Pilots and were politely but firmly thrown out of the building. Personnel would be in touch with the details of their severance package, if any. The survivors of the purge were told that they were safe for the time being, but harder work and longer hours were required.

The five-foot high silver stools were sold on eBay for $600 apiece; the $2,000 light bulbs in the lobby obelisk were not replaced, leaving it looming like a single structure from Stonehenge, a monument to faux Right Livelihood and the demise of this dot.comedy of errors.

The boyish CEO still globetrotted in his corporate Lear Jet trying to woo increasingly skeptical venture capitalists. Second, third, and fourth waves of layoffs followed, and the dream ultimately died with a Chapter Seven bankruptcy.

What can we learn from this? Right Livelihood is a noble principle, but extremely hard to implement in the modern era. When companies try to force the issue, or create the illusion that they are warm and fuzzy, please be advised that the bottom line, not enlightenment, is the Nirvana they seek. You will find that many in the business world who speak of Right Livelihood are merely corporate wolves in Buddhist robes.

CHAPTER 22

The Forgotten Philosophers

As you have been reading this book, you may have come to the conclusion that philosophy is strictly the purview of that misunderstood and unfairly maligned minority known as "dead white men." While it is true that many of the famous philosophers were European men, and most of them are dead, this chapter will endeavor to give an overview of African philosophies as well.

"Primitive" Cultures

These other philosophies are commonly, and perhaps condescendingly, called "primitive" cultures. While much of this philosophy is mixed with mythology and spirituality, there is a rich tradition of wisdom to be gained from the philosophies that originated in Africa and the native inhabitants of North America.

Africa is a diverse land of cultures, beliefs, and philosophies. It is believed that the first hominids, the ancient ancestors of you and me, first stood upright on the African continent, so in effect, until proven otherwise, it is the birthplace of all humankind.

What follows is by no means a comprehensive dissertation, but merely a general overview of the basic philosophical and spiritual concepts that have emerged from the African continent.

African Philosophy

The African philosophy, in very general terms, involves a deep connection with nature and an understanding and respect for the inexorable cycle of life. Man is part of the Big Picture that is Nature and the cosmos. Man does not live by reason alone in the African worldview. Intuition and imagination are regarded as valid, and logic is not stressed as the path to wisdom. Emotion plays a more important role.

Western philosophy has engaged in much debate about the existence of God. Ontological arguments, inductive and deductive reasoning, and proofs about the Immovable Mover do not figure into African philosophy. The fact that there is a "Force" is a given, as well as the fact that there is a spirit world that coexists with the realm of physical reality.

The typical African philosophy maintains that there is an order to the cosmos. The higher powers (gods) are at the top of the hierarchy, followed by man, animals, and inanimate natural objects.

No Philosophical Debates

There is no conflict between Rationalism and Empiricism; all the great philosophical debates are rendered moot. The world is neither an idea in the mind of man; nor is it only to be understood through sensory experience. This dueling Dualism is not present in African philosophy. There is no either-or mentality or conflict of opposites that permeates Western thought (and the East for that matter—consider the Yin and the Yang of Buddhism).

ESSENTIALS There is no "dualism" in African and Native American culture. Life is a seamless cycle, and we are all one with Nature. The Western tendency to establish a conflict of opposites does not exist in this world.

The seamless harmony and flow of nature is at the heart of African philosophy. Death is not an end; it is simply a part of life and a journey into a new phase of existence of the spirit—though this belief is true of religious people from all cultures. There is also the healthy mind-body-spirit connection that is now more accepted in other societies. A human is one organism, and disease of the soul can become a diseased body. This is the basis for holistic medicine, which has grown very popular in the Western world.

It's about Time

African philosophy views mankind simply as part of a harmonious whole, not as the exalted center of the universe or as a malignant accident of nature. And time was not measured by the clocks and other timepieces; the sunrises, sunsets, and the changing of the seasons measured it. There was no discussion of Heraclitus's theory that everything is a constant state of flux or Parmenides's notion that change is an illusion and that permanence is the natural state of reality.

The other great European time controversy was between Sir Isaac Newton and Gottfried "Monads" Leibniz. Newton, the great seventeenth-century scientist and mathematician who "discovered" gravity, determined that time was not a sequence of events that comprise life; rather it was absolute and mathematical and occurred in and of itself. Leibniz believed that the succession of events is what constitutes time. Our old friend

Aristotle believed that time was part of the innate course of all things from potentiality to actuality.

FACTS

Traditional African and Native American cultures do not measure time the same way. They are not slaves to the ticking clock. Time is measured by sunrises and sunsets, as well as the changing seasons.

The African belief is that time is simply the life process. Again, harmony and wholeness was the philosophy of Africans for many millennia. Of course, in this age of industrialization and the Internet, Africans have adopted many Western ways, just as the West is continually intrigued by the philosophies that have emerged from Africa, and the traditions of the American Indians.

Native American Philosophy

Like the Africans, the Native Americans are not a monolith. There are more than 700 nations, and many more tribes within these nations. Though there is much diversity within this people, there are common cultural philosophies.

The Same God

Traditional Native Americans believe that no matter what name or characteristics people give the Creator, Christian, Muslim, Jew, or Native American, they are all referring to the same deity. They believe that just as you are what you eat, you are what God made you. There you stand, now go out and make the most of life. You are not stained with Original Sin, you are not inherently wicked (after all, God made you), and therefore you do not need a savior to redeem you. Remember the old poster in schools that read, "I know I'm special 'cause God don't make no junk?" This is Native American philosophy.

The Vision Quest

One intriguing expression of Native American spiritual philosophy is the Vision Quest. This is a private ritual that is rarely discussed with others in the tribe, let alone outsiders. The person usually goes alone into the wilderness with little or no supplies and through prayer and meditation, receives messages from the Creator, often in the form of an animal spirit that becomes his guide.

Story Time!

Like all so-called primitive cultures, Native American history, spirituality, and philosophy have been transmitted though an oral tradition. Very little was ever put in writing. Everyone loves a good story, and the best stories endeavor to explain universal truths and try to show who we are and how we got here. This rich mythology contains many basic truths and deep wisdom, presented in an entertaining manner. Storytelling, rather than dogma or didactic lecturing, is regarded as the best way to get your point across.

Very little, if anything, was put in writing in African and Native American cultures. They have a rich oral tradition, and history, mythology, spirituality, and philosophy were passed down from generation to generation through storytelling.

Native American stories, like their African counterparts, describe a world where animals and humans are equals in the cycle of life. The animals, though hunted and killed, are revered for their sacrifice, and their spirits are worshipped, because without them the humans would perish. There is no sense that mankind has been given dominion over the earth and the other creatures of the earth, as in the Old Testament tradition. The Native American sense of time is also based on natural rhythms of the seasons, cycles of the moon, and their own body clocks.

An Afterlife

Ours is not the last word on the real world, according to American Indian tradition. There are other places of existence, replete with spiritual life, and there is constant interaction between these worlds. Spirit guides visit humans, and humans can, if they know how, visit other dimensions through, among other means, astral projection.

Black Elk Speaks

Black Elk Speaks is a contemporary classic of Native American philosophy and spirituality, as interpreted by poet John G. Niehardt. It tells the extraordinary story of a remarkable man and expresses the philosophy of a people. Published in 1932, it is based on the conversations between Neihardt and an old Sioux Indian named Black Elk.

Black Elk lived through a tumultuous time in the history of America, a time that saw the decline and fall of his people and their way of life. He was a teenager at the Battle of Little Bighorn, the last stand of the Sioux where General George Armstrong Custer and his troops were massacred. Though they won the battle, the Sioux, and all Native Americans, lost the war, and they were sent to reservations where their posterity remains to this day. Though some have entered the casino business, the conditions are for the most part less than satisfactory.

A Broken Man

In the 1880s, Black Elk was a performer in Buffalo Bill's Wild West Show, which toured the Eastern United States and Europe. After a few years of celebrity, he returned to his people only to witness the horrible and notorious massacre at Wounded Knee in 1890. A broken man after this event, he converted to Roman Catholicism out of resignation rather than a valid conversion experience. For thirty years, he served his people as best he could on the Pine Ridge Reservation, teaching a faith that was not his and putting aside the visions and insight he had experienced in his youth. He dressed like a white man and gave up his shamanic religious practices for Catholicism. But Black Elk's native spirituality could not stay dormant forever. As Jung spoke of the shadow, such things will surface when the right impetus is there to spur them.

Black Elk's vision was of a scared hoop of all the peoples of the world living together in peace. He was exhorted by the Great Spirit to go forth among the people and spread this message, but he kept it to himself for many decades. The ancient saying that "When the student is ready, the teacher will appear" goes both ways, and in 1930, Black Elk met a student to help him fulfill his divine mandate.

A Spirit Revitalized

American poet John G. Neihardt interviewed Black Elk as a historical source for an epic poem he was writing on Wounded Knee. Black Elk saw something in Neihardt and believed that he had been brought there for a reason. It became a mutually beneficial relationship and a lifelong friendship. The poet met a great man and produced a profoundly spiritual work; Black Elk put on his native dress and returned to the "center of the world" where he had received his first vision, Harney Peak in the Black Hills of South Dakota.

Witnesses recall that during Black Elk's prayer, clouds formed, thunder rumbled, and a drizzle fell upon those present. When the prayer ended, the skies cleared. It was a prayer of forgiveness and atonement for not remaining true to his beliefs, but Black Elk more than made up for his hiatus of despair as he did the work of the Great Spirit by spreading the word to all who would listen.

The Medicine Wheel

A common philosophical tradition among Native Americans is the belief system called the *Medicine Wheel*. The symbol of the wheel represents the cycle of life, both macrocosmically (the world) and microcosmically (the individual). The four spokes of the wheel are the four directions of the compass—north, south, east, and west. Each direction has its own philosophy, a symbolic animal, and a color.

The Meanings of the Spokes

East is considered the beginning, because the sun rises in the east. The color is gold, and the animal is a golden eagle. The philosophy is one of seeing the world as it really is, with clarity and without illusion.

The south is represented by the color green, and the symbolic animal is the mouse. The mouse represents the striving and curious nature that is to be encouraged. Most of us think of the mouse as an icky nuisance, but the traditional Native American sees a shrewd, savvy, and dogged explorer. Think about that the next time you see one of the poor little critters on a glue trap.

SSENTIALS

The Native American concept of the Medicine Wheel is similar to Carl Gustav Jung's notion of *individuation,* which is the successful integration of all the disparate aspects of your body, mind, and spirit to create a wholeness and harmony.

The west is where the sun sets, and the color is black. The animal is the bear. The bear is a nocturnal creature and hibernates in a cave. These Native American amateur psychologists saw the bear as the symbol for introspection. Most of our minds are subconscious, and those who traverse these darkened realms, as the bear prowls the night, indulge in introspection and are more likely to find illumination. This indicates a highly sophisticated understanding of the human mind.

Finally, the north represents winter. The color is the whiteness of the snow and the totem animals are the wolf and the buffalo. These animals represent intelligence and insight, things that often come too late, in the winter of one's life.

The Center

All four spokes come together at the center. If you reach the center in your life, you will have incorporated in a perfect balance all these qualities. The concept of the Medicine Wheel is similar to Carl Gustav

Jung's notion of individuation, which is the successful integration of all the disparate aspects of your body, mind, and spirit.

Some Native American nations have a very enlightened sense of criminal justice. The Navajo regard a criminal as a sick person, not an evil person, and healing rituals and ceremonies and rehabilitation are encouraged and the person is welcomed back into the tribe. This is not the primitive form of knee-jerk liberalism, however. A repeated offender who is deemed beyond redemption and remains a threat to the lives of the rest of the tribe is usually dispatched with finality.

Summary

The Native American philosophy can be summed up as follows. Everything is connected, and humans are just one small part of the cosmic Big Picture. Like Heraclitus, the Indians believe that the cycle of life is one of constant change, but not chaotic or meaningless change. Everything is happening for a purpose, even if we do not understand what that purpose may be. People have a body and a spirit, and there is a spiritual world that is as real as the world we see and experience with our five senses.

FACTS

Some Native American nations had an enlightened sense of criminal justice. The wrongdoer was treated as a sick person and an attempt was made to heal them and reintegrate them back into the tribe. Of course, the extremely violent, murderous members incapable of rehabilitation were dispatched with finality.

We are here on this earth to learn. The optimum conditions for learning require a balance of the physical, mental, emotional, and spiritual aspects of our nature. We will be given help from the spirits if we ask for it. Achieving your maximum human potential is where it's at, and the only real sin against God is failure to use whatever gifts God has given you for your own good and the good of the community.

A Famous Letter from Chief Seattle

We will close with a famous letter from Chief Seattle to the "white man" about selling the land to them. It distills the Native American philosophy with poignant eloquence and reminds us of the crimes committed against this noble race of deeply spiritual philosophers.

"The President in Washington sends word that he wishes to buy our land. But how can you buy or sell the sky? The land? The idea is strange to us. If we do not own the freshness of the air and the sparkle of the water, how can you buy them? Every part of the earth is sacred to my people. Every shining pine needle, every sandy shore, every mist in the dark woods, every meadow, every humming insect. All are holy in the memory and experience of my people. We know the sap which courses through the trees as we know the blood that courses through our veins. We are part of the earth and it is part of us. The perfumed flowers are our sisters. The bear, the deer, the great eagle, these are our brothers. The rocky crests, the dew in the meadow, the body heat of the pony, and man all belong to the same family. The shining water that moves in the streams and rivers is not just water, but the blood of our ancestors. If we sell you our land, you must remember that it is sacred. Each glossy reflection in the clear waters of the lakes tells of events and memories in the life of my people. The water's murmur is the voice of my father's father. The rivers are our brothers. They quench our thirst. They carry our canoes and feed our children. So you must give the rivers the kindness that you would give any brother. If we sell you our land, remember that the air is precious to us, that the air shares its spirit with all the life that it supports. The wind that gave our grandfather his first breath also received his last sigh. The wind also gives our children the spirit of life. So if we sell our land, you must keep it apart and sacred, as a place where man can go to taste the wind that is sweetened by the meadow flowers. Will you teach your children what we have taught our children? That the earth is our mother? What befalls the earth befalls all the sons of the earth. This we know: The earth does not belong to man, man belongs to the earth. All things are connected like the blood

that unites us all. Man did not weave the web of life, he is merely a strand in it. Whatever he does to the web, he does to himself. One thing we know: Our God is also your God. The earth is precious to him and to harm the earth is to heap contempt on its creator. Your destiny is a mystery to us. What will happen when the buffalo are all slaughtered? The wild horses tamed? What will happen when the secret corners of the forest are heavy with the scent of many men and the view of the ripe hills is blotted with talking wires? Where will the thicket be? Gone! Where will the eagle be? Gone! And what is to say goodbye to the swift pony and then hunt? The end of living and the beginning of survival. When the last red man has vanished with this wilderness, and his memory is only the shadow of a cloud moving across the prairie, will these shores and forests still be here? Will there be any of the spirit of my people left? We love this earth as a newborn loves its mother's heartbeat. So, if we sell you our land, love it as we have loved it. Care for it, as we have cared for it. Hold in your mind the memory of the land as it is when you receive it. Preserve the land for all children, and love it, as God loves us. As we are part of the land, you too are part of the land. This earth is precious to us. It is also precious to you. One thing we know—there is only one God. No man, be he Red man or White man, can be apart. We ARE all brothers after all."

ESSENTIALS   *Black Elk Speaks* is a wonderful twentieth-century interpretation of Native American spirituality. It is the memoir of a *shaman,* or medicine man, as told to a noted American poet. It should be considered required reading for anyone who wants to understand Native American culture.

CHAPTER 23

Twelve Steps to a Better Life

The curse of addiction has afflicted mankind since the dawn of time. One of the most ravaging and ruthless of these addictions is alcoholism. It adversely affects millions of people, destroying countless lives, both of the drinker and those around him or her.

Alcohol in Society

The consumption of alcohol has been a socially and culturally accepted custom for thousands of years. While Muslims and some other societies eschew alcohol, it is entrenched in most others. And why not? It's an icebreaker. It can liven up a party and lift deflated spirits (though make no mistake, alcohol, as chemicals go, is a depressant, not a stimulant).

Alcohol is also ruthlessly habit forming. While most folks can take it or leave it and indulge in its many delights without any deleterious effects (save the New Year's Day hangover), for others, alcohol is nothing less than a cocked and loaded pistol poised to blast the abuser into oblivion. For these poor unfortunate souls, drinking is what Hamlet called "a custom more honored in the breach than the observance." In other words, they should stay away from the stuff. One is too many, and a hundred is not enough, as the saying goes.

The Affects of Alcohol

Alcohol kills multiple thousands of people a year. Drunk driving is an obvious example, but heart attacks, strokes, suicides, homicides, tragic accidents, and even some types of cancer can be directly attributed to alcoholism. Nowadays, alcoholism is acknowledged and treated with less of a stigma than in years past. Most medical plans cover treatment programs, and many employers will give alcoholics a second chance if they take advantage of such programs and demonstrate that they can stay on the straight and narrow. Rehabilitation programs and facilities are a big business. And in all likelihood, they will remain so, because as long as there are human beings inhabiting the planet, a certain percentage of them will abuse alcohol and other substances.

The Path to Rehabilitation

Easy access to treatment and the current social empathy to alcoholism were not always the case. In fact, alcoholism is a very recent phenomenon. There was once little recourse for the alcoholic other than to find solace, succor, and possible redemption in religious groups and temperance associations. Organizations such as the Salvation Army helped many a destitute soul. Many Catholics would visit the parish priest and "take the pledge," a vow to swear off the demon grog. This was usually at the urging of a beleaguered spouse. The active alcoholic, if he or she ended up on skid row, was regarded as a pathetic pariah. Even if the attempt was in earnest, the recovery rate was extremely poor. Staying sober for any length of time was rare, barring white-knuckled stubbornness and religious conversion.

FACTS

Alcoholics Anonymous came into being in 1935 and, after a rocky start and a humble beginning, it has helped millions of people all over the world battle the crippling addiction of alcoholism.

One refuge for the alcoholic in need was the Oxford Group. It was a nondenominational Christian evangelical organization formed in the early twentieth century. This group sought to emulate the practices of the very early Christian Church, when Christianity was a ragtag band of persecuted outcasts. They were not in the recovery business per se, but fallen men and women seeking a design for living and plan of action to combat their "failings" were welcomed.

One member of the Oxford Group sought treatment from the legendary Dr. Carl Jung. The eminent psychologist was baffled by the insidious enigma of alcoholism. After lengthy treatment and repeated relapses on the part of the patient, Dr. Jung acknowledged that the man was powerless over alcoholism and told the patient that only a spiritual conversion experience would help him. Such had been the case for centuries, and it looked like the status quo would not change anytime soon.

New Hope for the Alcoholic

There was no philosophy, no program geared specifically to the singular situation of the alcoholic—that is, until a series of happy coincidences in 1935 brought together a swaggering New York City stockbroker and a humble Ohio doctor and together they ushered in a new hope for the suffering alcoholic.

Bill Wilson was a World War I veteran, an ambitious and driven man who returned from the trenches to make his mark on the world. He enjoyed great success in the stock market during the Roaring 20s, while sinking deeper and deeper into the morass of alcoholism. When the stock market crashed and America was flung into the Great Depression, Wilson was one of the many casualties, and his escalated drinking sent his life into a maelstrom more chaotic than the plunging Dow Jones. Wilson and his long-suffering wife Lois went through a living hell. He was in and out of hospitals, staying sober for brief spasms, and relapsing with an ugly vengeance. There seemed to be no hope. His doctors told his wife to prepare for the worst. Wilson was written off as a man destined to die miserably or end up in the madhouse.

A Timely Visit from an Old Friend

Wilson was visited by an old friend who claimed to have found religion. He was a member of the aforementioned Oxford Group. He was an old drinking buddy, and Wilson was inspired by his story. He was struck by his friend's talk of a concept of a power greater than ourselves. Many people who were resistant to organized religion had a problem staying sober through the auspices of those who would insist you "listen to the sermon" in order to get the assistance. Whether it be for reasons of pride, prejudice, or principle, many people couldn't get past "the God thing." Bill Wilson was one of these men, but beaten down as he was, a desperate alcoholic who had lost it all and was in danger of losing his life, it was suddenly not much of a leap of faith to conceive of something, *anything* greater than the great "I am." He found strength in his friend's message and committed himself to sobriety.

Bill's Crisis

But wait, we have yet to begin at the beginning. On a business trip to the Midwest, Bill Wilson had a crisis. He was craving a drink yet struggling desperately not to take the first one because he knew that once he took the first drink, all bets were off. The cocktail lounge in the hotel lobby was awfully tempting, but instead he desperately called around town with what was then a strange request: He was looking for another alcoholic to talk to. He wasn't in the proselytizing business. He had no desire to save the man's soul. He was motivated by enlightened self-interest. Talking to another alcoholic was therapeutic for him.

Bill Wilson was introduced to Dr. Bob Smith on that fateful day. Smith, who also had exposure to the Oxford Group in his hometown, reluctantly granted a few minutes of his time. The two men then ended up gabbing for several hours. And thus one of the most influential and beneficial movements of the twentieth century was born—Alcoholics Anonymous (AA).

The Birth of Alcoholics Anonymous

The premise of Alcoholics Anonymous is a simple one: Get a group of people together who are simultaneously struggling to combat a common problem. People who have shared the same experiences can gain strength from each other and find hope for the future. The notion of a sober alcoholic helping a down-and-out drinker for his own benefit was new. Certainly, an element of compassion and altruism was present, but the primary motivating force was in the individual's recovery. The act of kindness was rewarded with the strengthening of one's own commitment to staying sober.

This motley confederation of recovering alcoholics started slowly in Akron, Ohio, and New York City. But what kind of philosophy could they devise to stay alive and thrive, to save themselves and offer their message of hope to the multitudes of people suffering from this terrible affliction?

The Philosophy Behind AA

While it is true that the founders of Alcoholics Anonymous and most of its early members were white men and their bent was decidedly Christian, we must not hold that against them, no matter how fashionable that may be in this day and age.

One of the mainstay philosophies of Alcoholics Anonymous is the concept of "one day at a time." Of course, AA did not invent this concept. Nor did it come about via a 1970s sitcom of the same name. It's an ancient philosophy that transcends East and West. The Buddha exhorted people not to dwell on the past or brood about the future. The wise man focused on the Now. A sense of mindfulness, awareness of the present moment without being assaulted by distractions from a past you can't change and a future that remains a mystery, is a great way to stay focused and sane.

St. Augustine's notion of God as residing in the Eternal Now, unaffected by the vicissitudes of linear time, is also a model. And Augustine's seminal work, *Confessions,* was read by Bill Wilson, who gained strength from its powerful message of a profligate personage's pilgrimage toward prominence.

No Cure

Members of AA do not consider themselves "cured." To do so is actually a dangerous belief, because the malevolent menace that is alcoholism lays dormant within a person. Recovering alcoholics merely maintain that they will stay sober "today." Today they will not pick up the first drink. This philosophy allays the fear and crippling mind games an addict plays on himself. Stop, smell the flowers, and don't take the first drink. Hardly original, but when applied by an alcoholic to his situation, the results can be miraculous.

ESSENTIALS

Members of AA feel there is no cure for alcholism. They stay away from the first drink "one day at a time." This philosophy is not unique to AA. It is an ancient tradition that goes back millennia and transcends East and West.

The Serenity Prayer

The noted medieval philosopher (and animal lover) St. Francis of Assisi, several centuries before Bill met Bob, inadvertently provided AA with one of its foremost philosophies, in the form of what is known as the Serenity Prayer. The prayer offers a guide for living that promotes positive peace of mind, be you a tippler or teetotaler, or former tippler-turned-teetotaler. In other words, everyone can benefit from practicing its principles.

Alcoholics Anonymous uses the Serenity Prayer of St. Francis of Assisi as a meditation to reflect upon and a source of succor: *God grant me the serenity to accept the things I cannot change, the courage to change the things I can, and the wisdom to know the difference.*

The Meetings

AA meetings usually take place in an inexpensive meeting place, often a church basement—not for any other reason than the landlord is empathetic, and the rates are reasonable. There are no dues or fees, but they do pass the basket to pay for the room and the coffee. The meetings take several forms. Some are discussion meetings, where an informal leader will speak for a few minutes and then go around the room, offering any in attendance the opportunity to share their thoughts about the topic of discussion. Themes such as "acceptance" or "gratitude" are discussed, but they are merely a springboard to spur the free and open discussion of alcoholism. Some attendees take the opportunity to "dump" or blow off steam about a situation that's currently bothering them. This is usually politely indulged, but an emphasis on alcoholism and recovery is stressed. It is, after all, the reason why they are all assembled.

At step meetings, one of the twelve steps is read and discussed. (The Twelve Steps of Alcoholics will be discussed later in this chapter. They are a plan for living devised by Bill Wilson.) Big Book meetings entail reading a passage from the Big Book and commenting about its practical application. The Big Book is simply the nickname for the book *Alcoholics Anonymous,* written by Bill Wilson, with a little help from his friends. The first part of the book is Wilson's story and a plan of action for the recovering alcoholic. The latter section of the book contains diverse personal stories of other people who found help through Alcoholics Anonymous.

FACTS

Until Alcoholics Anonymous, most alcoholics stopped drinking through stubborn determination or a religious conversion. AA offers another method, a design for living that enables the alcoholic to stay away from the first drink and also find the serenity that eludes the suffering alcoholic.

Open meetings are, as the name suggests, open to the public. Usually, three speakers address the assembly. Though the other type meetings are generally regarded as closed, there is no membership list. No attendance is taken, and no one will ask your name. The fact that you are there implies a desire to stop drinking. Nonalcoholics who may have a strange desire to "crash" an AA meeting can do so without fear, though one wonders why they would want to.

A Sponsor

The newcomer hooks up with someone, known as a *sponsor*. The sponsor is a person who has been around the block vis-à-vis recovery. Often (but not necessarily) older, this person guides the newcomer through the early stages of recovery, answering any questions he or she may have, accompanying them to meetings, and being available for advice and support. This harkens back to the age-old tradition of the mentor. As the Academicians looked to Plato and the Lyceumites hung on the words of Aristotle, newcomers look to their sponsor. However, these men and women do not claim any special wisdom; they merely know what worked for them and help themselves by helping out the next fellow. They are midwives in the Socratic tradition, humbly helping to bridge the chasm from the depths of despair to the heights of hope.

The Twelve Steps

The Twelve Steps of Alcoholics Anonymous were structured by Bill W. and company, and they are derived from several millennia of rich philosophical and spiritual traditions. It is fair to say that Bill Wilson didn't write the steps; he numbered them. But it was the right philosophy espoused in the right way at the right time to have socially transforming results. Looked at objectively, they are a sound guide for living, even for the nonalcoholic.

The Actual Steps

The first three steps are taken by the individual. The alcoholic owns up to the fact that booze has gotten the better of him, that he is powerless in its grip, and that he needs help to extricate himself from his predicament. AA calls it a "power greater than yourself" that can restore you to sanity. The alcoholic then decides to surrender his will to that power.

QUESTIONS?

Do you think you are an alcoholic?
Check out an AA pamphlet called 44 Questions and take the test. Or use this general rule: If you think you have a problem, then you do. The very fact that it weighs on your mind indicates you have a problem.

The fourth and fifth steps involve a "coming out" of sorts. It is recommended that the alcoholic make what is called a "searching and fearless moral inventory" of themselves. They take stock of their lives and try to see where they went wrong and how they can make things right. In the fifth step, they share this highly personal information with another human being, usually their AA sponsor. For many people, this is one of the most difficult things they will ever have to do. The rewarding element is that they find that they are not alone, and that the person they share the information with most likely will have had similar experiences. In the sixth and seventh steps, the alcoholic asks God to remove these "defects of character" identified by the alcoholic and his sponsor or confessor.

Steps eight and nine also do not come naturally to the alcoholic, or anyone for that matter. The alcoholic is advised to make a list of the people he or she has harmed during his or her drinking days. This usually involves family members, employers, employees, and various and sundry loved ones. This can be an embarrassing and painful process, but again self-interest is the primary motivating factor. If confession is good for the soul, making amends is even better. It is a weight off the shoulders and a burden lifted from the guilty conscience.

Steps ten through twelve are what are traditionally called "maintenance steps." The alcoholic continues monitoring those pesky character defects, prays and meditates for guidance from his High Power, and, very importantly, carries the message through service and helping the newcomer, giving back what has been freely given him or her.

The Issue of Surrender

Many newcomers have a big problem with this business of surrender, the admission of powerlessness, and the concept of the High Power. While most of the early AA members were Christians and that influence is heard in the language, AA is as much akin to Eastern thought as the Judeo-Christian tradition—plus a healthy dose of pragmatic and positive selfishness.

AA and God

The constant references to God may lead one to believe that AA is some sort of religious cult. AA insists otherwise. They say that you can make anything your Higher Power. People should not be put off by the language, written in the 1930s. Nor is it a cop-out or a semantics game to make appropriate substitutions in the language. Many people make the philosophy of AA their Higher Power without bringing a mystical element into the mix. AA has the power to help people stay sober. It is a power that the alcoholic lacks when left to his own devices. Ergo, it is a power greater than himself. Sophistry? Well, this is an instance where the philosophy of "whatever works" can actually do a great deal of good.

Despite the controversy, AA is not a religious organization. It is a spiritual program of recovery, but belief in God is not a requirement for membership. The only requirement for membership is the requirement to stop drinking.

Twelve Traditions

In addition to the Twelve Steps, which serve the individual, AA also has Twelve Traditions, which are designed to optimize the health and wellness of the organization as a whole. Why twelve, you may ask? An amazing coincidence that there just happened to be Twelve Steps *and* Twelve Traditions? Of course not. Bill and friends numbered them to conform to the significance of the number: twelve apostles, twelve members on a jury, and so on.

Anonymity as a Philosophy

Anonymity is a philosophy that is often difficult to practice. When you have turned your life around, you want to shout it from the rooftops and tout your accomplishments to all the world. Given that the relapse rate is very high, it is not a good idea to blow your own horn when you may find yourself back on a barstool in short order. In the early days of AA, there were a few celebrities who went to meetings and publicly pronounced that they were now living the clean and sober life courtesy of this great new organization called Alcoholics Anonymous. A little while later, the press reported their latest drunken scene at the Stork Club. Not good public relations.

There was also a stigma against alcoholics. It was considered a moral failing and a sign of low character, and attempts at recovery were not respected. They were often considered the last-ditch efforts of a scoundrel. Ironically, people were fired from jobs if the employer learned that they were in AA. Fortunately, that's a far cry from these more compassionate times.

There is also the connection between anonymity and humility. A distinction should be made between humility and humiliation. As Aristotle observed, the truly unselfish act must be done willingly, not to score points and impress people and enhance your reputation. AA urges its members to place "principles before personalities." The importance of this philosophy cannot be underestimated. The principles of Alcoholics Anonymous are noble and life-affirming. People being people, sometimes self-important egotists can monopolize a meeting, feeding their hubris with vainglorious efforts to establish themselves as the authority on AA and recovery. Such prima donnas must be shunned by a newcomer. They are the antithesis of midwives in the Socratic tradition. They cross the line from humble philosopher to cult leader wannabe. After all, people did not happily sashay through the doors of an AA meeting because life was wonderful and they were totally together, deep, and wise thinkers. AA represents a cross-section of the population—the Idiot Factor is as present as at your job or local diner.

Recovery, especially in the early stages, is a deeply difficult and personal struggle, and it is best to make the effort amidst the friendly confines of an AA meeting room where you can draw on the fellowship of like-minded folks.

Remaining Financially Independent

Another important AA tradition is the philosophy of financial self-reliance. Early in AA's history, Bill Wilson met with John D. Rockefeller to seek a grant. Rockefeller turned him down flat, but not out of a miserly streak. As a businessman, he knew that he who controls the money always calls the shots. Rockefeller told Wilson that he had a good thing going with AA, and he should keep the capitalists out of it. Had this not happened, AA probably would have not survived, or you would be able to spot a recovering alcoholic on the street by the various logos he or she was sporting on his or her clothes like a Nascar racer.

With the advent of rehabilitation facilities becoming a profitable industry, there are many other programs that promote sobriety, for a fee. There are plenty of people who have found help through them, but even these programs suggest that once their patients return to the real world, they attend AA meetings. There are also some AA members who become CACs (Certified Alcoholism Counselors). They are essentially akin to the Sophists. They are charging a fee for a gift that has been freely given to them. Socrates, as you recall, never made a dime off his philosophizing and thought it was inappropriate to do so. Wisdom should be freely available to all who seek it. In fact, it dwells without the human soul waiting to be accessed by those who take the time and have the inclination to do so.

FACTS

Hundreds of Twelve Step programs have borrowed from AA to help others with assorted addictions, including everything from drugs to overeating, from compulsive gambling to sex addiction.

AA has, for the most part, remained unspoiled. It has helped millions of people and remains the most successful way to achieve and maintain sobriety—one day at a time, of course.

Adaptation by Other Organizations

Many other organizations have co-opted the Twelve Steps of Alcoholics Anonymous and adapted them to their ends. Ancillary groups such as Alanon and Alateen offer support for the families of the alcoholic. Bill Wilson's long-suffering wife, Lois, in fact, founded Alanon. Their names are legion: Narcotics Anonymous, Overeaters Anonymous, Adult Children of Alcoholics, Sex Addicts Anonymous, and literally hundreds more. All follow the principles of the Twelve Steps, a positive philosophy of psychological and spiritual attitude adjustment that is one of the most successful action plans for self-improvement devised by the mind of man, with a little input from the Higher Power (as you understand it, of course).

CHAPTER 24

Everything Old
Is New Age Again

The phrase New Age evokes many impressions and emotions. Some see its practitioners as enlightened men and women on the cutting edge of spiritual evolution, helping to usher in a brave new world. Others see them as a collection of tree-hugging kooks. Perhaps they are a little bit of both.

So Just What Is New Age?

Actually, there is no group of people banded together under a banner emblazoned with the words "New Age." New Age is a convenient term applied by sociologists and the media to describe a diverse and eclectic cross section of the citizenry practicing diverse and eclectic lifestyles and disciplines.

If most people with little interest in or knowledgeable about New Age subjects were asked to name the quintessential New Ager, they would probably say Shirley MacLaine. Indeed, this Hollywood star is responsible for making things like reincarnation, astral projection, and channelers more widely known to the general public. But there is much more to this loose confederation of seekers, and the first thing we should be aware of is that there is nothing "new" about any aspect of this so-called New Age.

It's Not New at All

The New Age movement encompasses many facets: past lives, soul mates, charkas, Tarot cards, astrology, numerology, astrology, and many other schools of thought, tools of divination, and quests for answers in these troubled times. There is nothing new about them, however. All elements of the so-called New Age are age-old beliefs and practices, most of which were inspired by the great thinkers and philosophers of antiquity. The philosophers of ancient Greece and the mystics of the mysterious East were all aware of and studied the various ideas that now reside under the very generic umbrella of the New Age.

Reincarnation

Considered a fanciful New Age notion by contemporary Americans, reincarnation is a foundation of the religious faith of much of the rest of the world. More people currently extant on the Planet Earth believe in reincarnation than do not. They take it very seriously and plan their behavior in this life with an eye on the ramifications it will have on the next one.

An Age-Old Tenet

Reincarnation is a basic tenet of Hinduism and Buddhism, as well as many other religions. Early Christian sects believed in reincarnation until the church dogma was codified some 400 years after the death of Jesus. Reincarnation, along with many other spiritual beliefs, was subsequently removed from the official scrolls and deemed to be heretical thought.

Plato believed in reincarnation. Voltaire wrote of it as a possibility. He said that if you are born once, why not again and again? General George Patton was surprisingly candid about his belief. He believed he was always being reincarnated as a warrior of some sort, from a belligerent cave man to a Roman soldier to one of Napoleon's officers, up to and including his most famous military incarnation. One wonders what army he is currently "being all he can be" in?

Pythagoras and his followers also believed in reincarnation. They believed that both humans and animals had souls that reincarnated after death. They also believed that, based on our behavior in this life, we would come back as another human or take an evolutionary step backward to a lower life form. Pythagoras and his followers did not use the word karma, but it is essentially the same thing as the Hindu/Buddhist concept.

Reincarnation has captured the imagination of people since the dawn of time. It is comforting to believe that if you don't quite get it right in this life, you will have an opportunity to try again the next time around.

It's All about Karma

Hindus and Buddhists believe in karma. As discussed in an earlier chapter, karma is the belief that there is a cosmic scorecard that keeps track of our comings and goings during our living and dying. Rewards and punishments are doled out based on our behavior. If you are a thoroughgoing S.O.B. in this lifetime and feel that you have gotten away scot-free when you give up your ghost, think again. Karma knows what evil lurks in the hearts (and deeds) of men and women. Payback is horrible, and inevitable. There is no escaping your karma. And, conversely, if you are a perpetual victim in this life, or a kindhearted and magnanimous soul, you will be rewarded in the next life based on your clean living and good deeds in this incarnation.

Writings on Reincarnation

Today, there is great interest in past lives among Europeans and Americans. While for Hindus and Buddhists, reincarnation is part of their faith, for those in the Western world, it is more of a secular pursuit. An Amazon.com search results in more than 700 reincarnation-related books. And not all of them are written by Shirley MacLaine!

Dr. Brian Weiss has a series of books about past lives and the intermediary period between lives, which in the *Tibetan Book of The Dead* is called the bardo state. This is the place where the "life review" occurs. The newly deceased takes a long hard look at the life just lived, sees what he or she can learn from the experience, and prepares for the next go-around. In this bardo state, according to Dr. Weiss's books, we meet the Ascended Masters, who also appear in Buddhist tradition. They are enlightened spiritual beings that once lived on earth and now guide and teach those of us remaining on the earth plane. Dr. Weiss is an M.D. and psychiatrist who, through hypnotizing patients to uncover buried traumas, ended up discovering their past lives and their encounters with the Masters, who are quite opinionated and vociferous for dead people.

Criticism

Lest we become too flippant, reincarnation is taken seriously by a great many people, and much of the criticism is unfair. For example, a common snipe is that everyone who believes in reincarnation claims to have been Henry VIII or Shakespeare or Marie Antoinette. Nothing could be further from the truth. The fact is that most past lives recalled are pretty pedestrian peasant existences. They confirm cranky old Thomas Hobbes's credo that life is nasty, brutish, and short. It certainly describes the overwhelming majority of past lives recalled by contemporary people. And this makes perfect sense because until very recent times, the majority of the residents of this planet lived harsh, hazardous, and hardscrabble lives.

One of the main themes in Weiss's books is the reuniting of soul mates. This is another popular aspect of the New Age that is actually a very old idea.

Soul Mates

This intriguing and romantic New Age belief has its philosophical roots in our old friend Plato. On a psychological level, soul mates reuniting is akin to Dr. Jung's collective unconscious and theory of the anima and animus.

Who has not wished that their mate be their true soul partner? Who has not, gazing up at the starry night, held out hope that their "other half" is out there somewhere, gazing up at the same heavens and dreaming of them? It is a deeply romantic notion to believe that you and your beloved were brought together by a divine plan, that destiny has deemed you to become One once again.

Plato's Theory

Plato's theory is a mythic story that says that many, many moons ago, the human species was made up of androgynous creatures, meaning they embodied both male and female sexuality. The gods split these creatures into two parts, creating male and female humans. The belief is that each one of us, on a deeply subconscious level, knows that something is missing within ourselves, and we seek wholeness.

German Idealist Schopenhauer said that polarity, or the sundering of a force into equal and opposite halves, is a fundamental type of all the phenomena of Nature, from the "crystal and the magnet to man himself."

Many theories on the soul mate differ from Plato's. Purists and romantics at heart agree with Plato that the true soul mate is your other half, also called a "split-apart" or "twin soul" or "twin flame."

The Quest for Soul Mates

Contemporary interest in the soul mate, or soulmate as it is also spelled, is found throughout the Internet and in the New Age and/or relationship section of your local bookstore. A search on Amazon.com results in more than sixty books with the words soul mates in the title. These books suggest that you can find your Twin Flame everywhere from the workplace to the Internet.

A small sampling of the lengthy list includes

- *Twin Souls: Finding Your True Spiritual Partner*
- *Hot Chocolate for the Mystical Lover: 101 True Stories of Soul Mates Brought Together by Divine Intervention*
- *Edgar Cayce on Soul Mates: Unlocking the Dynamics of Soul Attraction*
- *Soulmates: Following Inner Guidance to the Relationship of Your Dreams*
- *Caution Soul Mate Ahead!: Spiritual Love in the Physical World*
- *21 Ways to Attract Your Soulmate*
- *Soul-Mates: How to Find Them and Keep Them*
- *Soul Mates: Understanding Relationships Across Time*
- *Friends, Lovers and Soul Mates: A Guide to Better Relationships Between Black Men and Women*
- *Love Lost and Found: True Stories of Long-Lost Loves—Reunited at Last*
- *Soul Dating to Soul Mating: On the Path Toward Spiritual Partnership, How to Find Mr. or Ms. Right: A Practical Guide to Finding a Soul Mate*
- *The Ascended Masters on Soul Mates and Twin Flames I and II: Initiation by the Great White Brotherhood*
- *Internet Soul Mates*

As you can see, the quest for soul mates is a big business. Counselors offer to help people find their soul mates, New Age Dolly Levis (the matchmaking diva of *Hello, Dolly*) assure you to, as Dolly would bellow, "just leave everything to them."

Lest the alternative lifestyle community feels left out, books and services and Web sites claim that they can help you find your gay or lesbian soul mate. People also purport that they can help you find your soul mate of color, or your rich soul mate. Because the soul is an ethereal element that transcends race and socioeconomic class, one wonders if these people are not guilty of New Age sophistry.

FACTS

Though regarded as a kooky New Age notion by many in the Western world, reincarnation is a spiritual tenet of Hinduism and Buddhism. Although your friends may laugh if you say you've lived before, more people on the planet believe in reincarnation than do not.

The psychologically inclined say that your soul mate is closer than you think. Those who endorse the Jungian theory of the anima (inner woman) and animus (inner man) that dwells within the psyche of every man and woman suggest that this is your true soul mate. And you had better have a good relationship with them, otherwise all sorts of psychological dysfunction may occur.

Many people claim to have found their soul mate, often using the phrase in a most convenient and cavalier fashion. It is interesting to note that more than one middle-aged New Age guru has found his soul mate on the beaches of southern California. Their soul mate was not their first wife who stood by them during their salad days and is the mother of their grown children. The woman they publicly pronounce to be their soul mate, the Twin Flame that traveled with them from the lost continent of Atlantis through Egypt and Shakespeare's London, as passengers on the Titanic with Leo and Kate, right up to this lifetime, is usually a woman who auditioned for the cast of *Baywatch* and is young enough to be their daughter. How lucky these guys are to have won the karmic lottery!

The Down Side

In this age where people are finding it hard to connect and forge lasting relationships, the idea of the soul mate has its negative aspects. This cosmic quest can prevent people from being happy with the person they are with and from finding joy in the little things—the normal, nonmystical, and humdrum yet beautiful things that couples must do to make a relationship work.

For the single men and women out there, the idea of a soul mate can make men more commitment shy and the women more finicky than they already are. Why settle for the dork who leaves the toilet seat up or the woman who snorts when she laughs, when the buff and perfect knight in shining armor or the princess bride is out there waiting for you?

The belief in and search for a soul mate can create unrealistic expectations of what true love and romance are all about. Your soul mate is not likely to be the Cleopatra; the Queen of Sheba; a bodice-ripping, swashbuckling pirate; or a brooding Byronic poet of the Romantic era. Your soul mate may be the guy or gal in the next cubicle or in line at the supermarket. It could even be a person you meet in an online chat room (but talk to them on the phone before you make plans for the house with the picket fence!).

I Ching

The *I Ching* is used by many people today as a popular parlor game, but it also has its roots in a rich spiritual and philosophical tradition. The two most influential Chinese belief systems, Taoism and Confucianism, can be found within the *I Ching*. Lao-Tzu, the first Taoist to whom the writing of the *Tao Te Ching* is attributed, was inspired by the *I Ching,* and Confucius is believed to have written the commentaries that comprise about half of the text.

The *I Ching* can be translated into English as the "Book of Changes," the "Classic of Change," and the "Oracle of Change." It is said to be more than 5,000 years old—3,000 of those years in written form. This makes it one of the oldest written documents in the world. Like Tarot cards and Rune stones, it had greater significance in its ancient past, but its potential power has not diminished. It is the spiritual nature of mankind that has sadly deteriorated. People used to be more in tune with the unseen realms and have an open mind to the fantastic.

For those with an open mind, there is much to learn about yourself from fooling around with the *I Ching*. Whether it taps into something already within you and gives you food for thought, or whether divine properties are at work, who knows? Either way, there is much wisdom and insight to be gleaned. If it worked for the eminent Dr. Jung, it can work for you.

Some New Age teachers believe that we have many soul mates. In fact, we travel through lifetimes in herds, playing different parts: the husband one time, the wife the next, the child in another, and so on. These people believe that the soul mate can be of the same or the opposite sex, and not necessarily a romantic partner.

Jung, in his memoir *Memories, Dreams, Reflections,* recounts how he would sit for hours at a time under a tree posing questions and looking up the answers in the *I Ching*. He found the answers were always applicable to the questions and stimulated further reflection on the problems and situations with which he was concerned. Granted, the maxims and aphorisms in the *I Ching* are, as is the case with much Eastern thought, cryptic in nature and open to interpretation, and perhaps they tap into our collective unconscious. That is why the *I Ching* has had the staying power to last five millennia.

Cynics would reduce the *I Ching* to the level of the fortune cookie in a Chinese takeout joint, but it goes far deeper than that. And if it is merely a tool to get you thinking about something, so be it. That has great value in this age of decreasing attention spans and insular, provincial thinking.

Astrology

There is much more to Astrology than horoscopes online and in the newspapers. While perhaps it is possible that a self-satisfied, toga-clad Roman bachelor tried to score with a Vestal Virgin by asking, "What's your sign?" astrology was taken more seriously in ancient times.

In the old days, astrology was the royal and aristocratic classes that charted the stars, and every respectable potentate had his court astrologer. It was a good job with excellent benefits, until, of course, things went awry, and the astrologer found himself the subject of the ancient tradition of killing the bearer of bad news.

Its Greek Roots

The earliest records reveal that astrology was practiced in the ancient kingdom of Mesopotamia. It was also practiced in ancient Greece, and the earliest philosophers were familiar with stargazing and attempts to divine human behavior and the future by looking to the heavens. It was Socrates who changed the focus of the philosopher by making it an inward journey into the souls and minds of men and moving away from external forces.

Aristotle's famous pupil Alexander the Great spread Greek culture throughout the known world, astrology included. He named a city after himself, Alexandria in Egypt, and in between the fall of Greece and the rise of Rome, it was the cultural capital of the civilized world. Alexandria was where astrology thrived and the zodiac was codified, and astrologers began to make their trade via creating star charts for paying customers. The most famous astrologer of this epoch was Ptolemy.

Astrology and the Roman Empire

Astrology was big business in the Roman Empire. In the classic BBC miniseries *I, Claudius*, a disgruntled Tiberius, cooling his heels in exile, regularly consults his harried and high-strung personal astrologer. He is impatient to hear portents that he will return to Rome and become the emperor, which eventually happens, but not before he is about to have the astrologer tossed off a cliff for perpetual bad readings. This hapless astrologer is saved at the eleventh hour by good news from Rome.

Astrology During the Renaissance

Astrology became a closet activity during the Middle Ages, when the Church was establishing itself as the new kid on the block, and a micromanaging, control freak of a kid at that. Astrologists were subject to persecution and worse for their practices, which were regarded as heretical. Like almost everything else, astrology found renewed interest and revived practice during the Renaissance.

FACTS

In the book *The Planets Within* about Renaissance astrologer Marsilio Ficino, the author proposes that Ficino was not charting the stars. He was actually an early psychologist who was attempting to navigate the human soul, or psyche.

The most famous Renaissance astrologer was Marsilio Ficino, the whiz kid of the Florentine Academy in Florence, Italy. He wrote a vicious attack on astrology early in his career, but then spent much of his time studying it. Contemporary author Thomas Moore (not to be confused with the Renaissance Humanist Thomas More, who lost his head so Henry VIII could get a divorce) has written a very interesting book called *The Planets Within* about Ficino. This book proposes that Ficino was in fact not charting the stars. He was actually an early psychologist who was attempting to navigate the human soul, or psyche. Moore suggests that the planets and the characteristics assigned to those born under them are actually personality traits that dwell within every man and woman. They are in fact what Jung would call archetypes of the collective unconscious.

Astrology Today

Astrology became fashionable again in the twentieth century and continues to enjoy popularity today. No major tabloid newspaper is without a horoscope section, and online services like America Online have their interactive Internet equivalent. So the next time a geeky guy tries to suavely inquire about your sign, remember that he is lamely misrepresenting and trivializing a once respected ancient tradition. Tell him so and send him on his way.

Numerology

This popular New Age form of divination has several ancient sources, but its philosophical source is our old friend Pythagoras. The Presocratic Greek philosopher believed that reality could be reduced to numbers and mathematical principles. He also invented the stringed musical instrument called the lyre and studied astrology, but he is most famous as a numbers man.

How It Works

Pythagoras said that the letters of the alphabet corresponded to certain numbers. This is the principle of numerology. Of course, Pythagoras's alphabet was different than our own, hence some adaptation was required in different cultures and languages. Pythagoras was one of the first to suggest that, based on numerology, your name can tell you much about your personality. Just as astrologers believe that the stars can shape your character, Pythagoras and contemporary numerologists believe that the letters in your name and the corresponding number they generate can explain who you are. Legend has it that Pythagoras changed his name from time to time in order to see how aspects of his personality would change.

FACTS

In the post-Renaissance age, the Scientific Revolution and Galileo's telescope created the science of astronomy. As astronomy grew, astrology lost some of its reputation as the mystical poor relation of the exalted newfound science.

In numerology, each letter of the alphabet has a corresponding numerical value, and these have a particular cosmic vibration. The combination of letters and numbers is said to create a unique vibration that reveals much about the person, and numerological readings can be used to understand the present and plan for the future.

A Sample Profile

Pythagoras did not have the advantage of the Internet for a quick reading of himself. For the purposes of research, the author of this book visited a Web site that offers free numerology readings and entered his name and birth date and received an instant personality profile. Here is a thumbnail numerological sketch of the author of this book:

You appear dignified and poised, intellectual, and somewhat aloof. When first meeting someone, you appear hard to know, but are friendly and a good talker when better acquainted. You emit a strong sense of self-knowledge.

(Quite flattering. The author likes to think so, yet others may have a different opinion.)

You live in an old, beautifully restored house; your library is full of precious and rare books and your study is adorned with classic art.

(Those who have seen the author's small New York City apartment would chuckle at this observation.)

You have a practical point of view and constantly work to put more order into your environment. In ventures or new directions, you like to look ahead, plan carefully, then apply yourself with concentration and good management. Once you have a goal in mind, you are persistent in its accomplishment.

(Many who know the author are having a big laugh at this. The author is a notorious procrastinator.)

You have a cosmic connection with spiritual wisdom. The Ancients are no stranger to you. In fact, you share their knowledge. You are known for who you are, and people seek you out to hear your words of wisdom.

(That, dear readers, is for you to decide!)

It would seem that numerology is not an exact science.

Mandala Drawing

Mandala drawing is a popular New Age activity that is designed to help you, through a form of art therapy, engage in self-analysis and hopefully get in touch with good stuff. Again, it is a very old tradition.

What Is a Mandala?

A *mandala* is a circular-shaped diagram, usually ornately filled in with colorful images from the culture of the person who drew the mandala. The word mandala is Sanskrit for circle, and it was a Hindu and Buddhist device to enhance meditation. A mandala is a pictorial representation of the universe. Though the word mandala is associated with Eastern religions, every culture puts it own spiritual spin on the sacredness of the circle. To the philosophically and spiritually inclined, the circle is much more than a simple geometric shape.

Plato believed that the soul was circular in shape. Jung called the circle the most powerful religious symbol. Life is an endless cycle of birth, death, and if you believe in reincarnation, rebirth. It is the Alpha and Omega, the beginning and the end. Round and round we go—what's it all about? Nobody knows.

What Does Drawing Do?

The act of drawing a mandala was said to be a scary experience. Museums are filled with lavish mandalas through the centuries. But the contemporary New Age activity of mandala drawing is perfectly egalitarian—anyone can draw a mandala and paint a picture of their soul.

The objective is to draw a circle and think about and reflect upon the different values in your life. The images that you draw will be summoned from deep within your psyche, primordial archetypes like the ones that are found on cave walls or Tarot cards. As you draw, you learn more and more about yourself. What ends up at the center of your personal mandala is supposed to represent the thing that is the priority in your life. It is an artistic effort to pull the scattered aspects of yourself together and find the focus.

Ancient Hindu and Buddhist mandalas are representations of the universe, replete with gods and goddesses and all manner of bliss, chaos, and mayhem. These represent the macrocosm, the big picture. Your personal mandala represents your microcosm, your internal universe. The objective is to keep the macrocosm and the microcosm in harmony; the vastness of the universe and the finite nature of the individual in tune and on the same wavelength.

QUESTIONS?

What's your sign?
The next time some smarmy geek asks this question, tell him that he is trivializing an ancient tradition that goes back many millennia. Mankind has always looked to the stars for inspiration and answers to life's burning questions.

What we see through the five senses is only a small part of what really comprises the universe. This is something the Greek philosophers and the Eastern spiritualists speculated upon time and again. Mankind, after his fall from grace (whether you believe in the Book of Genesis or any of the many other very similar creation myths from every culture in every corner of the globe), lost touch with the other realms. They appear to us like the flickering shadows of the rock wall in Plato's Myth of the Cave.

Chapter 25

Philosophy and the Couch Potato

Perhaps many of you find philosophy to be a daunting and academic affair, devoid of wit and warmth. You may feel that philosophy has little or no entertainment value, or makes your brain hurt in this age of the abbreviated attention span. In this global village of ours, everyone can be a philosopher.

Philosophy Beyond the Classroom

Philosophy is not like a Platonic Form, a nebulous blob out there in the ether. It is more like an Aristotelian Universal, embedded in the zeitgeist of our times. Philosophy exists beyond the classroom or the dusty shelves of an unfrequented library. It is a living, vivid force.

Philosophy can be found on your television screen. Not on MTV, or any of the "reality" TV shows—of these you can ponder the age-old question, "What is reality?" And if these shows and the people on them are representative of the populace at large, then perhaps Armageddon is indeed at hand.

No, you have to be a little discriminating in the search for philosophy on the tube, but it is there to be gleaned. Some of the best sources to find deep philosophical questions asked and deep thoughts pondered are the science-fiction shows of yesteryear. Science fiction and fantasy are ideal vehicles to discuss the provocative and complex questions that have intrigued and baffled mankind over the millennia.

Star Trek

The most famous science-fiction program that has stood the test of time and continues to reinvent itself is *Star Trek.* For our purposes, we will limit our discussion to its first, and in many ways best, incarnation, the original *Star Trek* from the 1960s, now known as Classic Trek. *Star Trek* is more than a mere "space opera." It is a thoughtful and thought provoking television show that is rich in philosophical insight.

For those of you not from Planet Earth, *Star Trek* chronicles the voyages of the U.S.S. *Enterprise,* a starship in the United Federation of Planets that is exploring the galaxy in the twenty-third century. Captain James T. Kirk, First Officer Mr. Spock, the irascible Dr. McCoy, and the rest are pop culture icons and contemporary archetypes, the stuff of modern mythology. You all know its mission statement by heart: to explore strange new worlds, to seek out new life and new civilizations, to boldly go where no man has gone before.

Of course, this mission statement was changed to "where no *one* has gone before" in *Star Trek: The Next Generation*—though Captain Kirk says it as the last line in *Star Trek VI: The Undiscovered Country,* the last film to star the original cast. This cleverly makes Kirk the first person to say it, bridging the generations.

Captain Kirk and Humanism

This concept of men (and women) boldly going in search of knowledge, insight, and wisdom is the cornerstone of Renaissance Humanism. Indeed, the predominant philosophy that weaves its way through all the incarnations of *Star Trek* is Humanism. Humanism, you will recall from an earlier chapter, is a celebration of mankind in all his splendor and the many exploits we can achieve in our human endeavors. It places the onus and the credit for achievement and accomplishment squarely on the shoulders of Herculean and Homeric men and women, not on any divinity dropping down with a deus ex machina solution to our problems.

In the *Star Trek* universe, World War III was fought in the 1990s (Next Generation moved it up to the 2050s). The nihilism that many people felt during the Cold War, and that many feel today as we enter what is shaping up to be a not-so-brave new world, came to fruition in *Star Trek:* a nuclear conflagration in the immediate future, but the best and the brightest survived and thrived, creating a high-tech Utopia where all racial barriers dissolved, all diseases are cured, and mankind en masse begins a great journey of discovery. The tag line for the first *Star Trek* feature film was "The Human Adventure Is Just Beginning." What better clarion-call for the Humanist philosophy?

Deities are not treated with much respect in Star Trek. They are usually false gods who do much harm and little good, or godlike creatures who represent the "Trickster archetype," cosmic mischief-makers who bedevil the mere mortals. The Trickster is a mythological figure that appears in the myths and legends of every culture. This impish demigod loves to cause havoc among humans, but often the nuisance is designed to teach and assist mankind.

The notorious Q from *Next Generation* is basically a variation on General Trelayne, a character in the Classic Trek episode "The Squire of Gothos." These characters torment Captains Kirk and Picard, but humanity and human values triumph in the end. In the *Star Trek* universe, super-intelligent beings are also intergalactic fops.

The "gods" encountered by the Starship *Enterprise* are beings that thwart the potential of the creatures they serve and turn them into virtual slaves. In "The Apple," the inhabitants of a paradise-like planet worship a "god" called Vol. These primitive people live in an Eden where all their needs are provided for, given they periodically pay tribute to a fire-breathing cave god. Captain Kirk and company arrive on the scene and promptly function as the snake in the Garden of Eden. They destroy paradise for the simple folk, and they are better off for it, because mankind is meant to strive, to seek, to find, and not to yield.

Another dysfunctional god is found in the episode "The Return of the Archons." Here the *Enterprise,* while searching for a missing starship, arrives at a planet where the inhabitants resemble dour, puritanical New Englanders (some of them complete with the regional accent) who live in what looks like a nineteenth-century small town. They are passive and placid as if on Prozac until the night of "Festival." Festival is an orgiastic explosion of sex and violence. Property is destroyed, men are beaten with clubs, and women are raped. Festival is a mandatory affair, except for the elderly. One old coot who cannot attend chastises the *Enterprise* crew for refraining from participating in the Festival.

ESSENTIALS

The "gods" that appear in Star Trek are usually false gods and meddlesome, if not downright hostile forces that try to prevent mankind from "boldly going." This is another expression of Humanism.

The Festival is Star Trek's way of speaking to Dr. Carl Gustav Jung's notion of "the shadow." The shadow represents our unconscious drives of lust and aggression, and unless these elements are integrated into the whole personality, the shadow will surface unbidden, usually with antisocial results.

It turns out that this planet is ruled by a highly moralistic supercomputer that functions as God for the citizenry. Kirk plays God by deciding that this society is stagnant and sterile because of its God, so with the aplomb in an avowed humanist, he makes good on Nietzsche's axiom that God is dead by talking the computer-god into shutting down.

The most notorious "anti-God" and pro-Humanist stance is expressed in one of the *Star Trek* feature films. *Star Trek V: The Final Frontier* deals with nothing less than the crew of the Enterprise boldly going on a quest for God Himself. The starship is hijacked by Spock's messianic and completely crazy half-brother, who believes that God resides on a planet in the center of the galaxy. This leads to an anticlimax for both the crew and the viewer. They do find a powerful entity that manifests itself as a white male with a white beard, but it is a demonic creature. Kirk, Spock, and McCoy barely escape with their lives, and Kirk later offers a "final thought" that God resides "in the human heart."

FACTS

The dominant philosophy expressed in *Star Trek* is Humanism, the belief that mankind's mandate to "boldly go where no one has gone before" is his and his alone to achieve. Mankind can do just fine without divine intervention.

Man versus machine is another expression of Humanism in Classic Trek. One of Captain Kirk's many gifts is his uncanny ability to be able to talk computers into self-destructing. In several episodes, including the aforementioned "Return of the Archons," Kirk gives Landru the computer-god a good talking-to, prompting it to blow itself up. And in "The Ultimate Computer" the *Enterprise* becomes fully automated, and Captain Kirk is in effect rendered obsolete. Of course, the computer goes awry and destroys a couple of other Starships. Kirk is able to convince the computer to commit suicide to atone for its crimes.

Recall that the Deists believed that God was akin to an impersonal cosmic grandfather clock that kept things running smoothly, but with no interest in the affairs of humankind. The god of the Deists is no warm and reassuring omnipresence. Transfer the analogy to the *Star Trek* universe, and the clock would be a supercomputer. Not an indifferent celestial computer, however, as was the Deist's clock. Computers and false gods are malevolent forces in the Humanist universe of *Star Trek*.

One of the grand old Greeks takes a hit in an episode called "Plato's Stepchildren." The *Enterprise* comes upon a civilization of aliens who visited earth in ancient times and modeled their own society after Plato's *Republic*. These aliens (who like almost every species the Star Trekkers encounter, look just like humans and speak perfect English) revere Plato, wear togas and laurel crowns (though this is more Roman than Greek), and devote themselves to contemplation and introspection. Unlike the ancient Greeks, these devotees of Plato have telekinetic powers. Oh yes, they also torture and humiliate the one misfit in the community who is unable to defend himself, a dwarf named Alexander. These sadistic pseudo-philosophers then subject Kirk and Spock to all manner of indignity, from causing Kirk to repeatedly slap his own face to making Spock do a flamenco dance over the prone Kirk, poised to stomp the good Captain's head. Kirk eventually saves the day and gives the haughty leader of the aliens a taste of his own medicine.

In Plato's *Republic,* there is a rigid caste system where the worker classes are given short shrift and limited enjoyment of what society has to offer. It is a flawed societal role model within which not too many of us would want to be a citizen, and *Star Trek* shows the flaws of absolute power corruption absolutely. Speaking of which, this is another recurring philosophical theme in *Star Trek*.

In the episode "Where No Man Has Gone Before," Captain Kirk's best friend is affected by a spatial anomaly and begins to develop superhuman mental and physical powers. Does he become benevolent and godlike, and all-around cosmic muffin? No, he becomes a dangerous and diabolical megalomaniac who Kirk has to kill after a knockdown, drag-out fistfight. That Kirk! He can even defeat godlike supermen via the manly art of pugilism. However implausible the plot, the philosophical principle is a universal truth.

No discussion of *Star Trek* supermen would be complete without mentioning Khan, who appeared in the episode "Space Seed" and the movie *Star Trek II: The Wrath of Khan*. Khan is a genetically engineered superman who ruled one-quarter of the world between 1992 and 1996. Did you miss that on CNN? Khan is the perfect example of Nietzschean "superman" run amok. With both physical and mental prowess, often overweening hubris is attendant, and Khan Noonien Singh is no exception. Fulfilling your maximum human potential is one thing. That should always be encouraged. However, an aggressive contempt for your fellow citizens and a wanton disregard for civility and decorum should not be the byproduct of physical and mental superiority. A kinder, gentler superman is what we should strive to be, should we look to Nietzsche's superman as a role model.

Mr. Spock and the Objectivists

Even though Captain James T. Kirk is the swashbuckling hero of Star Trek, Humanist and babe magnet extraordinaire, his sidekick Mr. Spock embodies many philosophies, from Stoicism to being a poster boy for the Objectivists.

Star Trek's Mr. Spock is a hero for many Objectivists. He is the quintessence of the Rational Man, who despite internal struggles remains the epitome of logic.

Mr. Spock, the half-human, half-Vulcan First Officer of the *Enterprise,* embodies the Stoic ethic. Vulcans long ago eschewed emotion, believing that logic is the path to the Truth. It is not that they are without emotions; they repress them through will power and discipline. The Stoics consider this a good thing. Passions were an unnecessary distraction and complication in leading a good life. Of course, the Jungian theory of the Shadow is present here. The emotions repressed by years of practice and discipline resurface from time to time. Every seven years, Vulcans must return to their home planet to mate (like the salmon on Planet Earth or the flying eels of Rigel IV). And emotions are also brought to the surface by space viruses and evil aliens.

These episodes reveal the inner torment of Mr. Spock and show that in many ways, he is more human than his earthling shipmates. This struggle with self-control and idealization of Reason had made Mr. Spock popular with Ayn Rand's Objectivists. Spock is a hero to those who value Rationality as a prime virtue. He embodies the heroism and drive that the Objectivists set as a standard for what it means to be a fully realized hero in a hostile world, or in Spock's case, a hostile universe. He also embodies the virtues of the Enlightenment in this regard. And, for those mere mortals attempting to emulate this ideal, Spock is a powerful example because it is never easy for him. He struggles to maintain his logical nature despite profound internal and external struggles. Half-alien and half-human, he embodies the existentialist belief that much of life is a sense of "alienation," and he is also, to quote the title of one of Nietzsche's books, *Human, All Too Human.*

The Prisoner

The Prisoner is one of the most bizarre and unique television series ever produced, and it is rich with a variety of philosophical traditions that create a compelling viewing experience.

A surreal and allegorical tale, *The Prisoner* is the story of a secret agent who suddenly and surprisingly resigns from the agency, only to find himself kidnapped and transported to a strange community called the Village. He is addressed as No. 6 and subjected to a series of interrogations—some severe, some subtle—to determine why he resigned. The powers-that-be do not accept that it was simply a matter of conscience.

The Prisoner covers a lot of philosophical ground, and its devoted fans continue to debate its many meanings through conventions, fan clubs, and Web sites. The Individual versus Society is the main philosophy that weaves through the seventeen episodes of the show. No. 6's defiant shriek, "I am not a number! I am a free man!" followed by the derisive laughter of his latest nemesis opens almost every episode.

No. 2 is the manager who runs The Village, and he or she reports to the never seen No. 1. There is a new No. 2 in every episode, because they are replaced when their efforts to break No. 6 have failed.

The Village is a microcosm for the real world. It is never clear where the Village actually is. In some episodes, it is an island. In others, it is on the coast of Lithuania, and in the final episode, it appears to be a short drive from the city of London. These are not egregious plot flaws common to many television series. The geographic locale of the Village appears to be irrelevant. We are all residents of the Village, a Big Brother society where, as a character on the *X-Files* called it, the "military-industrial-entertainment complex" rules the world. The figurehead No. 2 is a mere lackey for the unseen forces that really rule the world, and the truly individualistic are broken, usually through nonviolent means, i.e., providing creature comforts and mindless entertainment. People cannot tell you where, let alone what, Kosovo is, but they can name all the cast members of each new version of *Survivor*. This is the society that The Prisoner was commenting on and warning against, and this is the society that we have become.

QUESTIONS?

Are you being watched?
In *The Prisoner,* The Village is a community where the residents are under constant audiovisual surveillance. This was science fiction in 1967, but in this age of cameras everywhere from tollbooths to public streets and thermal cameras that can "see" through walls, life imitates art.

The Prisoner was science fiction thirty-five years ago, but life has imitated art in many ways. A giant database provides instant access to all personal and private information on residents of the Village. Constant surveillance is maintained through hidden cameras. Today, some communities, with the consent of many and the outrage of others, have cameras set up on public streets, and they feed the image of your face into a supercomputer's databases.

The symbolism in *The Prisoner* has philosophical implications. At one point, people are playing chess on a playing field-sized board with people as the chess pieces. Is life merely a game, or are we puppets with unseen forces pulling the strings?

In an episode called "The Schizoid Man," No. 6 is brainwashed into believing he is a double of himself sent to drive himself crazy. The philosophical question of identity is posed in the classic '60s TV format of giving the hero an evil twin. (Captain Kirk had his share over the years.)

The final episode asks many philosophical questions, but does not answer them. SPOILER ALERT: Do not read the following few paragraphs if you have not seen the series and do not want to know the ending.

In the final episode, No. 6 is apparently being rewarded for his unrelenting individualism and his ability to maintain it despite constant pressure. He is feted in a formal celebration and offered the alternatives of leaving the Village or becoming its new leader, No. 1. When he finally meets No. 1, he is confronted by a masked person in a robe. He rips off the mask to find a mask beneath the mask—a rubber gorilla mask. He removes that mask and sees . . . himself! The other No. 6 runs off, and the original No. 6 destroys the Village in an explosive, shoot-em-up finale. He returns to his own home in London. The door is automated and opens with the same sound that accompanied all opening doors in the Village. Is he free even now? Is the "global village" as much a prison as the place from which he just escaped?

It is certainly one of the strangest and confusing endings to a television show, and fans have been arguing about the philosophical implications for thirty-five years. Is reality a prisoner? Can one man change the world, and if not, can he at least maintain his individuality and control his own destiny? In many ways, No. 6 is a classic existentialist hero, but Ayn Rand's Objectivists also see him as a role model. Perhaps the message in the final episode is that there is no message at all; life is something you must make up as you go along. Maybe it was reaffirming one of the mottos displayed in the Village: Questions Are A Burden For Others; Answers A Prison For Oneself.

The Fugitive

The best pop culture expression of existentialism is the classic drama *The Fugitive* starring David Jansen—not the movie with Harrison Ford or the deservedly short-lived TV update, but the moody original. Dr. Richard Kimble is a man falsely convicted of the murder of his wife. When fate moves its huge hand (as the show's narrator tells us), he manages to escape and lives a life on the run. Not only is he eluding the relentless policeman ever hot on his trail, he is on a quest to find the mysterious One-Armed Man, whom he saw leaving the scene of his wife's murder.

The black-and-white episodes create a dark view of small-town America, a hopeless landscape through which the solitary fugitive wanders. Society is an oppressive and malevolent enemy. The Fugitive has no friends, only strangers that he meets and who, if they discover his true identity, betray him. For a man on the run, he has his share of romance, but given the nature of his lifestyle, he is a commitment-phobe.

The world is out to get you despite that fact that you have done your best to live a good life. This is a theme of existentialism and a grim fact of life that Richard Kimble lives with. A law-abiding pillar of the community, through circumstances beyond his control, he loses everything and is forced to run for his life. Even when evidence surfaces that he is innocent, the cop on his trail remains unmoved. Lieutenant Gerard is an automaton who symbolizes the ruthless and uncaring society.

Alienation is a key facet of existentialism, and who is more alienated than a fugitive? Richard Kimble can never remain in one place very long, never get close to anyone, and never trust anyone.

Richard Kimble is TV-land's answer to the "Myth of Sisyphus." He regularly gets close to catching the real killer, but circumstances thwart him, and he finds himself back on the run, on to another town and a new identity and the never-ending story of his quest.

Emma Peel: Feminist Icon

The contemporary Feminist movement began in the 1960s, with writers and activists such as Gloria Steinem and Betty Friedan. As we have seen in previous chapters, however, the principles of feminism go back many centuries. Yet as with civil rights and gay rights and many other groups seeking rights, the swinging '60s were an epoch of social transformation. It may seem frivolous to some, but no less a social critic than Camille Paglia has cited the character of Emma Peel from television's *The Avengers* as a quintessential feminist icon.

Emma Peel, as played by Diana Rigg, was and is a role model for the modern woman. Independent, educated, and eminently stylish, she is everything the well-dressed super-spy ought to be. In recent years, Xenia the Warrior Princess became an icon, but Emma Peel embodied more sophistication and finesse. She is not simply a woman who could beat up men, though she did this in just about every episode. She is a woman of genius-level intelligence, remarkable physical prowess, and financial and social independence. She is a civilian who periodically teams up with John Steed, a dapper dandy member of British Intelligence, and together they battle all manner of diabolical masterminds out to conquer the world. This female James Bond never relies on her feminine wiles to thwart her opponents; she is a martial arts mistress who can bang heads with the best of them.

FACTS

Emma Peel, the karate-chopping yet ever-stylish heroine of TV's *The Avengers*, was, for many in the women's movement, a feminist icon of the swinging '60s when modern feminism was coming into its own.

It is no surprise that this character came at a time of sociocultural upheaval and a time when women were fighting for equality. Emma Peel was more than the equal of any man without sacrificing her femininity. A woman who fights for her rights yet ends up adopting the characteristics of the men who kept her on the other side of the glass ceiling has achieved a hollow victory. Today's women should watch the reruns of *The Avengers* to see a feminist role model in action.

Appendix A

Glossary of Philosophical Terms

A

Absolute, The—Hegel's name for the ultimate reality.

Aesthetics—The school of philosophy that ponders the nature of art and beauty. Schopenhauer recommended it as one of the ways to keep earthly passions at bay.

Alienation—The feeling of isolation, of not being part of society. Expressed by Hegel, Kierkegaard, and the Existentialists.

Altruism—Looking out for the next fellow and trying to do good works. Some philosophers believe altruism is impossible, because all actions, even charitable ones, are motivated by self-interest. The Objectivists think it is a downright foolish practice.

Angst—Deep anxiety, which many philosophers, including Hegel, Kierkegard, Sartre, and Camus, believe is an unavoidable emotional state for any thinking man or woman.

Anthropomorphism—Assigning human qualities and characteristics to nonhuman things, including nature and God.

Ápeiron—The Greek word for Boundless, this was Anaximander's way to describe the ultimate reality, as opposed to the other Monists who made one of the elements the basis for all reality.

Aphorism—Nietzsche's main technique for philosophizing. A pithy observation that can vary in length from a few lines to a few paragraphs.

A posteriori—Literally meaning "after." A statement, concept, or idea that is determined after the fact, based on experience or observation.

A priori—Literally meaning "before." A statement, concept, or idea that is a given and does not need to be based on experience or observation.

Atomism—The belief of the Presocratic philosopher, beginning with Leucippus and Democritus, that everything could be broken down to tiny, indivisible particles called atoms. It turned out to be true (until scientists learned that the atom could be split into subatomic particles).

B

Behaviorism—The psychological school of thought that espoused that the best way to study humans is by observing their behavior, not delving into the depths of the unconscious. B. F. Skinner is the most well-known psychological behaviorist.

C

Calculus of Felicity—Jeremy Bentham's strange mathematical formula wherein we can calculate the pain/pleasure factor of an act before indulging in it.

Cogito, ergo sum—Descartes's famous "I think, therefore I am" proves that you can be certain of at least one reality in this crazy world: You exist because you are thinking thoughts right now.

Consequentialism—Another name for the Utilitarian philosophy. The consequences of an action determine its value. From a Utilitarian perspective, this philosophy means seeking pleasure and avoiding pain.

D

Dasein—Heidegger's word for what he called "Being There," a fully realized conscious approach to life, more than merely "stayin' alive."

Deconstructionism—The process of breaking down a thing (in Jacques Derrida's case, language) to show that what is being stated is in fact inherently false.

Deism—The religious faith that likens God to a Cosmic Watchmaker. The universe is an orderly, perfectly functioning yet impersonal cosmos. God designed it and now it more or less runs itself.

Dialectic—The Socratic Dialogue, a series of questions and answers to help the person discover the truth for themselves, rather than simply telling them.

Dualism—The view that each person is two entities, a mind with mental attributes and a body with physical attributes, instead of a single entity with attributes of both sorts.

E

Empiricism—The philosophy that maintains that all knowledge is gathered through sensory experience alone. The opposite of Rationalism.

Enlightenment—Also called The Age of Reason. The age of Voltaire and the other philosophers.

Epistemology—Another word for the theory of knowledge.

Eternal recurrence—Nietzsche's proposition that we live the same life, without variation, over and over again. He probably did not mean this literally. He was suggesting that we should make our lives such that we would not mind repeating it time and again.

Existentialism—The philosophy that expresses the belief that life is meaningless and absurd, and the best that we can do is try to lead authentic, heroic lives in a cold and uncaring world.

F

Forms—Plato's doctrine that Ideas independently exist beyond their physical and mental counterparts. For example, there is a Form of "Beauty" out there in the ether, and things of beauty we see in physical reality are mere shadows of the Form.

Functionalism—Emile Durkheim's theory that a society, in essence, takes on a personality of its own and can be objectively viewed the way a scientist or physician may regard a living organism.

H

Hedonism—The belief that the pursuit of pleasure and the avoidance of pain is the greatest goal of mankind. Social Hedonism was at the foundation of the Utilitarian philosophy.

I

Idealism—The belief that everything is "in the mind," and physical reality does not exist. Made famous by George Berkeley.

Illumination—Divinely inspired insight and wisdom. St. Augustine believed that this was a necessary ingredient to true knowledge.

Immanent—Something that is directly experienced. The opposite of "transcendent."

Innate ideas—Thoughts are observations that can come without benefit of sensory experience. This was the belief of the Rationalists, and the opposite viewpoint of the Empiricists.

L

Logical atomism—Russell and Wittgenstein's theory that language and concepts could, like physical elements, be broken down to their smallest particulars and thereby logically analyzed.

M

Materialism—The belief that reality is composed of physical matter. The opposite of Idealism.

Monism—The belief that one element or thing is the basic stuff of reality. The Presocratic philosophers were Monists.

N

Natural selection—Charles Darwin's theory of Evolution. Members of a species that are the "fittest" survive and reproduce, altering the species over time as those unable to adapt die off.

Nihilism—The ultimate in a despairing, negative worldview. Utter hopelessness.

Nominalism—The Middle Ages belief that opposed the Aristotelian theory of Universals.

Noumena—Kant's name for the metaphysical world, the reality that lies beyond our ability to perceive.

O

Objectivism—Ayn Rand's popular twentieth-century view that combines rugged individualism and laissez-faire capitalism.

Ockham's Razor—The philosophical version of the slogan: Keep it simple. The simplest solution to a problem or question is also usually the correct one.

Othering—Michel Foucault's name for the way people distinguish themselves from other people, usually in a pejorative way.

P

Pantheism—The belief that God is Nature, not an all-powerful entity in Heaven but a force that surrounds and permeates the world.

Paradox—A seemingly contradictory concept that, upon close examination, is not contradictory at all.

Phenomenology—The study of consciousness in and of itself, leaving the empirical world out of the equation altogether by a technique called "bracketing."

Philosophes—The name for the French philosophers of the Enlightenment. It is the French word for philosophers.

Philosophy—Literally the "love of wisdom," from the Greek words philos and sophia.

Polis—The Greek word for city-state. Athens was a city-state. The words "politics" comes from polis.

Postmodernism—The current state of philosophy falls under the label of Postmodernism. Perhaps future generations will have another name for this era.

Predestination—The belief that your fate is determined before you are born, and nothing you do in this life will make a difference as to whether you go to Heaven or Hell.

Presocratic philosophers—The group of philosophers, also called Monists, who offered theories that the nature of reality was composed of one thing (water, air, fire, numbers, and so on).

R

Rationalist—The philosophy of Descartes, Spinoza, and Leibniz. They believe that there are innate ideas in the mind, and not everything we know must necessarily be gathered through sensory experience.

Relativism—The belief that things such as morality vary from society to society and culture to culture, and none is better or worse than any other.

S

Social Contract—a relationship between the government and the people. It could be formally agreed upon or an unwritten, implicit agreement. Thomas Hobbes, John Locke, and Jean-Jacques Rousseau all had versions of what they felt was the ideal social contract.

Sophistry—The frivolous misuse of philosophy to teach how to win arguments and sway opinions via linguistic legerdemain.

Syllogism—Aristotle's logical argument that has two premises and a conclusion. The famous example is, "All men are mortal. Socrates is a man. Therefore, Socrates is mortal."

T

Tabula rasa—Latin for "blank slate." Many philosophers, including John Locke and Voltaire, believed that we are born with an empty mind, ready to have sensory experiences imprinted on our brains.

Things in themselves—This is Kant's name for the Noumenal world, the metaphysical reality beyond the limited reality that we can perceive, which he called the phenomenal world.

Transcendent—Something beyond the realm of ordinary experience. The opposite of immanent.

U

Universals—Aristotle's spin on Platonic Forms. He believed that the Forms were within the physical object, not separate entities in another dimension.

Utilitarianism—The philosophy of Jeremy Bentham and John Stuart Mill that suggests that the ultimate goal of individuals and society should be the maximization of pleasure and the minimization of pain.

APPENDIX B

Who's Who in Philosophy

ALFRED ADLER—Another of Freud's students, Adler believed that feelings of inferiority rather than sexuality were the main motivating unconscious force in people.

ANAXAGORAS—He took the theories of four roots a step further by declaring that reality can be reduced to an infinite number of "seeds." Not unlike Empedocles's hypothesis, these seeds contain elements of everything and are in everything, yet certain elements are there in greater abundance, creating life's myriad diversity. And in lieu of Empedocles's Love and Strife theory, Anaxagoras postulated on the existence of a Nous or omniscient yet impersonal Mind that gave order and constancy to the universe.

ANAXIMANDER—A younger contemporary of Thales, he didn't believe that it was one of the four familiar elements that was the basic stuff of the world; rather, all those elements and more all comprised a common element he, for lack of a better word, called "The Boundless." All things arise from The Boundless (ápeiron in Greek), and all things return to The Boundless. This foreshadows Einstein's dictum that "Matter can neither be created nor destroyed."

ANAXIMENES—A pupil of Anaximander who digressed from his mentor's theory by singling out air as the root of all things. We need air as much as water. He believed the soul was composed of air.

ANSELM OF CANTERBURY—A Benedictine monk and teacher who ultimately became the Archbishop of Canterbury, the highest religious office in England. He sought to distinguish between philosophy and theology. The famous maxim of Anselm was "Credo ut intelligam," which means "I believe that I may understand." He is most famous for his Ontological Argument, which "proves" the existence of God.

THOMAS AQUINAS—A primary Catholic thinker who sought to Christianize Aristotle similarly to the way that Augustine adapted Neoplatonism to Christian teaching, he also reconciled the dilemma of Faith versus Reason. He is famous for his five points that prove the existence of God, and he spoke of Universals, his revised version of that Platonic Forms.

ARISTOTLE—Aristotle studied under Plato as a student at the latter's Academy for twenty years. He was a prodigy and generally regarded as Plato's heir apparent.

However, he disagreed with the master on several key points. Aristotle is famous for the syllogism, which is a logical argument that takes two truths, connects them, and arrives at a third truth.

AUGUSTINE OF HIPPO—He was born and died in the last days of the Roman Empire and serves as a bridge between the classical and the medieval worlds. Augustine's candid autobiography, *Confessions*, chronicles his struggles with faith and earthly pleasures and contains the famous and ironic prayer, "God grant me chastity . . . but not yet." Augustine used Neoplatonic philosophy to defend, endorse, and affirm Christian theology. Augustine attempted to explain some of the many mysteries of Christianity through the philosophies of Plato.

MARCUS AURELIUS—He was a foremost Stoic whose collection of journal entries, written in between vanquishing barbarian hordes, *Meditations*, is a quintessential distillation of Stoic thought and practice.

FRANCIS BACON—This British politician and businessman took a scientific approach to philosophy. He studied the world as an empirical observer would and attempted to avoid bringing his preconceptions and prejudices into the proceedings. Bacon proposed that, in order to truly understand the world, we must first be aware of the various obstacles and distractions that prevent us from seeing things clearly.

ROGER BACON—Bacon was a Franciscan monk who is regarded as a forerunner of the modern scientist. He sought to incorporate the academic disciplines of mathematics and language into theology and philosophy through his book *Opus Major*. Bacon proposed that there are three ways to gain knowledge: authority, reason, and experience. He breaks experience into the realms of the internal and external. External experience is awareness of physical reality and the world of the senses. Internal experience is similar to Augustine's "illumination," a little help from the person upstairs.

GEORGE BERKELEY—He believed that everything was an idea, even physical matter. Only minds and the ideas they generate are real, according to this Irish clergyman. He is considered to be the founder of the modern version of Idealism, a belief that goes back to Plato in its original presentation. Unlike the closet atheism of Locke, Berkeley flatly states that God is responsible for the introduction and dissemination of perceptions into the human brain. These things we perceive do not exist outside the mind. They have no substantial reality of their own.

FRANZ BOAS—An influential anthropologist who sought to make anthropology more respectable, he believed in fieldwork, or living among the civilization you were studying for an extended period of time. He also rejected the ethnocentric and downright racist views of many of his predecessors. He trained a whole generation of anthropologists, and his work was the basis for the practice of cultural relativism.

ALBERT CAMUS—This French-Algerian man of letters wrote *The Stranger*, *The Myth of Sisyphus*, and other novels, plays, and nonfiction works. He, along with Jean-Paul Sartre, was a premier exponent of Existentialism. Camus was given the Nobel Prize for literature in 1957 and died tragically in a car accident in 1960. Although primarily known as a novelist and playwright, these fictional devices exposed existentialism to a wide audience.

CICERO—The famous Roman senator, lawyer, orator, and philosopher lived and died dur-ing some of the most turbulent times in ancient history. Cicero "Romanized" the Greek philosophers in Latin translations designed to bring the classics to the Romans. It is said he was inventive in his translations, and as a lifelong lawyer and politician, he had ulterior motives in his efforts to bring philosophy to the Roman Empire. Ever the pragmatist, he intended to use philosophy as a tool to further his political goals and advance the glory that was Rome. Though he was largely linked to the Roman branch of Skepticism, he was also a premier practitioner of Eclecticism.

AUGUSTE COMTE—This French philosopher is generally regarded as the father of modern sociology. Comte sought to employ the same methods that scientists had used in the investigation and exploration of the physical world and apply them to the study of human affairs.

CHARLES DARWIN—The most famous proponent of the theory of evolution, he proposed the theory of natural selection in his book, *On the Origin of Species*. This theory maintains that certain characteristics and qualities in a species enabled it to survive, and thus those characteristics were passed on to the progeny, over time altering the species in significant ways. Species went off in other directions while their progenitors remained stagnant or died away.

JACQUES DERRIDA—This contemporary French philosopher started the philosophical school called deconstruction, which is the process of breaking down something (in Derrida's case, language) to show that what is being stated is in fact inherently false. He thumbs his nose at traditional philosophy by saying that philosophy is logocentric.

RENÉ DESCARTES—This French philosopher is often called the Father of Modern Philosophy. He started out his career as a mathematician and is credited with discovering the concept of Analytic Geometry. He uttered perhaps the most famous sentence in the history of philosophy: "I think, therefore I am." Everything could be questioned, but one thing remained a fact: the thinking of the thinker.

EMILE DURKHEIM—He bridged the disciplines of sociology and the equally new notion of anthropology. Durkheim also founded the school of thought called *Functionalism,* which maintains that a society, in essence, took on a personality of its own and could be objectively viewed the way a scientist or physician may regard a living organism. He proposed that cultures have a *collective consciousness,* where the values and beliefs held by a culture direct the behavior of its members without them even knowing it.

RALPH WALDO EMERSON—Emerson was a writer and lecturer whose famous works include *Nature and Self-Reliance*, which expressed the Transcendentalist philosophy. He viewed every individual as having full and free access to the Over-Soul. We are all something like cells in the giant organism that is God/Nature. We can access this collective unconsciousness and experience total interconnectedness with our fellows and the natural world. He believed that evil is not a force unto itself but merely arises from the absence of good. He considered poets to be the modern mystics and prophets and directly influenced and inspired America's greatest poet, Walt Whitman. His influence in philosophy and literature had a profound impact on the American culture.

EMPEDOCLES—Empedocles can be compared to Pythagoras in that he combined the scientific and spiritual, yet his area of expertise was medicine rather than mathematics. He also offered the theory that it was not one element at the center of it all, but rather that the roots of all found elements—fire, air, earth, and water—could be found in everything. The four roots would exist in different degrees. Obviously, water would have a preponderance of water roots, but the others would be there to a lesser degree. And in an ancient Greek variation on the yin/yang belief of coexisting complementary opposites, he added that the entities he called Love and Strife were complementary forces that impacted on the world as they knew it.

EPICURUS—One of the most misinterpreted philosophers in the pantheon of great thinkers. His name and his philosophy became synonymous with wanton hedonism. Although Epicurus put great stock in the pursuit of pleasure, his definition of pleasure would be more akin to the delights enjoyed by the couch potato as opposed to the libertine. Epicurus led a restful, contemplative life, eating modestly, drinking moderately, and philosophizing for the most part from a prone position on his hammock.

MICHEL FOUCAULT—This recent French philosopher is considered a postmodernist. Foucault's major works include *Madness and Civilization,* wherein he chronicled Western society's changing views toward mental illness over the centuries. Foucault's other major work is called *Discipline and Punish,* wherein he critiques the world's various penal systems making the case that, in the Western world at least, the employment of torture and physical abuse in modern prison systems has merely switched the destructive emphasis from body to soul.

SIGMUND FREUD—One of the most famous and influential psychologists of the twentieth century, his name is known by even those who don't know much about psychology. Two of the techniques of Freudian psychoanalysis are the interpretation of dreams and free association. Freud also came up with the infamous theory of the Oedipus Complex.

GORGIAS—He didn't put much stock in the notion of virtue, but instead felt that the power of persuasion was key. His philosophy is summed up in this three-pronged theory: Nothing exists, if anything did exist we could not know about it, and if something existed and someone knew about it, he or she couldn't communicate that awareness to others.

MARTIN HEIDEGGER—His existential philosophy influenced Camus, Sartre, and many modern philosophers that followed. Unlike Nietzsche, who posthumously suffered the slander of being labeled a Nazi, Heidegger has earned the title fair and square. The German publicly endorsed Hitler and the Nazis in the 1930s. He shifted the focus from the examination of the conscious to experiencing the state of simply "being there," in his book, *Being and Time*.

HERACLITUS—Nicknamed "the Obscure," Heraclitus was a philosopher who was known as something of a downer. His theory that everything is composed of fire, if taken metaphorically, is expressed in his belief that everything is in flux. You couldn't even step into the same river twice, according to him, because the flowing water was not the same water you dipped your big toe into mere seconds before.

THOMAS HOBBES—This English philosopher rejected Descartes's dualism and touted the theory that ours is a mechanistic and materialistic universe. An attempt to synthesize Empiricism and Rationalism, it is also quite a pessimistic viewpoint and paints man as a less than noble piece of work. His most famous work is called *The Leviathan*. The titular leviathan of Hobbes's tome is a society without order. Hobbes felt that without order, society would violently self-destruct.

DAVID HUME—A Scottish philosopher who was influenced by and expanded upon the ideas of John Locke and George Berkeley, Hume not only denied the existence of the material substances of Locke, but also the spiritual world of ideas proposed by Berkeley. Hume also rejected the existence of the individual self. You do not exist. According to Hume, you are nothing more than what he called "a collection of different perceptions." He dismissed the scientific principle of cause-and-effect and stated that knowledge of anything as certainty is just plain impossible, except maybe mathematics.

EDMUND HUSSERL—The founder of phenomenology, this German philosopher endeavored to study the mind itself, not the outside world of things and events that the mind perceive. The proper study of consciousness lies in the mind, according to Husserl. He called this *phenomenological reduction*.

WILLIAM JAMES—The Father of American Psychology and the brother of the novelist Henry James, his two-volume *Principles of Psychology* was the bible for a generation of American psychologists. His approach was Functionalist, proposing that the important purpose of psychological study was to examine the functions of the conscious. This involved studying selected subjects over a lengthy period of time, which consisted of observation and tests and was called longitudinal research.

CARL GUSTAV JUNG—The most famous follower of Sigmund Freud, Jung's most famous theory is that of the collective unconscious. This is a shared memory of symbols, imagery, and memories that he called archetypes, which harken back to the dawn of human consciousness and are common in all cultures and civilizations. Jung also proposed that within every man there is an inner woman and within every woman there is an inner man.

SØREN KIERKEGAARD—He was a literary figure in Denmark who used irony to make his points. As a result, it is often hard to tell when he is being serious and when he is pulling our philosophical leg. Kierkegaard is considered to be the first existentialist. His views on alienation, the angst that plagues people, and the inherent absurdity of life influenced Jean-Paul Sartre, Albert Camus, and other twentieth-century existentialists. They, however, were atheists while Kierkegaard remained a Christian throughout his life.

GOTTFRIED LEIBNIZ—While Spinoza spoke of modes, Leibniz believed that reality was made up of what he called monads. Like Democritus and the Atomists, Leibniz theorized that the smallest particle was called a monad. It was indivisible like an atom was once believed to be, and each monad was as unique as a fingerprint. Everything, including people, is composed of monads, according to Leibniz.

LEUCIPPUS AND DEMOCRITUS—The first to theorize that the world was composed of tiny particles called atoms. These particles were invisible to the human eye yet ubiquitous and their myriad combinations, comprising what we commonly call reality. Democritus built on the theories of Leucippus by suggesting that atoms were indivisible.

JOHN LOCKE—Locke was a British Empiricist who believed that all knowledge was gained through experience. There was no such thing as innate ideas, as he called them. He is famous for the theory of the tabula rasa, which means "blank slate" in

Latin. Locke proposed that the human mind is a complete void upon birth and gradually accumulates data as it is exposed to life and its many sensory experiences.

KARL MARX—He was the architect of what became modern socialism and communism, ideologies that went on to change the face of the globe and the state of the world in ways that Marx himself may never have imagined. A student of philosophy, he, along with Friedrich Engels, is the author of the world-altering tome, *The Communist Manifesto.* He sought social reform to combat the injustices of the Industrial Revolution.

MONTESQUIEU—Montesquieu was a noted jurist who spoke of relativism as it pertains to the law. Relativism is the belief that what is good for the goose may not necessarily be good for the gander. Montesquieu also proposed the notion of a separation of powers in a government. He advocated a series of checks and balances in order to provide balance and thwart one element of government gaining more power than another.

FRIEDRICH WILHELM NIETZSCHE—Perhaps the most controversial and most misunderstood philosopher, he was as much a literary figure as a philosopher. He had no formal philosophy and basically ranted in the form of aphorisms, short pithy quips, and pungent observations. Some of these notions include God is dead, the advocacy of the Superman, the theory of eternal recurrence, and many more hot topics. His main targets were Western Civilization and Christianity. A sensitive soul plagued by health problems, he ultimately descended into madness and never recovered.

PARMENIDES—The anti-Heraclitus; he wrote in direct response to him. Simply put, he believed that there is no flux; in fact, everything is stagnant. "It is" was his credo. Being is immutable and constant, and change is an illusion.

JEAN PIAGET—His main claim to fame is the work he did with children. After years of working in schools and interviewing thousands of children, the Swiss psychologist identified four stages of childhood development. The sensorimotor stage, from birth to age two, involves the mastering of motor controls and learning to deal with the physical world. In the preoperational stage, from ages two to seven, the child focuses on verbal skills and communication. Children begin to deal with numbers and other complex concepts in what Piaget called the concrete operational stage, and logic and reason evolves in the formal operational stage.

PLATO—Plato was Socrates's most famous protégé. He continued the Socratic legacy while building on it with his own theories. Plato was a firm believer in Ideas or, as they are also called, Forms.

PLOTINUS OF ALEXANDRIA—The founder of Neoplatonist thought, he established a school in Rome. Neoplatonism was the last shout of ancient Greek philosophizing.

PRODICUS—A rhetorician who, according to most accounts, was unabashedly in it for the money. Plato frequently satirized him as a pedantic lecturer on the niceties of language above all else. Eloquent and popular as he was, the officials of Athens saw fit to execute him for corrupting the young.

PROTAGORAS—The first Sophist, he had a successful career and enjoyed great fame in his lifetime. "Man is the measure of all things" was his credo. This was not to suggest the nobility and evolutionary superiority of the species. It is actually an extreme case of relativism, moral and otherwise. "Anything goes" was the natural devolution of such a principle. If it feels good, do it. If it gets you ahead even at the expense of another, go for it.

PYRRHO OF ELIS—The founder of the Skeptic school of philosophy, he saw the road to happiness as doing as little as possible. Repose was the only recourse for the truly wise man. The only path to peace is to suspend judgment, because no worldview is any better than another. Do not believe anything you see or hear. Do not have any opinions. There is no such thing as good or evil. Rather than promote chaos and confusion, Pyrrho believed that to accept this is the only way to live.

AYN RAND—An American novelist and philosopher, she is famous for the novels *The Fountainhead* and *Atlas Shrugged*. Her philosophy is called Objectivism. She put reason before emotion, and individualism over groupthink, and thought egotism was a good thing and altruism was a negative character trait.

CARL ROGERS AND ABRAHAM MASLOW—The pioneers of what was called humanistic psychology, they were dissatisfied with the rigidities of psychoanalysis and behaviorism. Their theories, neither psychoanalytic nor behaviorist, came to be called the third force. These two men saw psychology as a means to help people fulfill their maximum potential. Rogers felt that all people are instilled with an innate drive to "be all that they can be," and it was the role of psychotherapy to facilitate this process. Abraham Maslow devised a hierarchy of needs, which is the path a person takes from the basic needs of survival on the road to the achievement of their potential. The lowest levels on the scale would be food and shelter, while further up the scale would be things like security and love. The top of the list of needs is what Maslow called self-actualization.

JEAN JACQUES ROUSSEAU—This French philosopher and social critic also was one of the earliest practitioners of the tell-all memoir. His candor was shocking in his day.

BERTRAND RUSSELL—A British philosopher, Nobel laureate, and one of the most influential philosophers of the twentieth century, Russell was also a pacifist. The fact that he also lived to the ripe old age of ninety-eight meant that he protested every major conflict from World War I to the Vietnam War. He did, however, take a patriotic stand during World War II, but in the Cold War, he remained a staunch antinuclear weapons activist. At the advanced age of eighty-nine, he was arrested at an antinuclear protest.

JEAN-PAUL SARTRE—The other French existentialist of the twentieth century was also a novelist and dramatist as well as the author of philosophical works and political polemics. He is more famous for the novel *Nausea*, the play *No Exit,* and the nonfiction work *Being and Nothingness*. He was also awarded the Nobel Prize for literature, but unlike his fellow French existentialist Albert Camus, he turned it down.

JOHN DUNS SCOTUS—Scotus was a Franciscan monk who endorsed many of the precepts of Augustine, yet differed on other key elements, including the necessity of "illumination." Humans have the intellect to comprehend God and his wonders without a celestial cheat sheet. Being a cleric and a man of his time, dogma rules as far as Scotus is concerned. He spins the notion of Universals by suggesting that they exist as Forms (to be found in the mind of God) and as part of the physical things they represent (as perceived in the mind of man). While Aquinas has the intellect pre-eminent over the human will, Scotus said that will is more important than intellect. This led to a great medieval debate known as the Thomist-Scotist controversy.

SENECA—The Roman playwright and noted Stoic took his own life when he fell out of favor with the notorious emperor Nero.

B. F. SKINNER—The most famous Behaviorist, he believed that people's behavior could be changed through the process of conditioning. The famous example of this involves the rat in a box (designed by Skinner and appropriately named the Skinner Box). The rat learned that if it presses a lever, a food pellet is released. This positive reinforcement ensures that the behavior will be repeated and is called operant conditioning.

SOCRATES—This dynamic and controversial Athenian figure spent a lifetime in the public square engaging in dialogues with the young men of Athens. His singular method of posing questions to his intellectual quarry and drawing responses is called *Socratic Dialogue.* This form of question and answer and the logical debate of opposing views is called *dialectic.* Socrates's motto should be every philosopher's raison d'être: "The unexamined life is not worth living. Doing what is right is the only path to goodness, and introspection and self-awareness are the ways to learn what is right."

HERBERT SPENCER—This British philosopher put his spin on the evolutionary theory by applying it to humanity and calling it survival of the fittest. This form of social Darwinism was often used to justify colonialism and the xenophobic European feelings of superiority.

BARUCH SPINOZA—Spinoza believed in *pantheism,* meaning that God is present in all things. Like Descartes, Spinoza wrestled with the idea of Substance. Descartes called the infinite substance God, while Spinoza called it Nature. His belief that God is Nature and that nature is one substance that can shape-shift into various forms that he called modes is not unlike the Monist philosophies of the Presocratics.

THALES—Thales of Miletus is often designated as the first "official" philosopher. He is regarded as the founder of natural philosophy. He proposed that everything is composed of water. Though Thales could not have known that the human body is composed of mostly water, he was on to something, simplistic as his theories may seem today. His rational approach of not attributing anything and everything to "the gods" paved the way for the scientific method. He was revered as a sage in his lifetime and long after his death.

HENRY DAVID THOREAU—Famous for the book *Walden*, a journal of his solitary existence in a cabin on Walden Pond, Thoreau was an eloquent spokesperson for the Transcendentalist philosophy. Another philosophy that Thoreau espoused, and was later made better known and practiced in the twentieth century, was civil disobedience.

VOLTAIRE—One of the most famous and infamous philosophers of the Enlightenment, he was a celebrity and a controversial figure in his lifetime. His satirical pieces landed him in the Bastille, the notorious French prison, on more than one occasion, but these incarcerations did not cause his quill pen to run dry.

MAX WEBER—He was a German thinker who also took a jaundiced view of capitalism and sought to understand its emergence in the Western World rather than in another culture in another part of the world. He linked the rise of capitalism with the Protestant Work Ethic. Whereas Marx believed that economics motivated human thought, Weber believed the opposite: Human ideas brought about particular economic systems. And while Marx spoke of class struggles and ultimately class warfare, the word Weber used to describe the division of societies was *stratification*. Weber also addressed the rise of bureaucracies in Europe. He actually liked them! He thought they were the ideal organizing principle in the new industrial societies of Europe in the nineteenth century.

WILLIAM OF OCKHAM—Famous for the theory that has come to be known as Ockham's Razor, Ockham believed that when all is said and done in this crazy world, the simplest answer is usually the right one.

LUDWIG JOSEF JOHAN WITTGENSTEIN—This Austrian philosopher studied with Bertrand Russell and became an influential advocate of analytic and linguistic philosophy. In 1918, Wittgenstein completed the *Tractatus Logico-philosophicus,* which he called the "final solution" to all problems of philosophy. However, in later years, he rejected his own conclusions in the *Tractatus* and wrote yet another seminal work of modern philosophy called *Philosophical Investigations.*

MARY WOLLSTONECRAFT—This was a woman truly ahead of her time. She wrote one of the most famous novels in the history of the English language *(Frankenstein)* and was a feminist rallying cry almost two hundred years before the modern Feminist movement came into being.

ZENO—Zeno is best known for a couple of famous paradoxes. The first one explains how, sitting in your room, you can never really reach the door. If the distance between two points is composed of an infinite number of points, then we can bisect that line. And we can keep bisecting the areas we previously bisected ad infinitum. Hence, you potentially have an infinite amount of space in a finite distance between two points and can never really get anywhere.

The second Zeno paradox deals with motion. When you move from one place to another, you reach the midway point before the final destination. And before you get to the halfway mark, you reach the halfway mark of the midway point. Ergo, you have to travel an infinite number of points in a finite amount of time. And that is impossible, right?

ZENO OF CYPRUS—Founder of the Stoic school, he used to lecture from his porch, which was called a *stoa*, hence the name Stoic. The word "stoic" has remained in the language and defines a person who accepts life's slings and arrows without whining about it.

Index

A

a posteriori/a priori judgment, 97
Absolute, Hegel's, 100
absurdity, 126, 129
Adler, Alfred, 160
aesthetics, 103
African philosophy, 208–210
afterlife, 211. *See also*
  reincarnation
air, 3, 34
Alcoholics Anonymous (AA),
  221–226
  James and, 160
  Twelve Steps of, 225, 227–231
alcoholism, 219–221, 227
Alcott, Amos Bronson, 122
Alexander the Great, 23, 28, 30,
  242
alienation, 126, 129
allegory of the cave, 18–19, 150
altruism, 78–79
analytical psychology, 155
Anaxagoras, 7
Anaximander, 3
Anaximenes, 3–4
angst, 125–126
anima/animus, 156, 239
anonymity, 229–230
Anselm of Canterbury, 45–46
anthropology, 146–148
  Durkheim and, 145–146
Antisthenes, 29
apathy, 35
ápeiron, 3
aphorisms, 106
Aquinas, Thomas, 46–49
Aristotle, 22–26
  Aquinas and, 44, 46–49
  ethics of, 24–25
  humility and, 230
  Plato and, 22–23
  Stoics and, 35
  Theory of Potentiality of, 23–24
art

Aristotle on, 26
  Hegel on, 100
  Plato on, 21–22
Art of War, The (Sun-Tzu), 174–176
ascetics, 103
astrology, 241–243
ataraxia (inner peace), 32, 35
Atlas Shrugged (Rand), 198–199
atomists, 7–8, 30
Augustine of Hippo, 39, 43–45, 224
avatars, 165
Avengers, The, 259–260
Averroist theory of the Double
  Truth, 46–47

B

Bacon, Francis, 74
Bacon, Roger, 50
bardo state, 236
Behaviorism, 158–159
  Skinner, 158–159
  Watson, 158
Being and Nothingness (Sartre), 131
Bentham, Jeremy, 112–113
Berkeley, George, 84–85
Beyond Good and Evil
  (Nietzsche), 107–108
Birth of Tragedy, The (Nietzsche),
  105
Black Elk Speaks (Hiehardt),
  212–213, 217
Boas, Franz, 148
body mind concept, 24
bracketing of existence, 124
Brahmanas, 165
breath (*pneuma*), 34
Bruno, Giordano, 56–57
Buddha, 167–168, 170, 224
Buddhism, 167–171
  reincarnation and, 236, 239
  Right Livelihood and, 199–200
  Shinto contrasted to, 180
  Zen, 171
bureaucracy. *See* government

C

Calculus of Felicity, 113
Calvin, John, 65–67
Calvinism, 67, 143, 144
Campbell, Joseph, 155–156, 203
Camus, Albert, 128–130
Candide (Voltaire), 90–91
capitalism
  Calvin and, 67
  Locke and, 83
  Marx and, 143–144
  Weber and, 143, 144
causes, Aristotle and, 24
cave allegory, 18–19, 150
Channing, William Ellery, 121
childhood development, 160–161
China, 170, 171, 179
Christian Church, 42, 184, 186–189
  Descartes and, 75, 77
  Epicurus and, 31
  Erasmus and, 61
  Kierkegaard and, 125, 126
  More and, 62
  Neoplatonists and, 39
  Nietzsche and, 104–105, 106–107,
    108
  Russell and, 135
  scientific revolution and, 56–57,
    69–70
  Stoics and, 35–36
  see also Protestant Reformation
Cicero, 37–39
civil disobedience, 120
collective consciousness, 145–146
collective unconscious, 155–156
communism
  Buddhism and, 170, 171
  Marx and, 143–144
  Rand and, 196, 197
Comte, Auguste, 142
Confessions (Rousseau), 91
Confucianism, 177–181
  Taoism contrasted to, 240
Confucius, 177–178

consequentialism, 112
Copernicus, Nicholas, 70
Council of Trent, 68
Counter-Reformation, 67–68
critical philosophy, 96
Critique of Dialectical Reason (Sartre), 131
Critique of Pure Reason (Kant), 96–97
cultural relativism, 148
Cynics, 28–30

D
Dalai Lama, 170, 171
Darwin, Charles, 147
deconstruction, 139–140
deism, 90
democracy. *See* government
Democritus, 7–8
Demon Hypothesis, 75
Derrida, Jacques, 139–140
Descartes, René, 75–77
Devi, 164, 165
dialectic
   of Hegel, 100
   of Socrates, 13
Diogenes, 29–30
Discourse on the Origin and Foundation of Inequality among Mankind (Rousseau), 92
dogma, 42
dot.com story, 203–206
doubt, 75–77
drama, 26
Dream Hypothesis, 75
dreams, 152
dualism, 77
Durkheim, Emile, 145–146
dystopia, 196

E
Eastern philosophies, 163
   Buddhism, 167–171

Confucianism, 177–181
   Hinduism, 164–167
   Shinto, 180–181
   Sufism, 181–182
   Taoism, 172–176
Ecce Homo, How One Becomes What One Is (Nietzsche), 109
Eclectics, 37–39
education reform, 93
Eightfold Path of Enlightenment, 169
Electra Complex, 153
elements, 2–6, 7
Emerson, Ralph Waldo, 118–119, 120
Empedocles, 6–7
Empiricism, British, 81
   Berkeley, 84–85
   concept of innateness, 82
   Hume, 85–86
   Locke, 82–84
   Russell and, 134, 135
Engels, Friedrich, 101
Enlightenment, French, 87
   Montesquieu, 89
   philosophes, 88–89
   Rousseau, 91–93
   Voltaire, 89–91
Epictetus, 35
Epicureans, 30–33, 38
Epicurus, 30–33
Erasmus, Desiderius, 61
eternal recurrence, 107
ethics, 103
ethnocentrism, 147
evil, 44–45
existentialism, 123, 124, 126–127
   Camus, 128–130
   in *The Fugitive*, 259
   Heidegger, 127–128
   Kierkegaard, 124–127
   Sartre, 128, 130–132

F
feminism
   in *The Avengers*, 259–260

Mill and, 114–115
   Wollstonecraft and, 115–116
Fichte, Johann Gottlieb, 98–99
Ficino, Marsilio, 54, 243
fieldwork, 146, 148
fire, 4–5
forms
   Aquinas and, 47, 48–49
   Aristotle and, 23
   Plato and, 19–20, 23
   William of Ockham and, 50–51
Foucault, Michel, 137–139
Fountainhead, The (Rand), 198–199
Four Nobel Truths, 168–170
Francis of Assisi, 224–225
free will, 44–45. *See also* will
Freud, Sigmund, 150–154
   personality development theory of, 151, 153–154
   psychoanalysis and, 151–152
friendship, 25, 32
Fugitive, The, 259
Functionalism, 145
Fust, Johann, 71

G
gadfly, 12
Galen, 150
Galileo Galilei, 70
Gay Science, The (Nietzsche), 106
gender, 156. *See also* feminism
God
   Alcoholics Anonymous and, 227, 228–229
   Anselm and, 46
   Aquinas' proof of, 47–48
   Aristotle and, 24
   Augustine and, 44–45
   Berkeley and, 84–85
   Descartes' proof of, 76
   Hegel and, 100
   Leibnitz and, 80

Native American philosophy and, 210–211
Neoplatonists and, 39
Nicolas of Cusa and, 55
Plato and, 20–21
Spinoza and, 79
in *Star Trek*, 253
Stoics and, 35–36
Transcendentalists and, 118–119
Voltaire on, 91
see also monotheism
gods
Antisthenes and, 29
Cicero and, 38
Hindu, 164–165
Protagoras and, 9
in *Star Trek*, 251–255
Gorgias, 10
government
Aristotle and, 25–26
Calvin and, 66–67
Hobbes and, 78
Montesquieu and, 89
Plato and, 16, 21
Socrates and, 16
Weber and, 145
Greek philosophy, 1, 11
Aristotle, 22–26
Plato, 18–22
Pluralists, 6–8
Presocratics, 2–6
Socrates, 12–18
Sophists, 8–10
see also Hellenistic period
group therapy, 159
groupthink, 125
Gutenberg, Johannes, 71–72

H
haiku, 171
happiness, 24–25, 201–203
Hedonism, 112
Hegel, George W. F., 99–101, 124, 125

Heidegger, Martin, 127–128
Heliocentrism, 56, 70
Hellenistic period, 27–28
Cynicism, 28–30
Epicureanism, 30–33
Neoplatonism, 39
Skepticism, 39
Stoicism, 33–36
see also Greek philosophy
henotheism, 184
Heraclitus, 4–5, 23
Hiehardt, John G., 212–213
Hinduism, 164–167, 239
Hobbes, Thomas, 77–79, 83–84
Humanism, 59–60
Erasmus, 61
More, 61–62
Petrarca, 60–61
in *Star Trek*, 251–255
humanistic psychology, 159
Hume, David, 85–86
Bentham and, 112
Kant and, 96
Rousseau and, 93
Husserl, Edmund, 124

I
I Ching, 179, 240–241
Idealism, German, 95
Fichte, 98–99
Hegel, 99–101
Kant, 96–98
Nietzsche, 104–109
Schelling, 99
Schopenhauer, 101–103
Idealism, of Berkeley, 84
Idols, Bacon's, 74
Illuminists. *See* Enlightenment, French
individuation, 157, 214
innateness, concept of, 82
inner peace (*ataraxia*), 32, 35
insanity. *See* mental illness

Institutes of the Christian Religion (Calvin), 66
intentionality, 124
Islam, 184, 189–192
Five Pillars of, 190–192
Sufism and, 181–182

J
James, William, 160
Japan, 171, 180–181
Jesus of Nazareth, 187–188, 189
Islam and, 190, 192
Judaism, 184–186
judgment, 96–97
Jung, Carl Gustav, 154–157
alcoholism and, 221
I Ching and, 241
individuation and, 157, 214

K
Kant, Immanuel, 96–98
Karma
Buddhism and, 170
Hinduism and, 166–167
reincarnation and, 235–236
Kepler, Johannes, 70
Kierkegaard, Søren, 124–127
knowledge
Anaxagoras on, 7
Aquinas on, 49
Bacon on, 50
Foucault on, 138
Kant on, 96–97
Plato on, 20
Stoics on, 33–34
Koran, 190, 192

L
languages
Derrida and, 140
Humanism and, 65
Wittgenstein and, 136–137
Lao-Tzu, 172, 175, 240

learned ignorance, 55
Leibnitz, Gottfried, 80, 90, 209
Leucippus, 7
Locke, John, 82–84
logic, 80
Logical Atomism, 136
logocentrism, 140
Luther, Martin, 64–65

M

MacArthur, Douglas, 181
Machiavelli, Niccolò, 57–58
Machiavellianism, 57
mandala drawing, 246–247
Manichaeanism, 43
Marcus Aurelius, 34, 35, 36
Marx, Karl, 101, 142–144
Maslow, Abraham, 159
mathematics, 134. *See also*
    numbers
Medici, Cosimo de, 54–55
Medicine Wheel, 213–215
Medieval philosophy, 41–42
    Anselm, 45–46
    Aquinas, 46–49
    Augustine, 43–45
    Bacon, 50
    Scotus, 49
    William of Ockham, 50–51
meditation
    Buddhism and, 168, 171
    Right Livelihood and, 202–203
Mencius, 178
mental illness
    Foucault on, 138
    Greeks on, 150
Mill, John Stuart, 113–115
modern/postmodern philosophy,
    133
    Derrida, 139–140
    Foucault, 137–139
    postmodern defined, 137
    Russell, 134–136
    Wittgenstein, 136–137

monads, 80
Monists, 2–6
monomyth, 156
monotheism, 183–184, 193
    Islam, 184, 189–192
    Judaism, 184–186
    see also Christian Church; God
Montaigne, Michel de, 71
Montesquieu, Charles-Louis, Baron
    de, 89
Moore, Thomas, 243
More, Sir Thomas, 61–62
Muhammad, 192
Muslims. *See* Islam
Myth of Sisyphus, The (Camus),
    129–130

N

Native American philosophy,
    210–217
    Black Elk Speaks, 212–213, 217
    Chief Seattle's letter, 216–217
    Medicine Wheel and, 213–215
Nausea (Sartre), 132
Neoplatonism, 39, 43–44
New Age movement, 233–234
    astrology, 241–243
    Eightfold Path and, 169
    I Ching, 240–241
    mandala drawing, 246–247
    numerology, 244–245
    reincarnation, 234–237
    soul mates, 237–240, 241
Newton, Isaac, 209
Nicholas of Cusa, 55
Nietzsche, Friedrich Wilhelm,
    104–109, 127
    eternal recurrence theory of,
        107
    Superman of, 104–105, 255
nihilism, 103, 127
Nihilist, the, 10
No Exit (Sartre), 131–132
nominalism, 50–51

nonconformity. *See* Cynics
nondoing, 173
noumena, 97
Nous (divine intelligence)
    Aristotle and, 24
    Neoplatonists and, 39
numbers, 4. *See also* mathematics
numerology, 244–245

O

Objectivism, 195–199
    in *Star Trek*, 255–256
Ockham's Razor, 50
Oedipus Complex, 152–153
On Liberty (Mill), 114
*On the Genealogy of Morals, A
    Polemic* (Nietzsche), 108
Ontological Argument, 46
operant conditioning, 158–159
Oracle at Delphi, 14, 15
original sin, 44–45
othering, 139
Over-Soul, 118, 119
Oxford Group, 221, 222, 223

P

pacifism, 134
pantheism, 35, 79, 119
paradox, 125
Parmenides, 5, 23
passive resistance, 120
pathe, 35
Pavlov, Ivan, 158–159
perception, 85
peripatetics, 23
Persona, 156
personality, Freud's theory of, 151,
    153–154
Petrarca, Francesco, 60–61
phenomenological reduction, 124
phenomenology, 123, 124
Philosopher-King, 16, 21
philosophes, 88–89

Montesquieu, 89
Rousseau, 91–93
Voltaire, 89–91
Wollstonecraft and, 116
Piaget, Jean, 160–161
Plato, 18–22
Aristotle and, 22–23
Augustine and, 43–44, 45
cave allegory of, 18–19, 150
Ficino and, 54
on insanity, 150
psychology and, 150
The Republic, 21–22
Socrates and, 13–14, 17, 18
Sophists and, 8
in Star Trek, 254
theory of soul mates, 237
pleasure
Bentham on, 112–113
Epicureans and, 30–33
Mill on, 113–115
Right Livelihood and, 201–202
Plotinus of Alexandria, 39
Pluralists, 6–8
pneuma (breath), 34
poetry, 22
polytheism, 164
positive reinforcement, 159
postmodern philosophy. See
modern/postmodern philosophy
Potentiality, Theory of, 23–24
predestination, 66, 67, 144
Presocratics, 2–6
Principia Mathematica (Russell
and Whitehead), 134
printing press, 71–72
Prisoner, The, 256–258
Problems of Philosophy, The
(Russell), 134
Prodicus, 10
Protagoras, 9
Protestant Reformation, 63–64, 189
Calvin and, 65–67
Counter-Reformation and, 67–68
Luther and, 64–65

Protestant Work Ethic, 67, 143, 144
psychoanalysis, 151–152
psychology, 149–150
Adler, 160
Freud, 150–154
humanistic, 159
James, 160
Jung, 154–157
Piaget, 160–161
Skinner, 158–159
Watson, 158
punishment/penal system
Foucault on, 138–139
Native Americans and, 215
Pyrrho of Elis, 36–37
Pythagoras, 4, 235, 244–245

R

Rand, Ayn, 196, 197, 198–199
rationalism, 77
reality, 97–100
Reformation. See Protestant
Reformation
reincarnation
Buddhism and, 169
Hinduism and, 164, 166–167, 169
New Age movement and, 169,
234–237
Pythagoras and, 5
relativism, 89
religion. See Christian Church;
Eastern philosophies; God;
gods; monotheism
ren, 177
Renaissance, 53–54
Bruno, 56–57
Machiavelli, 57–58
Medici, 54–55
Nicolas of Cusa, 55
Telesio, 55
Republic, The (Plato), 21–22
Right Livelihood, 195, 199–206
Rockefeller, John D., 230
Rogers, Carl, 159

Rousseau, Jean Jacques, 91–93
Rumi, 182
Russell, Bertrand, 134–136
Ryobo Shinto, 180

S

sacraments, Christian, 188
sage, 36
Sartre, Jean-Paul, 128, 130–132
satori, 171
Schelling, Friedrich Wilhelm Josef
von, 99
Scholasticism, 42, 43, 60
Schopenhauer, Arthur, 101–103,
104, 237
scientific revolution, 69–72
Scotus, John Duns, 49
self-actualization, 159
Seneca, 35
senses, 31–32
Serenity Prayer, 224–225
Sextus Empiricus, 71
sexuality, 139, 151–154
shadow, Jung's, 157
in Star Trek, 252–253, 255
Shinto, 180–181
Shiva, 164–165
Siddhartha Gautama. See Buddha
Sisyphus, myth of, 130
Skepticism, 36–37, 71
Skinner, B.F., 158–159
Smith, Bob, 223
Social Conflict theory, 143
social contract
of Hobbes, 78, 84
of Locke, 83–84
of Rousseau, 92–93
Social Contract, The (Rousseau),
92–93
Social Hedonism, 112
Society of Jesus, 68
sociology, 141–142
Durkheim, 145–146
Marx, 142–144

Weber, 144–145
see also anthropology
Socrates, 12–18
  belief system of, 15–16
  influence of, 17–18
  on insanity, 150
  trial and apology of, 14–16
Socratic dialogue, 13
sonnet, 60
Sophists, 8–10, 15, 39
soul mates, 237–240, 241
Spanish Inquisition, 68
Spencer, Herbert, 147
Spinoza, Baruch, 79–80
Stalin, Joseph, 128–129
Star Trek, 250–256
Stoicism, 33–36, 255–256
Subjection of Women, The (Mill),
  114–115
substances, 76
suffrage, 115
Sufism, 181–182
suicide, 35–36
Sun-Tzu, 174
Superman, Nietzsche's, 104–105,
  255
syllogism, 25

T

tabula rasa, 82
Talmud, 185
Tao Te Ching, 172, 173, 175
Taoism, 172–176, 179, 240
Telesio, Bernardino, 55
television, philosophy on, 250
  The Avengers, 259–260
  The Fugitive, 259
  The Prisoner, 256–258
  Star Trek, 250–256
Thales of Miletus, 2–3
theocracy, 66–67
third force, 159
Thomist-Scotist controversy, 49
Thoreau, Henry David, 120–121

Thus Spoke Zarathustra
  (Nietzsche), 106–107
Tibet, 170, 171
time
  Africans on, 210
  Augustine on, 44
Torah, 185
Tractatus Logicophilosophicus
  (Wittgenstein), 136–137
Transcendentalism, 117–118
  Channing, 121
  Emerson, 118–119
  Thoreau, 120–121
transmigration of souls, 166
truth, subjective/objective, 126
Twelve Steps of Alcoholics
  Anonymous, 225, 227–231

U

unconscious. See psychoanalysis
United States, philosophical basis
  of, 83, 89
Universals
  Aquinas and, 48–49
  Plato and, 23
  Russell and, 136
  William of Ockham and, 50–51
Upanishads, 165–167
Utilitarianism, 111, 122
  Bentham, 112–113
  Mill, 113–115
Utopia (More), 61–62

V

Vedas, 165
vegetarianism, 4–5, 164
Vindication of the Rights of
  Women, A (Wollstonecraft), 116
Vishnu, 164, 165
Vision Quest, 211
Voltaire, 89–91, 92

W

Wagner, Richard, 108
water, 2–3
Watson, John, 158
Weber, Max, 143, 144–145
Weiss, Brian, 236, 237
whirling dervishes, 182
Whitehead, Alfred North, 134
will, 101–102. See also free will
will to power, 107–108
William of Ockham, 50–51
Wilson, Bill, 224, 225, 229, 230,
  241–222
Wilson, Lois, 222, 231
Wittgenstein, Ludwig Josef Johan,
  136–137
Wollstonecraft, Mary, 115–116

X

Xunzi, 178

Z

Zen Buddhism, 171
Zeno, 6
Zeno of Cyprus, 33

We Have EVERYTHING!

Everything® **After College Book**
$12.95, 1-55850-847-3

Everything® **American History Book**
$12.95, 1-58062-531-2

Everything® **Angels Book**
$12.95, 1-58062-398-0

Everything® **Anti-Aging Book**
$12.95, 1-58062-565-7

Everything® **Astrology Book**
$12.95, 1-58062-062-0

Everything® **Baby Names Book**
$12.95, 1-55850-655-1

Everything® **Baby Shower Book**
$12.95, 1-58062-305-0

Everything® **Baby's First Food Book**
$12.95, 1-58062-512-6

Everything® **Baby's First Year Book**
$12.95, 1-58062-581-9

Everything® **Barbeque Cookbook**
$12.95, 1-58062-316-6

Everything® **Bartender's Book**
$9.95, 1-55850-536-9

Everything® **Bedtime Story Book**
$12.95, 1-58062-147-3

Everything® **Bicycle Book**
$12.00, 1-55850-706-X

Everything® **Breastfeeding Book**
$12.95, 1-58062-582-7

Everything® **Build Your Own Home Page**
$12.95, 1-58062-339-5

Everything® **Business Planning Book**
$12.95, 1-58062-491-X

Everything® **Candlemaking Book**
$12.95, 1-58062-623-8

Everything® **Casino Gambling Book**
$12.95, 1-55850-762-0

Everything® **Cat Book**
$12.95, 1-55850-710-8

Everything® **Chocolate Cookbook**
$12.95, 1-58062-405-7

Everything® **Christmas Book**
$15.00, 1-55850-697-7

Everything® **Civil War Book**
$12.95, 1-58062-366-2

Everything® **Classical Mythology Book**
$12.95, 1-58062-653-X

Everything® **Collectibles Book**
$12.95, 1-58062-645-9

Everything® **College Survival Book**
$12.95, 1-55850-720-5

Everything® **Computer Book**
$12.95, 1-58062-401-4

Everything® **Cookbook**
$14.95, 1-58062-400-6

Everything® **Cover Letter Book**
$12.95, 1-58062-312-3

Everything® **Creative Writing Book**
$12.95, 1-58062-647-5

Everything® **Crossword and Puzzle Book**
$12.95, 1-55850-764-7

Everything® **Dating Book**
$12.95, 1-58062-185-6

Everything® **Dessert Book**
$12.95, 1-55850-717-5

Everything® **Digital Photography Book**
$12.95, 1-58062-574-6

Everything® **Dog Book**
$12.95, 1-58062-144-9

Everything® **Dreams Book**
$12.95, 1-55850-806-6

Everything® **Etiquette Book**
$12.95, 1-55850-807-4

Everything® **Fairy Tales Book**
$12.95, 1-58062-546-0

Everything® **Family Tree Book**
$12.95, 1-55850-763-9

Everything® **Feng Shui Book**
$12.95, 1-58062-587-8

Everything® **Fly-Fishing Book**
$12.95, 1-58062-148-1

Everything® **Games Book**
$12.95, 1-55850-643-8

Everything® **Get-A-Job Book**
$12.95, 1-58062-223-2

Everything® **Get Out of Debt Book**
$12.95, 1-58062-588-6

Everything® **Get Published Book**
$12.95, 1-58062-315-8

Everything® **Get Ready for Baby Book**
$12.95, 1-55850-844-9

Everything® **Get Rich Book**
$12.95, 1-58062-670-X

Everything® **Ghost Book**
$12.95, 1-58062-533-9

Everything® **Golf Book**
$12.95, 1-55850-814-7

Everything® **Grammar and Style Book**
$12.95, 1-58062-573-8

Everything® **Guide to Las Vegas**
$12.95, 1-58062-438-3

Everything® **Guide to New England**
$12.95, 1-58062-589-4

Everything® **Guide to New York City**
$12.95, 1-58062-314-X

Everything® **Guide to Walt Disney World®,
Universal Studios®, and
Greater Orlando, 2nd Edition**
$12.95, 1-58062-404-9

Everything® **Guide to Washington D.C.**
$12.95, 1-58062-313-1

Everything® **Guitar Book**
$12.95, 1-58062-555-X

Everything® **Herbal Remedies Book**
$12.95, 1-58062-331-X

Available wherever books are sold!
To order, call 800-872-5627, or visit everything.com
Adams Media Corporation, 57 Littlefield Street, Avon, MA 02322. U.S.A.

Everything® **Home-Based Business Book**
$12.95, 1-58062-364-6

Everything® **Homebuying Book**
$12.95, 1-58062-074-4

Everything® **Homeselling Book**
$12.95, 1-58062-304-2

Everything® **Horse Book**
$12.95, 1-58062-564-9

Everything® **Hot Careers Book**
$12.95, 1-58062-486-3

Everything® **Internet Book**
$12.95, 1-58062-073-6

Everything® **Investing Book**
$12.95, 1-58062-149-X

Everything® **Jewish Wedding Book**
$12.95, 1-55850-801-5

Everything® **Job Interview Book**
$12.95, 1-58062-493-6

Everything® **Lawn Care Book**
$12.95, 1-58062-487-1

Everything® **Leadership Book**
$12.95, 1-58062-513-4

Everything® **Learning French Book**
$12.95, 1-58062-649-1

Everything® **Learning Spanish Book**
$12.95, 1-58062-575-4

Everything® **Low-Fat High-Flavor Cookbook**
$12.95, 1-55850-802-3

Everything® **Magic Book**
$12.95, 1-58062-418-9

Everything® **Managing People Book**
$12.95, 1-58062-577-0

Everything® **Microsoft® Word 2000 Book**
$12.95, 1-58062-306-9

Everything® **Money Book**
$12.95, 1-58062-145-7

Everything® **Mother Goose Book**
$12.95, 1-58062-490-1

Everything® **Motorcycle Book**
$12.95, 1-58062-554-1

Everything® **Mutual Funds Book**
$12.95, 1-58062-419-7

Everything® **One-Pot Cookbook**
$12.95, 1-58062-186-4

Everything® **Online Business Book**
$12.95, 1-58062-320-4

Everything® **Online Genealogy Book**
$12.95, 1-58062-402-2

Everything® **Online Investing Book**
$12.95, 1-58062-338-7

Everything® **Online Job Search Book**
$12.95, 1-58062-365-4

Everything® **Organize Your Home Book**
$12.95, 1-58062-617-3

Everything® **Pasta Book**
$12.95, 1-55850-719-1

Everything® **Philosophy Book**
$12.95, 1-58062-644-0

Everything® **Playing Piano and Keyboards Book**
$12.95, 1-58062-651-3

Everything® **Pregnancy Book**
$12.95, 1-58062-146-5

Everything® **Pregnancy Organizer**
$15.00, 1-58062-336-0

Everything® **Project Management Book**
$12.95, 1-58062-583-5

Everything® **Puppy Book**
$12.95, 1-58062-576-2

Everything® **Quick Meals Cookbook**
$12.95, 1-58062-488-X

Everything® **Resume Book**
$12.95, 1-58062-311-5

Everything® **Romance Book**
$12.95, 1-58062-566-5

Everything® **Running Book**
$12.95, 1-58062-618-1

Everything® **Sailing Book, 2nd Edition**
$12.95, 1-58062-671-8

Everything® **Saints Book**
$12.95, 1-58062-534-7

Everything® **Selling Book**
$12.95, 1-58062-319-0

Everything® **Shakespeare Book**
$12.95, 1-58062-591-6

Everything® **Spells and Charms Book**
$12.95, 1-58062-532-0

Everything® **Start Your Own Business Book**
$12.95, 1-58062-650-5

Everything® **Stress Management Book**
$12.95, 1-58062-578-9

Everything® **Study Book**
$12.95, 1-55850-615-2

Everything® **T'ai Chi and QiGong Book**
$12.95, 1-58062-646-7

Everything® **Tall Tales, Legends, and Outrageous Lies Book**
$12.95, 1-58062-514-2

Everything® **Tarot Book**
$12.95, 1-58062-191-0

Everything® **Time Management Book**
$12.95, 1-58062-492-8

Everything® **Toasts Book**
$12.95, 1-58062-189-9

Everything® **Toddler Book**
$12.95, 1-58062-592-4

Everything® **Total Fitness Book**
$12.95, 1-58062-318-2

Everything® **Trivia Book**
$12.95, 1-58062-143-0

Everything® **Tropical Fish Book**
$12.95, 1-58062-343-3

Everything® **Vegetarian Cookbook**
$12.95, 1-58062-640-8

Everything® **Vitamins, Minerals, and Nutritional Supplements Book**
$12.95, 1-58062-496-0

Everything® **Wedding Book, 2nd Edition**
$12.95, 1-58062-190-2

Everything® **Wedding Checklist**
$7.95, 1-58062-456-1

Everything® **Wedding Etiquette Book**
$7.95, 1-58062-454-5

Everything® **Wedding Organizer**
$15.00, 1-55850-828-7

Everything® **Wedding Shower Book**
$7.95, 1-58062-188-0

Everything® **Wedding Vows Book**
$7.95, 1-58062-455-3

Everything® **Weight Training Book**
$12.95, 1-58062-593-2

Everything® **Wine Book**
$12.95, 1-55850-808-2

Everything® **World War II Book**
$12.95, 1-58062-572-X

Everything® **World's Religions Book**
$12.95, 1-58062-648-3

Everything® **Yoga Book**
$12.95, 1-58062-594-0

Visit us at everything.com

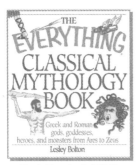